Bionomics of Behaviourism

Bhanuvikraman Nair

ATLANTIC

PUBLISHERS & DISTRIBUTORS (P) LTD

Published by
ATLANTIC
PUBLISHERS & DISTRIBUTORS (P) LTD
7/22, Ansari Road, Darya Ganj,
New Delhi-110002
Phones : +91-11-40775252, 23273880, 23275880, 23280451
Fax : +91-11-23285873
Web : www.atlanticbooks.com
E-mail : orders@atlanticbooks.com

Branch Office
5, Nallathambi Street, Wallajah Road,
Chennai-600002
Phones : +91-44-64611085, 32413319
E-mail : chennai@atlanticbooks.com

ISBN 978-81-269-1561-3

Printed in India at Nice Printing Press, A-33/3A, Site-IV, Industrial Area, Sahibabad, Ghaziabad, U.P.

Dedicated to

The everlasting memory of
My beloved parents

Foreword

In ecology, bionomics is the comprehensive study of an organism and its relation to its environment. In the present times, however, bionomics is widely used to mean ecology. Bionomics is one of the ways to bring economy (techno-sphere) into harmony with ecosystem (biosphere) and help mankind avoid ecological catastrophe. However, bionomics in the context of behaviourism, has less to do with ecology, but a lot to do with the behavioural patterns of a human being, which are governed by his mental activities. Psychology is the science of mind and behaviour and it explores the rôle of mental functions in the individual behaviour and his/her social interactions. Simultaneously, it also explores the physiological and neurobiological processes that underlie certain functions and behaviours. Myriad thoughts keep coming into the mind of every individual. These thoughts are generated due to the various types of imagination and emotion, which in turn are influenced and coloured by extrinsic factors such as time, place, environment, etc. and intrinsic traits of the individual such as selfishness, hypocrisy, hatred and many other negative factors. Such thoughts, *per se*, are not visible to others, but symptoms of their existence/appearance are manifested in the behavioural patterns of the individual. Therefore, it can be stated that behaviour of an individual serves as a "barometer" for measurement of thoughts behind it. This is the 'bionomics of behaviourism'.

I feel greatly privileged and glad to write a brief Foreword to the book entitled *Bionomics of Behaviourism*, authored by Shri Bhanuvikraman Nair, my friend of over two decades. In this book, he has, in his flippant, irreverent, frank and bold style, expressed his views on many of the patented human behavioural traits during inter-personal transactions and also during dealings with the various elements of Nature. An individual is perhaps not aware of the impact of his/her behaviour on other in such transactions/dealings. A sense of bionomics emanating from an individual behaviour is, in fact, a by-product of these transactions/dealings—the subject matter of this book.

I have read two of Bhanuvikraman's previous works, *Random Reflections —Psycho-Socio Ethos* and *Communication: A Circumspection*. His out of the box thinking and treatment of the subject matter, in his inimitable and unique style of presentation, are evident in the present book as well. He has sporadically used subtle humour and satire in various essays, which ensure easy and effective communicative equation and rapport between himself and his prospective readers. Here, special mention may be made of the last essay, "A Dog's Musings", which stands out as the only one in first person narrative, giving an autobiographical account of what a dog feels about the world around, particularly its human owners.

I am confident that the present book will substantially add to the existing knowledge of bionomics of behaviourism. The book would be of immense interest to sociologists, psychologists and behavioural scientists, who are constantly seeking the whys of human behaviour.

I wish all success to this endeavour of the author.

K. Ravindran
Wg. Cdr. (Retd.)

Acknowledgements

I am indebted to all beings of this beautiful globe, members of fauna and even flora, who have been my best teachers. Whatever bits of empirical knowledge that I could gather has mainly come about as a by-product of my childlike keen observations of their individualistic as well as collective behaviour at various stages and situations, and so also my interactions with them. The output of these observations and interactions has then been brought to micro-focus and analysed, to the extent of my capability, with proportionate tinge of real and virtual imaginative projections on them.

I profusely thank Shri K. Ravindran for having written Foreword to this book. Shri Ravindran is known to me for the last two decades. He is a voracious reader and a prolific writer. He has written a book, *Happy Living* which has been well-received by one and all. He has travelled widely. I do not think that there is any place on earth which he has not visited. Presently, he is engaged in compiling many a travelogue based on his visits. He is an active member of Retired Officers Forum, a platform which he utilises to champion the cause of senior citizens by appraising the concerned authorities and agencies of the Government. He is an enthusiastic social activist.

My thanks are due to my wife, Dr. Kanakalakshmi Nair, formerly Professor of Chemistry, MS University of Baroda and also my friends who directly or indirectly encouraged me during the course of preparation of this humble creation of mine.

Last, but not least, I would thank Mr. Harjeet Singh, Publishing Coordinator, Atlantic Publishers & Distributors (P) Ltd., New Delhi, for the interest evinced in publishing this book.

Bhanuvikraman Nair

Contents

Introduction

Millennia ago all members of the fauna were wild. Man too was wild with animal instincts. Humans used to live in caves or improvised huts in jungles. In fact, the earth used to be covered with either forests or naked deserts. Rivers used to flow through the forests. For their very existence, both flora and fauna needed water, besides air. Hence forests came up near water resources and the fauna settled down where both water and forests were available. That is why all human civilizations flourished alongside the courses of rivers. None of the members of the fauna could settle down in the deserts, for obvious reasons. All of them had the same kind of living style. They lived mainly on fruits and roots of plants; and some of them on their hunt-proceeds.

Most of the wild members of the fauna like the members of the feline species used to hunt and kill other animals and eat their meat for their livelihood. Most others like the mighty elephants and rhinoceros used to live on grass and other vegetation. In fact, a large majority of the fauna were vegetarians. Initially, *Homo sapiens* too were vegetarians; they used to live on fruits and roots of plants, but subsequently, with some hesitation they too took to hunting small animals and birds and started eating raw meat. Frequently, wild devastating fires used to cause mass destruction of flora, the main source of food for the humans. Small animals and birds too were either killed by these fires or they were forced to move out to safer locations. When they found that there was no food available, they started eating meat of small animals roasted alive in fires. They found that the roasted meat was tastier than raw meat. That marked the end of their eating raw meat. Ultimately they started eating both vegetarian and non-vegetarian food, depending on availability.

Humans were not physically as strong as many other animals in the jungle. Individually, humans had to face many problems which even threatened their survival. It was this survival instinct that had brought them together. Initially, they had felt the need to protect their young ones from other wild animals—a common animal instinct. Living as a family was the first step towards formation of societies. They had instinctively understood that union is strength. Gradually, they started grouping into families. Societies thus had been born. Similarly, all other members of the fauna too started living together as groups or some sort of societies. These processes were all part of grand natural organic evolution gradually taking place in the living world. Most important catalytic element in it had been communication. Their communicative skills developed, and with that their mental horizon became widened. All these developments occurred slowly and gradually, consuming many a millennium.

Human societies are thus formed by natural organic processes. Human beings too wanted them, when they were formed millions of years ago. They had to live together for mutual benefits at that time. It is true of the present times too. The role of the societies has not changed even a bit, despite a long passage of time. Societies are for sharing happiness and sorrow of individual members, notwithstanding other benefits. None is so much bothered about sharing happiness with others unlike in the case of sorrow where one finds it difficult to consume or absorb it. Man likes to share sorrow with other members of the society, because by sharing he would be able to dispel a large portion of it. He would feel relieved.

Here comes the role of the society. It absorbs sorrow. Thus, sorrow gets dissipated and its concentration gets rarefied by sharing, thereby one's burden is reduced qualitatively and quantitatively to a bearable level. This lessens its impact on that one person. The others' empathy is the essence of sorrow-sharing.

The meaning of the term 'environment' includes everything external to an organism; all the surrounding things, conditions and influences affecting the growth and development of living things. Environment could be abiotic or biotic. Abiotic environment includes non-living environmental factors such as soil, water, atmospheric and weather conditions and radiation. All of them have influences on one another as well as on the surrounding communities of living things, individually or collectively. Biotic environment includes food, plants, animals, and their interactions among one another and so also the influences of the various factors of abiotic environment. Abiotic as well as biotic environmental factors have a say in the matter of survival of all living organisms. The term 'environment' may thus be conceived in the widest of senses to include the entire worlds of fauna, flora and the very Nature itself in a holistic manner. 'Bionomics' or 'ecology' is the branch of science dealing with the interrelations and interactions between and among organisms and between the various organisms and their environment. It is thus a composite of the fundamental biological sciences, combined with some aspects of sociology, social psychology and ethology.

In the present treatise, I have ventured to focus mainly on certain individual characteristic traits of human beings that have social dimensions. It deals with ethology—the science of character—together with the genesis of human behaviourism, in certain realms within and without. Human behaviour reflects his internal constitution and chemistry. Efforts at understanding how human minds work are all directed towards observation of how they behave. The working of the mind depends on many factors, intrinsic and extrinsic. Intrinsic factors relate to inheritance and the extrinsic relate to his acquired ones, voluntarily or otherwise, from the dynamics of society and the entire environment. An analysis of the various intrinsic traits of humans would reveal the extent of their influence on their interrelations and transactions with the rest of the elements of the environment. Since humans beings exist in their environment, their interactions with it are a matter of interesting and intriguing study.

In the present study, which is both empirical and experimental, my humble imagination has been fused with the empirical inferences that I could gather. Most of the topics relate to psychological ethos and bionomics of the humans. Human behavioural syndrome is determined by their susceptibility to emotions as well as reasoning. Their emotions are volatile and transient and hence imperceptible and imperfect. I have dealt with certain intrinsic characteristics having overtones on the extrinsic: they have mutual inclusiveness. As a pre-requisite to developing the overall ethos of this subject, I have started with the human mind together with the system, in brief, of its working, and then highlighting many of the 'patented' characteristic ways of 'exercising' his mind. In this, to begin with, I have touched upon his trait of selfishness as well as the consequential behavioural output.

As a part of social living, man shares his expertise and wisdom by indulging in counselling others around him. His communicative interactions with others in his society as well as with the various elements of his environment have been focussed. Man is concerned about the welfare of the society of which he is a part. I have identified and focussed on a certain number of human traits, and then searched for their attributability to animals other than humans. Herein humans would get enough opportunities to deride themselves. Some people consume alcohol and become addicts, and alcoholics. Some resort to ragging their juniors in the organizations on the pretext of inculcating or improving cohesiveness in the working systems. People forget more than what they remember. Forgetfulness could more often be a curse, but sometimes a boon as well. In rare cases, even animals other than humans suffer from this disease.

Most of the traits that human beings manifest are inherited through their genes. They, therefore, can be considered as 'self-sprouted' or automatically germinated elements within their minds. They are capable of growing and developing well with the help of the 'food' stored in their 'seeds', taking an analogy from the flora kingdom. If and when these mini-plants are transplanted on the surface of a fertile earth, they grow very fast by drawing additional ingredients of food, manure, and the needed quantum of water through their roots, so also oxygen and carbon dioxide from the atmosphere. Each plant is an autonomous entity. They have expert cooks to cook their food. They enjoy living. Similarly, all the intrinsic traits of selfishness, jealousy, hypocrisy and the like take their birth in human minds and grow very fast to their full size by drawing additional nutrients from the society and the environment. There is no dearth of nutritive 'manure' in the society. Grateful creatures as they are, these human beings clear their 'debt' by returning the borrowed 'capital' together with interest thereon to the society for recycling. It is a great investment that the society makes! Society is happy that it could increase its net assets through each of such transactions. The process continues perennially. I have tried to analyse some of these human intrinsic traits together with their significant 'contributions', so to say, in the field of bionomics.

Human behaviour could be formal or informal. The formal is official and is governed by written or unwritten codes of conduct or rules prescribed by all governmental, cultural, corporate or social organizations, whereas the informal is unofficial and not governed by any such codes or rules, but well identified and recognized by parties involved. Both are required to be followed customarily and strictly by all concerned for sustenance and perpetuation of the organizational fabrics and edifice. Behaviour by people not conforming to these established systems in either case will be socially condemned. In both the types there is scope for hypocrisy; the one in the formal type is accepted and condoned to a great extent whereas, in the other, case is otherwise. Inter-personal relationships and behaviour between and among individuals are interdependent. It is such relationships that determine behaviour and it is the behaviour that determines relationships. Behaviour emanates from relationships and relationships are sustained from behaviour. Both are mutually inclusive. There are innumerable types of human relationships—parents and offspring, doctors and patients, legal practitioners and their clients, students and teachers, the rulers and the ruled, employers and their employees, humans and their pets, humans and other members of the fauna, humans and members of flora, humans and Nature and her elements and so on.

The present study should be useful to sociologists, psychologists and many others constantly exploring why humans behave the way they behave. It will substantially add to the existing knowledge of bionomics of behaviourism.

Bhanuvikraman Nair

Working of Human Minds: A Perspective

1

Understanding the working of human minds is very daunting task. Human minds offer themselves as one of the most intriguing and obscure subjects. There is no methodology to understanding this phenomenon called 'mind'. We are aware of the fact that there exists Force of Gravitation by experiencing its effects. We cannot see or perceive it by direct means in the ordinary sense. We could, therefore, adopt indirect approaches to know of it. We study the effects of it on everything in the universe and derive a feel or measure of it. Similar is the case with the human mind and its thought processes. Thought processes form the 'cause' and the behaviour their 'effects'. Efforts often oblige one with a vista of ways of human behaviour and offer key to analysing his interpersonal transactions with fellow beings in the society and also his behavioural approaches with the various other elements of the environment. Every mind works in different manner and hence it is very difficult to make out a generalized formula of universal application as to how all minds work. Herein I am making an effort to understand what constitute a mind and whereby obtaining a glimpse of the manner in which it works.

It is the mind that makes a person selfish. His propensities to be curious and creative, to become a hypocrite and a braggart, to get angry, to be loving and loved, to exhibit his sense of humour, and of his sportsmanship, to be sarcastic, deriding and insulting to others, to be mutually admiring and compromising, exploiting, terrorizing, superstitious and sycophantic form part of mind's play. He watches Nature and analyses its relevance to the existence of the fauna and the flora.

He tries to conceive about the existence of some grand supernatural power, much beyond his perception and even imagination, he names that 'God', controlling this perceivable universe of his. He thinks about God (and let us presume that He too thinks about him!). He could vertically divide and perceive the whole of the existence on the earth into two entities, the positives and the negatives. This helps him in understanding the world in a holistic manner, and so also in determining his location *in situ,* in multi-faceted context of the world or universe. He is able to look at himself from a distance and that is the way he would be able to view himself in a disinterested manner. These are some of the ways in which human minds work.

Managing mind is managing thoughts, because it is in this mind that all thoughts are generated. Minds may be conscious, or subconscious. Consciousness is awareness, having the feeling or knowledge of something. In this state all our activities are performed by our five senses, relating to sight, sound, smell, taste and touch, and so also time and space. Any thought or action by the conscious state leaves an indelible impression on the subconscious mind and has influence on our subsequent actions and thoughts. It is the seat of intellect, logic and reasoning, and works only when one is awake. Subconscious mind is the seat of intuition, creativity and emotions, and it works even when one is asleep. It does not relate to the five senses, time and space. The storage capacity of the conscious mind is quite meagre as compared to the subconscious mind which can store huge amount of information which becomes mental software. It is quite fascinating to see as to how Regression Therapists get to emptying-out the latent impressions stored since times immemorial in the subconscious minds of their clients.

Mind is a concept. It has neither corporal nor corporeal existence. According to some wise men, mind is the brain itself, to some others, it is a combination of both, brain and heart, *id est,* reason and emotions, operating in two diametrically opposite directions and planes. Thus it is the combination of non-combinable and uncompromising elements. These elements too should be thought of as conceptual ones. As we know the heart is nothing but a gadget functioning like a mechanical pump, pumping in and out blood for its circulation in the whole physical body, we can not conceive it to have any metaphysical task to perform except perhaps metaphorically.

The heart behaves like a very highly skilled, proficient and confident worker who does not like to get supervised by anyone. This worker is highly sensitive. If someone other than the 'wedded' one installed in the 'headquarters' gives even suggestion to do his job in a slightly different manner, it gets agitated and demonstrates total rejection of the suggestion. Such a worker may cause disruption in the proper functioning, either slows down or steps-up or even stops the pace of the working the whole system of which it is a part. If the heart gets excited or agitated, one knows what would happen. It all means that the heart is an organic one, a 'living pump' a sensitive one, quite different from its mechanical counterpart. The brain activates the various sensory organs on a 'living' body, similar to activation of any electric gadget by supplying to it the needed electric voltage or current, and it is through these sensory organs that the brain detects, discerns or perceives the world by analysing signals received back from them. The brain collects, collates and digests the inputs, and sends out some relevant information to the heart, after storing for itself the lion's share. Depending on the nature of these inputs thus received, the heart reacts by making scintillations; it beats hard or soft, makes its owner weep, laugh, smile or angry, leaving some residual impressions on the mind.

Well, the 'heart' can work in a metaphysical mode too, not merely a metaphorical one! It is this heart element that is conceived and conceptualized here in the context of mind. This serves as proof of existence of a sensitive organic living heart within the physical heart-mechanism. The physical and the metaphysical elements are entirely different; the latter is susceptible to emotional imbalances that the heart is subjected to. They create scintillations; the degree and extent of which depend on the chemistry and physiological system within the individual. Often these scintillations are responses to intrinsic as well as extrinsic stimuli; there being no guarantee that the quantum and quality of responses would be proportionate to those of the stimuli. There may not be any direct or overt linkage between the two. There are various contributory factors for such anomalous responses; some are easily explicable while some others are not.

In the context of minds, we assume that the 'mix' of heart and head elements contains only a small part of the former and a major part of the latter; the former having only a limited role to play in the working of the combination called mind. Theoretically, the combination should work in smooth and balanced way. The combining trend varies in respect of different individuals, and hence there are various types of people and personalities in the world.

Let us try to formulate classes of people on the basis of combining trend of both brain element, the centre of reason, and of the heart element, the centre that generates sentiments. For this purpose we may have seven combinations, (A) to (G) as shown below:

(A)	(B)	(C)	(D)	(E)	(F)	(G)
100/0	80/20	60/40	50/50	40/60	20/80	0/100

Here, the figures under the classifications (A) to (G) show the percentages of brain and heart elements, forming the combination of what is known as 'mind'; the first figure in each of the classes indicating brain element, and second, heart element. We may now imagine as to how these combinations work and produce variations in our personality traits which account for their behaviour. The data furnished are purely based on empiricism and imagination of the author. For the sake of brevity and convenience, and at the same time without causing any jeopardy to the quality of inference, we will club classes (A) and (B) together, similarly (C) and (D), and, (E) and (F), and (G) becoming a unique loner. Here (A) and (B) form the two extremes.

People belonging to (A) and (B) classes are 'very highly' to 'highly' rational, whose actions always will be according to the dictates of their brain, and hearts do not come to play in any manner. They dislike or hate music because music deals with emotions. Emotions are housed in the hearts. Since 'reason' is very strong, it could eject out 'emotions' from the partnership deed. The people accommodated in these classes are matter-of-fact people, who always call a spade a spade. They are usually boring, dry, egoistic, rude, rough, strict, tough, uncompromising, uncouth, unloving, and unmerciful. They are generally good in the subject of Mathematics. They like abstract things. Loving is an out-of-fashion affair for them. They may remain bachelors/ spinsters throughout their lives. If they get married, then it would be purely for materialistic, physical or physiological needs. Any planning is the work of the brain, hence they 'believe' in family planning! I had heard a true story wherein a soldier serving in the Royal Indian Army got promoted to the commissioned rank. After getting promoted, he came back home in his 'battle dress' and confronted his wife, asking, "I say, look here, you are a soldier's wife. I am an officer. How can you live with an officer? You had better quit. Tell me how much compensation you want." This soldier-turned-officer who, in normal parlance, is a 'heart-less man' should be placed in this class.

As far as classes, (C) and (D) are concerned, people in these classes are average, balanced, rational as well as emotional, sensibly loving. They generally have a clear view of the world. They are pleasant and mature people. Their decisions would be balanced and they don't hurt anyone. They are imaginative and they are given to empathy. They don't experience any sort of mental stress, as they have a built-in system to analyse situations and find out solutions for themselves. In short, they don't have many of the strong characteristic traits that we have seen in classes, (A) and (B). Here their heads tell them something, they listen to it; their hearts tell them something else, they listen to it also; and then finally, by taking both into consideration they take their decisions. These are balanced decisions and hence there is no chance of their going wrong. Here, in these classes, teachers, administrators and managers are given accommodation.

They all will have smooth and comfortable lives. They are mediocre in their romantic lives. They have love for music too.

People covered in classes, (E) and (F) obey mainly the dictates of their hearts rather than their head. They are very loving, sometimes platonic. Women are fond of having love-affair with men of such sort, they enjoy the flattery which such men shower on them, but definitely dislike marrying them. They are prone to mental stress and get under influence of fear psychosis, so also, likely to go mad. They are volatile, and with sudden surge of sentiments they go erratic in their behaviour. They will be given to prayers. They are immature, and they create problems for themselves and for others.

The people placed under class, (G) are highly volatile and create problems for themselves as well as for others. Since head does not play any role in their decisions or actions, they are highly erratic. Heart usually cheats a person, in the absence of head, which balances the scintillations of the heart. They get melted in love, and hence there are chances of their committing suicide in case their love fails. For women, such men are repulsive. Such men succumb to anger and go mad. Since they are unable to take or absorb any mental load, they easily 'give in'. Such people are intolerant and immature in their approaches. They must be subjected to psychiatric treatment.

The above classifications mainly pertain to men. In the case of women, they generally belong to classes (B) to (F), and classes (A) and (G) are generally not seen applicable. It does not mean that women are less intelligent nor are they less emotional; only thing is that their intelligence is not abstract and dry like what we observe in men. Women are less volatile in most of the circumstances; they have a suitably built-in emotional setting that, to a great extent, draws a balance between the abstract intelligence and high 'voltage' emotional upsurges. They are able to maintain some sort of equilibrium. Unlike men, they are capable of consuming and absorbing sorrows. Their inexhaustible lachrymal glands come to their rescue in controlling emotional upsurges. Men too have these glands, but they are dysfunctional due to non-utilization over long periods of time. There are many other characteristics that are peculiar to the females like shyness which bring about this equilibrium. Men too are shy, but their shyness is of a different type. Their shyness is restricted to their minds only not to their physique. Hence both men and women manifest different responses to the same stimuli and behave differently.

Women are physically weak and hence their minds are always alert and ever over-prepared, like delicate gazelles in the jungles, to face any impending eventualities and adverse situations. Some of such delicate animals in jungles and forests have large ears that rotate 360 degrees enabling them receive any noise from all directions—a gift from Nature. There exists in women a seeming pessimism clinging to them perennially and when they understand that their apprehensions are not well founded they are apt to switch to optimism without much ado. Even this pessimistic approach is also a defensive mechanism. They can adapt to situations more speedily than men can. It is interesting to watch their performing surveys and scans of rear and side vicinities by looking backwards and sideways especially while walking alone even in broad day-light. It is an involuntary action. The system works like a rotating radar scanner. Indications of a potential danger appear on the scan-screen. All these help them in evaluation of situations and resort to taking preventive or evasive actions. They are capable of telling an aggressor from a non-aggressor spontaneously. They have built-in efficient anticipatory syndrome. They can sense any impending danger. Nature has provided them with larger eyes with gift of wider peripheral view vis-à-vis their male counterparts. They are generally better managers of crises-situations.

It is interesting to watch infants behave. When a stranger with the sole idea of fondling and entertaining approaches an infant, the latter ascertains the genuineness and sincerity or otherwise of the former by intently looking into his eyes. The infant accepts the offer by smiling if the result of probing is positive and rejects it by loud cries if negative. In either case the reaction is spontaneous. They have no developed brain and mind at that stage to analyse the inputs thus gathered. There may be some inputs of information of the 'instant' variety provided to the infant through genetic channels which aids it in its impulsive and intuitive decision-making process. We can only imagine about these things in the absence of concrete and conclusive evidence. There are rare cases wherein human infants are friendly with stray dogs, monkeys and snakes, the latter doing no harm to the former. The infants, as though, are having some sort of spontaneous scanning and resolution techniques inherent in them.

Mind may be considered 'strong' and 'hard' and 'weak' and 'soft'. These classifications pertain to psychological realms. A mind, in fact, is neither of them; it is made to appear so. A mind is considered strong or hard when it can take bold, practical, unbiased, ruthless, unwavering, unpleasant, substantive and hard decisions. It is possible only if the 'head' element in the mind is more prominent than the 'heart' element forming the mind. Conversely, a mind is considered weak and soft when it takes decisions that are weak, substandard and biased. There are many reasons why a mind functions that way. When a mind is under the spell of a series of misfortunes, miseries, stresses, traumae, panic, terrorism and other adverse situations in the life of its 'owner', then the performance of thinking system in it falls short of its usual levels of qualitative out-put. In such situations, the mind contracts debilities and ailments; all these render it weak. Highly knowledgeable and educated people become more philosophical than those less educated and knowledgeable, rendering the former more vulnerable and weak. It sounds paradoxical. Decisions made by such people are usually erratic and substandard. Reason for this is that such people analyse situations thoroughly, focusing on pros and cons of the decisions that they are about to take and get themselves into a mess. The uneducated and the less educated do not possess this 'faculty' and hence they take abrupt and bold decisions. Here is a case in point. If a highly mature and educated bomber pilot goes on an offensive mission into enemy territory, before pressing the 'button' he analyses the ill-effects that his bombing might bring about to innocent people and hence he decides to land back without accomplishing his mission. It is a cowardly act. A pilot who is not very mature and less educated, on the other hand, accomplishes the mission. He has courage to perform because he does not analyse the after-effects of his action unlike in the case of the former. That is the reason why people with high levels of imagination and with philosophical bend are not employed in any fighting arm of the forces. There are many such examples we can come across in many a realm. Most of the problems are self-created by wild and rampant imagination and hallucinations. They have emotional dimensions. They render such people weak-minded and ineffective.

Imagination is another gift as a part of the mind. It can be a fancy, fantasy, conception or notion, related to real or unreal objects or situations. It may have a positive or negative, constructive or destructive or productive or unproductive dimension. It all depends on 'who' is behind it. Imagination is the ability to form mental images; it helps providing meaning to experience and understanding to knowledge; it is a fundamental facility through which people make sense of the world. The power of imagination influences and controls the working of the mind. Whatever intrinsic traits possessed by the mind are being cultivated and cultured by imagination, and the imagination is influenced by the environment. There is mutual inductance between them. The mind generates thoughts. Thoughts generate actions leading to their output; we can call it behaviour. It is very 'rare' that one behaves with oneself; he behaves with others in the society and the total environment. Thus there are inter-relationships among thoughts, imagination and behaviour.

The purpose of the foregoing discussions is to highlight and focus the behavioural patterns exhibited by people while interacting with others in the society as well as environment. The resultant behavioural output depends on the role 'head' and 'heart' combination or the 'mind', as we call it, plays. People behave in different fashions depending on the working set-up in their minds. It is unhealthy to obey either only head or heart. Ideally they should have a '60-40' combination, i.e. Class (C). Even people having a '50-50' combination, placed under Class (D) are also somewhat desirable. People must observe themselves their behavioural outputs *vis-à-vis* the situations they are confronted with. It is a healthy habit to look backwards after each step that one takes forward, in order to analyse and review the impact of his behaviour during the previous step. This should be a constant and continuing drill to be followed. That is to say that one should be 'self-possessed', so that he gets his course properly guided. Life is given to one and it is up to him to enjoy it, and make others too to enjoy it. In the ultimate analysis, it is the 'MIND' that creates pleasure or pain for individuals.

Management of thoughts offers the greatest challenge in this world. The complex and unpredictable nature of the process of thinking makes the job very difficult. Thoughts can't be governed or harnessed; they are like wild horses. They have wings and fly about, wander wantonly in the wild wilderness with speeds surpassing that of even light-rays. Hence manoeuvring or managing the thoughts can be done only by a system built-in, just in the mind itself beside the thoughts-manufacturing unit, just like a pilot controlling his flying machine in the air while in flight. Sometimes it may become necessary to invoke operation of the controlling system on the spot at the same time as the thoughts themselves are originated. They are to be designed to operate concurrently. The services of a 'resident controller' are required. No 'remote controlling' system installed elsewhere will be adequate to manage such instantaneous, spontaneous and ponderous overflow of thoughts. As for example, let us imagine that a person from Delhi had visited the city of London a few years ago and now all of a sudden, sitting at Delhi, he thinks about that city. He could make several repeat-trips to places in that city he had visited at that time, through his imagination, within a fraction of a millisecond.

There is no restriction whatsoever on the quantum or quality of the output of thoughts from one's mind, as long as it does not affect adversely anyone else. The tax-laws of all countries have granted exemption of tax-levies on these abstract products, despite its uncontrolled mass-production. But at the same time Law does not permit any use of these which ultimately results in harm to anyone else. In fact, punishment awarded to anyone for any crime perpetrated is a case in point. It is the *mens rea* that is punished, because of its involvement in various ways at various stages from conceptualization to execution of the crime. Since the punishment is awarded to the mind, it is it that suffers too, even when corporal punishments are awarded. Physical body *per se is* incapable of 'picking-up' any type of feelings. Pain out of such corporal punishments will be felt only with the 'permission' of the brain which is merely one of the departments of the mind. A punishment like 'confinement in a jail' for a term is in effect a punishment for the mind, and not for the body. The body does not 'exist' in the real sense in the absence of its master, the mind.

'Mind is like a monkey', it is said. Monkeys are good creatures; with due apologies and without despising them, we are apt to adopt and employ only their seeming fickle-mindedness for the purpose of comparison. Monkeys, we can observe, jump from one branch to another, one tree to another, incessantly all over the area at will, with full freedom, manifesting some sort of restlessness. In this business, they eat variety of leaves, flowers and fruits that the Nature offers in the jungle. Here we take this jumping behaviour for comparison with the behaviour of human minds. The human minds work like the ways the monkeys do, but the latter's behaviour is sans the complexities of the former's. The manner in which the human minds move about is not even known to their 'owners'.

There are mainly two disturbing elements in our body-system, the tongue and the heart. The tongue executes the commands or wishes of the heart. The tongue wags inside the mouth and vomits out abuses on someone who in turn, as a reaction, replies in terms of blows on the face of the former. The tongue after perpetrating the mischief chooses to hide inside the mouth where it enjoys full protection. It has nothing to lose. Again, it shows eagerness to devour any tasty food with the least consideration either for the capacity of the stomach to digest the same or if that tasty food is actually required for the body for its maintenance or sustenance. It might result in ailments, but the tongue does not bother. Thus both of them behave irresponsibly at times and cause embarrassment to the body-system. The mind plays an infinitesimal role only in these. The behaviour of the tongue could be related to residual impressions of past experiences warehoused in some corner of the mind otherwise heart-component of the mind is the main player.

In order to managing one's mind, he has to plan, organize and control his 'thought processes'. For this, one has to depend upon techniques of self-analysis and introspection. By practising these techniques the person will become mature, peaceful and sagacious, and he is sure to undergo significant changes in his attitude towards others and things. He will be able to understand his strengths and weaknesses, whereby he can make necessary adjustments. He is sure to become more refined and mentally developed. He would get rid of undesirable traits like selfishness, egoism, cynicism, wickedness, meanness, jealousy, hypocrisy and other parochial thoughts. He will thus be good to himself and to the society at large.

All pervading through the Hindu texts and scriptures are the subjects of mind and soul. All through the *Bagavat Gita,* Lord Krishna educates Arjuna on the various aspects of the working of the mind and the need for keeping it purified and focused; only through such a mind would one be able to serve the *Jeevatman* (Soul or Spirit), an infinitesimal part of the eternal divine Glow, conceived as *Paramatman* (God), existing in every living being. The ultimate aim of *Jeevatman* is to re-unite with the *Paramatman,* and for this, the former has to be preserved pure, for, the latter does not accept impurities. Only through *Satwik vichara and satkarma* (noble thoughts and actions) can one preserve its purity. This re-union is conceived as *Moksha* (salvation or emancipation of the soul), the antithesis of re-birth. Great souls like those of Jesus, Shankaracharya, Vivekananda had departed their human bodies well before forty years of their earthly existence, by which time they could finish their "allotted" *Karma* (work or tasks) on the earth and release their souls for the ultimate re-union with God.

Selfishness as a Trait

2

Man is selfish, a fact which he is rarely aware of. Even if he is aware of it he cleverly manages to camouflage and conceal it by hypocritical methods. The genetic route starts from his parenthood and genes. As he grows-up in a society, he learns and acquires more of selfish ways; he confirms for himself that the selfish traits he has inherited are the threshold assets and hence are to be genuinely required to be preserved and fostered, and so also to be supplemented by proficiently acquiring more from the society which is ready to offer any variety of it ex-stock. Thus he gradually becomes a 'perfect' selfish person. An infant is most selfish, probably because his being selfish helps him in his struggle for existence and survival. A child is a natural 'product' and he behaves in an uninhibited and non-hypocritical manner. All of his actions or activities at that stage are directed at fulfilling his personal requirements and desires. He wants to satisfy his basic needs like food and sleep irrespective of the fact that his parents or older brothers or sisters in the family are deprived of these. This is the way the Nature wants him to behave. As he grows-up, he learns how to camouflage and conceal his selfishness in public presence by resorting to hypocrisy. If one asks a child, for example, to part with the only piece of chocolate-bite he is having, he refuses to oblige anyone including the one who gave it to him a while ago. When he grows-up, he would be giving it away telling, "Uncle, have it", willingly or otherwise. The initial behaviour is the natural one whereas the subsequent one, an artificial demeanour, is due to some sort of manipulative conditioning by society.

A selfish person is bound to manifest his selfishness in all his dealings with others in the society and the environment involuntarily. The built-in selfishness casts its shadow on all his actions and inactions. In order to avoid detection he employs his hypocritical skills in various ways and struggles a lot, in vain, in order to conceal this trait while interacting with others. The others too are not different from him. It is very interesting for anyone to watch from a distance in a circumspective and disinterested manner all of their struggles in this direction. Since it is an invisible trait, we can not photograph it in the normal way, but an 'X-ray' footage of spectrum of the entire web of societal selfishness existing can be availed which would provide very interesting revelations. Selfishness as an intrinsic trait has direct linkage with bionomics.

A selfish person does not consider his having this trait as something to be ashamed of, for, it has already become his second nature: he seldom realizes or acknowledges that he is selfish, for, he knows that it is a trait that is something undesirable. This epithet, however, would be carefully preserved for ascribing to others. A beautiful arrangement! Selfishness thus is a part of intrinsic behaviourism that spills over and assumes extrinsic dimensions, having a final say in his bionomical behaviour. He behaves so with others in the society, and society is a part of environment. It is definitely an undesirable personal quality though discernible in everybody, every human being on this earth, which, of course, includes the one who is ascribing it to others. It implies one's own concentration upon oneself for gratification of his needs and wants. Here all the interests converge to one point where his self is seated. All actions are designed to be performed on one's own benefits. It is self-centricism. Selfishness is, therefore, antonym of self-abnegation. 'Self' is the ultimate in many of us. There from sprout some of the enemies of mankind like jealousy, hypocrisy, greed, egoism and wickedness.

Jealousy is one of the worst kinds of diseases, and, they say, 'there is no cure for jealousy and baldness' even though there is no co-relationship between them. Jealousy is the outward showing of some serious disorders or complications in the internal system of persons. One wants to feel superior to others in this materialistic world. This brings about competition, and according to individual perceptions this competition may be rendered healthy or unhealthy. A healthy one turns to an unhealthy one if players are deprived of fulfilment of their primary notional or conscious motives. Competition and frustration cohabit and jealousy is the offspring. Jealousy, expressed or unexpressed gives the envying person some sort of sadistic pleasure. This is the reward awarded to him as a negotiated compensation for the frustration he has faced. Jealousy generally does not occur between strangers due to non-generation of sadistic pleasure for the person feeling jealous. This feeling is never communicated directly to anyone, but its presence in the internal system finds expression in terms of his behaviour towards others. If a person is less jealous by nature, he would be able to conceal it by hypocrisy, but if the quantum is more, it overflows in terms of his behaviour towards others. The quantum and quality and the extent of out-throws of behaviour give enough indication of the 'inside story'. Thus bionomics becomes the measuring meter for this trait.

'Jealous' means, 'suspicious at rivalry, envious, solicitous'. What is the reason that one feels jealous over another person? It is then when one thinks or feels that everything he thinks or feels 'good' should be owned by him only, and none else. If both the individuals are possessing equal amount or equal number of 'good' things, then jealousy is minimal, but not a naught. If one is having a good amount of good things, and another is having fewer amounts, then the former is happy. He would have been happier if the other person is having good things even much less than that also. Here comparison is made mainly only about good and desirable things.

One envies another, if he must, by comparing quantum of misfortunes that has befallen on each other, and if it is less than what has befallen on him. But, if the quantum of misfortune is more on the latter, the former will be feeling happy 'internally', but definitely would be shedding 'crocodile tears' on the other. Similarly, all persons do the same thing in their respective cases. The main criterion for one's feeling happy *vis-à-vis* another is that one should be equal or higher-up in cases of good things; equal or lower in case of bad things. Both jealousy and happiness move in opposite directions, and are keenly watching each other; and each waiting to snatch and occupy the only chair vacated by the other, in their 'musical chair game'. They also envy each other! Self-diffidence is a cause for jealousy. Self-diffident people are more prone to being jealous. It is maximized when two people only are involved; if more people are involved at the same time, it gets diluted. Jealousy frequents on people who obey their hearts more. Reason can eliminate it by proper analysis. Hypocrisy is another indicative symptom of selfishness. People utter untruth or exaggerate or suppress truths in order to gain twin advantage of self-importance in the eyes of others on one side, and at the same time an opportunity to condemn others. Why should anyone lose this opportunity? This is an expression of sheer selfishness.

Selfishness brings up greed. Greed is to amass anything by any means. Here one would think of 'ends' only, and not the 'means' by which he would resort to fulfilment of his greed. One is not satisfied with his legitimate possessions only. He wants more in order to satisfy his imaginative needs as well. So he grabs them from anywhere shamelessly. After that he gets a feeling of satisfaction but this feeling is quite transient. Greed drags him further forward to satisfy more and more of imaginary needs. One is unable to tell genuine needs from the ungenuine ones at that stage. There is no end to it. He never gets 'satisfied'. Greed takes one to wilderness and renders him restless and even mad. This predicament may carry on till he ceases to exist. What a situation this greed has taken him to!

It is the malady of egoism that creates and fosters selfishness. This fact will be amply and vividly understood when we analyse the various manifestations of selfishness, namely, jealousy, hypocrisy, greed, wickedness, untruthfulness and so on. Selfishness is a curse on individuals as well as humanity at large. This is a very serious disease, and can be cured, if one comes to be aware of it and is seriously desirous of getting rid of. He should himself be given to sedulous unbiased self-analysis. This willingness may not come about automatically, but through an accidental turnaround of events in one's life, or due to some advice by some influential person, or due to some serious untoward disaster that one is forced to face. Whatever may be the cause, we can say that one is moving in the correct direction and he may be able to get rid of it partially at least, if not totally. At best, it can be considered as a positive trend. It is easier said than done.

On the moral front, selfishness is considered undesirable since it is not conducive for growth of the existing social set-up. On spiritual front, one will be deprived of self-realization and the eventual emancipation of the soul. Many wise men have taught us that mind has to be free from such parochial inclinations, if self-realization as well as emancipation of soul is what is sought for and to be realized. Society prescribes and allows certain level and degree of selfishness to its members. It is of a notional value and cannot be measured even in terms of milligrams or millimetres. It is all left to the judicious judgement of individual members. A certain level of selfishness is required to create and sustain oneself as individuals, and as a member of a family and of society. For this, one need not become a thief, a thug, a cheat, a wicked, jealous or selfish man. What he has to do is just working hard honestly and go forward, keeping his overall duties and obligations to everyone always in mind.

3

Curiosity and Creativity in Organisms

Curiosity is the quality or state of being inquisitive; the disposition to seek explanation and information. It seeks to answer how and why does a phenomenon occur, exist, vanish and or recur, and even why one does not occur at all. Curiosity denotes mental activity; it is mover of mind. It is 'rust preventive' measure for the mind. It is a harbinger of creations; it serves as a motive force for the mind; provides kinetic energy to the mind; a propellant for inquiry, exploration and investigation. It indicates thirst for knowing and learning of the usual and the unusual phenomena that the world offers. Curiosity is synonymous with inquisitiveness.

Curiosity is any natural inquisitive behaviour evident by observation in many human beings, and is the emotional aspect of living beings that engenders exploration, investigation and learning. It is a state in which you want to learn more about something. If somebody is curious, it reflects a lot about his personality. A curious person is always more well-informed as, because of this curiosity in his nature, he is able to explore more about the world and is able to well-connect the different facts to form a more logical reasoning for objects and situations encountered by him.

The Why's as well as 'Whys of Whys' of some occurrences or non-occurrences of certain situations and phenomena and existence or non-existence of objects form the subject matter of what we call curiosity. Curiosity is one of the most important aspects of life. It is through curiosity, a desire to find out something, that life promotes itself, keeps itself alive, reproduces itself, and gathers resources more effectively. Lack of curiosity can lead to lack of life, a lacklustre predicament, rather than the opposite. All creatures capable of being more than mere mechanical responders to stimulus are curious. That is, they explore their world rather than just respond to its stimuli. The biological pressures to develop curiosity are immense for several reasons, based on the biological drives of self-preservation, reproduction, and greed. In order to survive, animals above the primitive level must understand or be aware of the niche in which they live. In addition, they must discover any changes in that niche to be able to respond to those changes. Since it is his personal survival that the individual is most concerned about, the changes in his immediate vicinity that could affect it are the most important. The most effective way to discover changes is to go looking for them. Thus, a noise in the bushes draws the cat's attention, followed by a slow, stealthy stalk. It might be prey, it might be predator, it might be the automatic lawn sprinkler coming on. This curiosity can lead to a meal, a timely escape, or an inadvertent bath. In any case, it must be investigated. Investigating the unusual creates new pathways in the brain; the more pathways, the more possible responses to stimuli, the more possible responses, greater the likelihood of a proper response to another novel situation. Curiosity strengthens these learned responses.

Curiosity is common to human beings at all ages from infancy to old age, and is easy to observe in many other animal species such as apes, cats, fish, reptiles and insects as well as many others. Many aspects of exploration are shared among all beings, as all known terrestrial beings share similar aspects: limited size and a need to seek out food sources. Though curiosity is an innate capability of many living beings, it cannot be subsumed under category of instinct because it lacks the quality of fixed action pattern; it is rather one of innate basic emotions because it can be expressed in many flexible ways while instinct is always expressed in a fixed way.

Curiosity is emotional intelligence, a mind-game, that causes natural inquisitive behaviour such as exploration, investigation, and learning, evident by observation in human and many animal species. Mind is a concept; a combination of elements of heart and head. Curiosity emanates from this combination called mind or 'emotional intelligence'; both the heart and the head have a role to play. The term, curiosity, can also be used to denote the behaviour itself being caused by the phenomenon of curiosity. As it represents a drive to know new things, it is the fuel of science and all other disciplines of human study. Human being is always of curious nature. Since beginning it is his desire to know all about the things in all the subjects that made him touch the heights of developments.

Strong curiosity is the main motivation of many scientists. In fact, in its development as wonder or admiration; it is generally curiosity that makes a human being want to become an expert in any field of knowledge. The end result of any curiosity is creativity and creation. Though humans are sometimes considered particularly very curious, they sometimes seem to miss the obvious when compared to other animals. What seems to happen is that human curiosity about curiosity itself (i.e. meta-curiosity or meta-interest), combined with the ability to think in an abstract way, lead to mimesis, fantasy and imagination—eventually leading to an especially human way of thinking. This we may call "human reason", which is abstract and self-aware, or conscious. One particular mark about a scientist is that he keeps wondering why things work. We all had been observing that things fall to the ground from above the ground level; they come to their 'resting' place, so to say. There is nothing new in this, for all of us, except for Sir Isaac Newton who wondered, became curious and enquired seriously as to why they fall always to the ground. He came up with one of the greatest discoveries, 'Law of Gravity'. Einstein wondered, became curious and enquired as to why when falling, one could not feel his own weight and he came-up with the 'Theory of Relativity'. Similarly, Pasteur wondered as to why people got sick and he came up with 'Vaccines'. Scientists always find a question and search for the answer. Their curiosity never stops.

Curiosity is an important trait of a genius. One can not find an intellectual who is not a curious person. It is the curious people who take to adventures. Curiosity is very important because it makes mind active instead of passive. The presence of this quality makes a living man 'live' and absence makes a living man 'dead'. Curious people always ask questions and search for answers in their minds. Their minds are always active. Since the mind is like a muscle which becomes stronger through continual exercise; the mental exercise caused by curiosity makes the mind stronger and stronger. Secondly, curiosity makes the mind observant of new ideas. When one is curious about something, his mind expects and anticipates new ideas related to it. When the ideas come they will soon be recognized. Without curiosity, the ideas may pass right in front of him and yet he misses them because the mind is not prepared to recognize them. It would be interesting to think how many great ideas may have been lost due to lack of curiosity. Thirdly, curiosity opens up new worlds and possibilities which are normally not visible. They are hidden behind the surface of normal life, and it takes a curious mind to look beneath the surface and discover these. Fourthly, it brings excitement into life. The life of curious people is far from boring. It is neither dull nor routine. There are always new things that attract their attention; there are always new 'toys' to play with. Instead of being bored, curious people have adventurous lives.

Since being curious is very important for a good active life, we should develop it. Curiousness is dynamism. It is advisable to keep an open mind to learn, unlearn and re-learn. Certain things we know and believe might be wrong, and we should be prepared to accept this possibility and change our mind accordingly. This is very important. We should try not to take things for granted. If we just accept the world as it is without trying to dig deeper, we are sure to lose the 'holy curiosity'. Try to dig deeper beneath the surface of what is around us. A sure way to dig deeper beneath the surface is asking questions: *What* is that? *Why* is it made that way? *When* was it made? *Who* invented it? *Where* does it come from? *How* does it work? *What, why, when, who, where, wherefrom, whereto* and *how* are the best friends of curious people. Another important thing is that we should not declare anything to be boring. Whenever we do that, we are closing one more door of possibilities. Curious people are unlikely to call something as boring; instead, they always see it as a door to an exciting new world. Even if they do not yet have time to explore it, they will leave the door open to be visited another time. We must consider learning as fun. If we see learning as a burden, there is no way we will want to dig deeper into anything. That will just make the burden heavier; but thinking otherwise will make us want to dig deeper. So we should train ourselves to look at life through the glasses of fun and excitement and enjoy the learning process. It is advisable not to spend too much time on just one world; we should take a look at other worlds too. It will introduce us to the possible excitement of the other worlds which may spark our interest to explore them further. One easy way to do this is through reading diverse kinds of books or magazines on new subjects which will enable us to enter into new realms and vistas.

Curiosity can be triggered by observing others. We all need to innovate to stand out from the crowd. The key to innovation is *becoming an observer*. By observing how we and other people do things, we will spot opportunities for improvements. The more we observe, the more opportunities we will find. We can then work to provide solutions for some of the problems. By becoming a good observer, we will recognize the problems confronted by many people and gain a lot from their experiences. There is an ardent need latent in all of us for our growth and effectiveness. For this we have to become observers of what and how others do things. Even though all situations falling upon others might not be identical with those on us, we can always assimilate and emulate their ways of doing things, their actions and reactions, at least in similar cases and situations that we might face. One should not feel shy to observe others, for, shyness is due to self-created inhibitions and mental blocks. Knowing their ways of approach vis-à-vis their problems can provide us inspiration and impetus. Those who venture to reach the bottom of the sea only can see the pearls and take them too. One should treat learning as great fun, enjoyment and excitement and not as boredom or burden. Orienting mind to new vistas will keep the mind away from boredom and exasperation, for that, variety has to be offered. Mind will start craving for more ideas; sign of inculcation of curiousness. "Let noble thoughts come from all sides", the *Rigveda* of the Hindus says so.

"An idle mind is a devil's work-shop"; and logically we can say that an alert and active mind is an angel's. Only a creative mind can become curious and only curiosity can bring forth creativity as well as creations. Both of these are inter-dependent and mutually inclusive. If we have to be creative, we must minimize or eliminate hibernating and idling time. We have to determine never to be idle. Idle time is the time we spend on something other than what we are supposed to do. We know we should do something, but we procrastinate doing it or get distracted by something else. Idling is non-productive. It can be physical or mental. Physical idling influences or induces mental idling, and *vice versa;* the mental one being the worse kind. None should have occasion to complain of the want of time. None ever loses it, anyway. It is wonderful how much can be done if we are always doing. We lack time not because there is not enough time but because we lose too much of it. If we determine never to be idle, we will minimize lost time and make every moment valuable. We often lose or waste time by being idle without realizing it. So if we determine never to be idle, it will help us isolating and identifying idle time; the consciousness of it will bring us back to the state of doing. It is very difficult to eliminate idling, but it can at least be minimized. In order to minimizing, first of all, we must have a clear idea of what are considered 'not idle'. If we set our daily tasks and routines systematically, priority-wise, we will be able to identify and tell the 'idle' from the 'non-idle'. Anything outside the pre-determined schedule is idle time. Reading e-mail when it is time to do something else, engaging in unnecessary conversations, too much thinking before taking action, watching TV more than we should and lying on bed unless we decide to take rest are examples of idleness. We can also see this strategy of minimization from a positive point of view. Instead of seeing it as minimizing idle time, we should see it as maximizing 'doing' time. A half-filled glass is half-empty as well. We should be able to perceive as well as say that the glass is half-full and not half-empty. This is the positive approach. What we should do is to maximize our share of **doing time** each day. It is worth to remember that Time is **inelastic.**

Just as curiosity can **aid in self-preservation**, so can it aid in reproduction. However, in this case, the investigations and learning are aimed at finding a suitable member of the opposite sex and mating. For example, a man sees a woman across the room. Her appearance raises his curiosity, and he decides to make contact with her to satisfy that curiosity. The woman, on the other hand, depending upon how he approaches her, can become curious about him, or not wish to find out about him. Similarly, curiosity can aid greed. Greed is an animal's desire to possess more of whatever it needs to survive and reproduce. Curiosity can help an animal gather more resources. A curious animal, for example, may investigate a sound or a smell that a food source may be making; it will be richly rewarded.

Certainly, curiosity has aided humans in gathering resources. All inventions and discoveries are incidental or accidental. Sometime in the unknown past, some proto-human discovered that when two rocks struck each other, there occurred sparks of fire. Thus they learned how to create fire which they found very useful in many ways. Then they found that one of rocks after such strikes was occasionally left with a sharp edge that was useful in gathering resources. This proto-human was curious whether he could do it deliberately, and found he could, beginning tool-making. About ten thousand years ago, some curious person noticed that if seeds drop on the ground when conditions were a certain way, a few weeks later plants containing the same kind of seeds grew on the same spot. He was curious about how that happened, and tried deliberately sowing the seeds. This was the beginning of the agricultural revolution. Ever since such events, curiosity has led people to find other ways to gather resources. Much of human life is based on, or is the result of curiosity. With our ability to remember the far past and project into the far future, we may be the most curious creatures on earth. We constantly explore our world and everything in it. Often, these explorations are for the purpose of increasing resources, such as the search for minerals, fuels, plants, etc.

However, beyond these resources is the search for information for its own sake. Humans want to know everything like: who we are, who others are, where we came from and when, what's on the other side of the hill, the shape, size, composition, longevity, distance of everything from quarks to the universe. For most animals on earth, curiosity is the search for immediate answers to immediate stimuli. The cat doesn't search for what might appear later or try to discover a mouse's motivations; it tries to find out what made that sound or smells like that now. Since we think in abstractions, we can be curious about not just our immediate vicinity and immediate stimuli, like what the cat does, but can wonder about things that perhaps do not exist. In fact, we will speculate about things that do not exist, and formulate answers on the basis of little or no stimulus or information; we jump to conclusions. Curiosity may kill the cat, but it has made humans the most successful species currently on the earth.

Human beings are bestowed with two important faculties in abundance, imagination and intelligence. They become curious to know more about the earth they live on and many of the objects they observe above it like the sun, other planets, the moons, stars and others. They want to know more and more about the universe of which they form a part. As one moves forward through one's thoughts, duly aided by imagination, from his immediate vicinity to his country, continent, the earth, the solar system and to the universe, his relevance in existence diminishes and as he returns to himself through the same path, he realizes that he is a very insignificant speck with respect to this macrocosm. This is the starting point of his philosophical pursuit. Then he looks inward with the simple questions, "Who am I?", "Am I this body or any part of this body that I have so far been considering as I?", "What is the purpose of this life", "What exactly is the concept of God, of heaven or of hell?." To get answers for these, one has to spend his whole life time in introspecting, mostly in vain. Someone tells the doctor, "My hand or leg is aching. My stomach is upset." None says, "I am aching." This only shows that he is different from his body. Then, where is "I"? This is the beginning of spirituality. This is curiosity; curiosity begetting curiosity. There may be a few occasions when curiosity reaches saturation point; one feels frustrated when one reaches nowhere by pursuing curiosity. But for a curious mind, the road never reaches dead ends; curiosity is a hardened habit.

One can also express curiosity where one has no reasonable expectation of ever having the curiosity satisfied; for example, one can be curious about whether intelligent life exists on other planets, which may or may not be part of a larger philosophical quest to understand one's place in the universe. Some may insist that any human curiosity is an expression of the desire for a larger understanding about the "purpose of it all". But this is an *a priori* claim that seems to conflict with plain facts. Many people, curious to know about things, do not see themselves as questing for wisdom and may even express a modern existential sensibility that denies the existence of any larger purpose in the world. The burden of proof is on those who claim that what is really going on is different from how these people experience their own desires. A challenger might insist that such people still are searching for wisdom about how to live well, but it is far-fetched to think that curiosity about geology or other natural phenomena is connected to insight into the good life.

The philosophers possess two skills and two qualities that enable them to make important contributions in many specific fields, despite their lacking of specialized knowledge or information in them. They compensate their inadequacy of actual specialized knowledge with the skills and qualities they possess. The two skills are, on the one hand, an ability to analyse complex issues logically and conceptually and, on the other, an ability to document their conclusions in clear and persuasive language. And the two qualities that they possess are curiosity, on the one hand, and scepticism vis-à-vis all claims that they haven't examined themselves, on the other.

CURIOSITY AND CREATIVITY VIS-À-VIS WOMEN

Traditional tests have neglected the competencies important to real-world performance, thereby neglecting the competencies of most women. The intelligence testing movement originated in attempts to predict the academic competence of men and so concerned itself with the prediction of school performance. Using familiar situations with prior knowledge and reasoning may be sufficient in school and on intelligence tests, but it is not very effective in solving real world problems or meeting the challenges of everyday life.

Daily we are required to use our creativity to deal with the unexpected and ever changing world. We know very little about the creative processes of everyday life. Most creativity research has focused primarily on men and exceptional or extraordinary creativity, not the kind we use everyday. Consequently, we know very little about the creativity used everyday to navigate life and survive. And we know very little about the creativity of women. A substantial body of evidence indicates that males and females perform at similar levels on tests designed to measure creative potential. IQ tests are based on learning cultivated and valued by men, therefore traditional learning settings are generally not the best learning environments for females.

A balance of feminine and masculine intellectual and personal qualities appears basic to creative endeavours. Our overemphasis or misplaced emphasis on sex roles is a serious block to the development of many talents, especially creative talents. Creativity, by its very nature, requires both sensitivity and independence. In our culture, sensitivity is a feminine virtue while independence is a masculine virtue. Girls are encouraged to speak quietly, avoid mathematics and sciences classes, value neatness over participation and appearance over intelligence. Rarely do women become scientific discoverers, inventors or composers. Very few women have made contributions to theories of creativity. There is little doubt that the attitudes and treatment towards girls and women by society influences their creative development and behaviour. Many areas of experiences are placed-off limits to girls which interferes with their natural gifts. A comparison of highly creative women with less creative women would reveal that the former are more ambitious, confident, having a stronger sense of purpose and need partners and relationships that support creativity.

Let us consider an uneducated, poor, a full-time housewife and mother who was not considered creative by traditional standards, and yet she was a marvellous cook, mother, wife and homemaker. With little money, her home was somehow always beautiful. She was a perfect hostess and the meals she made were exquisite. Her taste in linen, silver, glass and furniture was impeccable. She was original, novel, ingenious, unexpected and inventive in all of these areas. They are all signs of her having a very creative mind. Her sense in preparing a first-rate soup is much superior to that of a painter who makes a second-rate painting or a poet who writes a trash of a poem, but we are apt in refusing to face facts. Ideas of creativity are to be seen in wider perspective.

Creative innovation is facilitated by certain social roles which are not usually available to women. Creativity investigators have concerned themselves only with creative men and masculine areas of interest or with the question of why women are not creative. Male judges of creative contributions tend to favour work similar to their own. Women's contributions do not customarily receive the same recognition. Creativity may be more of a social process, dramatically affected by social environments and institutions, than simply a psychological trait inherent in individuals. Until recently, most publicized and depicted roles for women were those of tradition—housewife, secretary, nurse, telephone operator. Only recently have women begun to reach levels of recognized success in roles previously off-limits to women—professional basketball player, CEO of a company, film-maker and director, commander in military organization, poet, senator, investment broker, doctor, governor, prime minister or president of a country and the like. These success stories are not to be considered as mere exceptions, but as thin end of wedge.

By excluding women from the textbooks we study and the stories we tell, women have been relegated to a status of second class citizens. The perception is that women must not have contributed, for example, to scientific discoveries prevails since they are not included in the textbooks or the stories that are told. Women become invisible and are perceived as being incapable of such contributions. Despite the increasing number of women entering into the public arena, they remain relatively rare in the elite levels of the arts, sciences, letters, finance, politics and ranks of the eminent.

Human experience has traditionally been defined using the patterns of the male experience. Male attributes are valued, studied and articulated while those associated with the feminine tend to be ignored. The analytical, masculine style of most school and work environments generally do not encourage nor foster relational learning thereby denying many girls and women equal opportunities for learning.

Women have grown up with historically and culturally ingrained definitions of womanhood in which women, like children, should be seen and not heard. The majority of voiceless students in typical college classrooms are women. Women in college and university classes speak less and are interrupted more. Many women fear that others will condemn or hurt them if they speak, that others won't listen or understand, that it is better to be "selfless" and give up their voices to keep the peace. By not speaking, women are giving up a powerful instrument and channel that connects the inner and outer worlds. Women typically approach adulthood with the understanding that the care and empowerment of others is central to their life's work. Tradition teaches women that getting something for herself is selfish and will deprive others since her role is that of caretaker and nurturer who sacrifices her needs for those of her family and others. In everyday and professional life, women often feel unheard or discouraged from pursuing unfeminine work or roles.

For centuries, women have been considered incapable of achieving creative success. Women's creative products and achievements have been underrated or ignored in history. Women have historically been encouraged to marry and raise families exclusively. Only with the help of mentors, women have been encouraged to pursue creative achievements or to think of themselves first. As a consequence, we know very little about the creativity of women and only of the creative achievements of a very few courageous women.

It is observed that men are more creative than women. Men outnumber in the fields of art, music, engineering and science and many others. It is probably because the human societies have been 'man-made' and 'man-dominated'. Women have not been getting enough opportunities in a man-dominated system to express themselves in these fields, and that is why we come across only a few artists, artisans, musicians, engineers, sculptors, literary authors, scientists, CEOs, politicians and heads of states among women. Their physical as well as physiological structure and their role in society are mainly responsible for this predicament. Women are intelligent, some of them even more imaginative than their male counterparts, but the society is not able to utilize and exploit their intelligence and imagination optimally. Moreover, their priorities in life and the *raison d'etre* too are different *vis-à-vis* men. Hitherto women have been playing her role in home management and bear and rear children only, and men looking after outdoor duties. There have not been adequate opportunities for developing the 'accepted brand' of curiosity and creativity in these realms. This trend is undergoing changes, but the evolution is very slow due to inherent factors. One thing is sure, if any faculty is not put to use for a long period of time, that faculty gets 'rusted', redundant and dysfunctional, and this is what has happened with women. Gradually their faculty of curiosity and creativity has been maimed and sidelined.

Consequently, there continues to be an unequal ratio of successful women to men in creative fields. This can easily be seen in the large numbers of highly successful, recognized creative men in traditionally feminine pursuits, such as fashion design, hair styling, art, interior design, cooking and the likes. The reverse is not true. There are very few successful, recognized creative women in traditionally masculine pursuits, such as politics, law, medicine, business, and the like.

Women have been cultured to stay in the background and follow the male lead. Women tend to attribute their success to luck while men attribute their successes to ability. The longstanding tradition of excluding women from public life has meant that women's experiences have been largely overlooked in research and theories of talent development. Educational emphasis must be placed on nurturing the creativity of girls and women. Creativity is not a gender specific ability, but its recognition, acknowledgement and development are.

CURIOSITY AND CREATIVITY VIS-À-VIS CHILDREN

Why is the sky blue? Where do babies come from? What makes dogs bark? and thousands of such questions are asked by children. We need not tell anyone that kids are curious! Curiosity fuels the imagination and leads to creativity and confidence and sometimes diffidence. We have only to help them develop this natural instinct.

Children, before they begin their traditional learning experiences, they are expert learners who use all of their senses and capabilities to learn. They learn by experiencing, seeing and comparing. All of them begin life as experiential and relational learners. It seems logical then to believe that education must validate these processes of learning in order to meet the needs of all learners, not just those who do well on pre-determined standards. Children are experts in creative ways of learning and self-expression. They have considerable experiences in questioning, inquiring, searching, manipulating, experimenting, creating, exploring and playing. However, as children enter school, many restrictions are placed on their manipulativeness and curiosity. Schools target the cognitive and intellectual areas for development, with the areas of intuition, affect and self-expression being left to develop on their own. As a consequence, many children do not learn to express themselves or their creativity and do not learn to deal with personal difficulties in a healthy manner.

One of the most consistent findings in creativity research with children is that discontinuities in creative development often result in loss of interest in learning, increased behavioral problems and increased emotional disturbances. These periods are at times so extremely stressful that an individual's creativity is inhibited, reduced or unnecessarily lost as the child ages. As a child ages into adulthood there are more obstacles to the development of her/his creativity and self-expressiveness. These obstacles include pressure to conform, ridicule of unusual ideas, the drive for success and rewards based on other's demands and standards, and the intolerance of a playful attitude. It is far too common for people to grow up and lose touch with their creativity and inner potentials.

Learning by doing should not be left to mere chance, but should be part of the guidance we give to learners of all ages. We need to offer opportunities for learners to explore and examine core subjects creatively. Creative thinking and learning involve such abilities as evaluation, redefinition, analysis, divergent production and problem solving abilities. Creative learning is a natural, healthy human process that occurs when people become curious or excited about understanding or knowing more.

Children are bestowed with abundant capacity of curiosity. They are highly curious about the world and its multifarious manifestations. Curiosity is defined in the dictionary as 'an eager desire to know', and so is certainly a useful disposition to encourage it in young children. Curious children actively explore the world around them. They ask questions about what they see and make predictions about why things happen in a particular way. They test out their theories, interpret the results of these investigations and share their discoveries with others. This is exactly the same scientific process that a scientist engages in when carrying out experimental work. Curiosity in young children gets displayed in many different ways, not just through the questions they articulate. Young children, particularly those who are not yet proficient in language, demonstrate their curiosity through their facial expressions, body language, stance and posture. They also demonstrate their interest and involvement through the length of time they spend investigating a particular object or activity. In younger children curiosity tends to be impulsive as their interest is taken by a succession of new experiences, objects or situations.

"Curiosity in children is nothing but an appetite for knowledge. The great reason why children abandon themselves wholly to silly pursuits and trifle away their time insipidly is because they find their curiosity blocked and their inquiries neglected" (John Locke). It is the duty of teachers and elders to help them explore ways to use this faculty in positive ways that will render them self-motivated independent learners. For this, learning to communicate is very important. Young children have a naturally investigative style of learning and an equally natural urge to communicate their discoveries. By communicating their ideas, children are able to demonstrate their curiosity and express their creativity. The science and technology aspects of knowledge and understanding of the world as they perceive provide an ideal opportunity to help them develop and express their own ideas about how their own world works, and make choices for investigations. This is why teaching science should not be about giving children information, but giving them questions. Curiosity in children should be fostered, for, it will remove the ignorance they were born with; which, without this busy inquisitiveness, will make them dull. A great mistake of teaching science is that teachers do not let the students ask questions. It is all about awakening the curiosity of the students. That is what they need. Curiosity leads to inquest and investigation which lead to creativity and further in turn to innovation, inventions and discoveries. As a reverse process, creativity creates curiosity.

As children grow older, curiosity tends to become more focused; they pay more attention to details and begin to look for explanations for the things they see and experience. Posing questions is one of the very common ways in which we begin discussions with children, helping to establish what they already know about a particular subject. Open-ended questions which invite a comment or response from the listener are the most useful sorts of questions to be used in this context. Open-ended questions don't have a right or a wrong answer and therefore invite responses which can lead to further discussion and investigation. Open-ended questions often begin with, 'How do you think...?' or 'What might happen if...?' Encourage children to give explanations when they put forward an idea or a theory. By continuously asking, 'Why do you think...?', we will help them to make connections in their learning and develop their thinking skills. As children's enthusiasm for investigation and exploration develops they often become absorbed and concentrate for long periods of time. In addition they may want to revisit an experience several times while they extend and consolidate their learning. Young children exploring the world around them will experience the joy of discovering things for the first time. Children often invest a great deal of emotion in the thinking behind the ideas and theories they come up with. Their observations can be very profound at times and demonstrate deep thinking of a spiritual nature. Respecting and valuing this awe and wonder and helping children to communicate it will encourage them to be even more curious and creative.

"It is, in fact, nothing short of a miracle that the modern methods of instruction have not entirely strangled the holy curiosity of inquiry." said Albert Einstein.

CREATIVITY AND CREATIVE THINKING

Creativity is the ability to think; generation of new ideas seeking to serve solving of problems. All human beings are born with this ability, but all are not bestowed with it in uniform degrees and measures. There is no equitable distribution of this faculty among all human beings. It gets developed as one utilizes it; by constant practice it will become one's second nature. It gets diminished or totally eliminated in due course if not cultivated and cultured. If a person keeps working in routine stereotyped fashion, he does not have to utilize whatever creativity he has brought with him as inheritance. He can safely instate this faculty in the dormant mode. In such cases, he loses his initiative which is an integral ingredient of creativity. Society prescribes certain norms governing the behaviour of its members. Society insists on compliance of such norms by a system of rewards and punishments. Similar is the case with one's own familial norms and stipulations that are imposed on individuals. Both these institutions thus try to indoctrinate their members; there is no escape from this situation. Any sorts of indoctrination will harm or kill creative thinking. There is an absolute need for intellectual independence for sharpening creative thinking. Since none can question or go against these built-in culture, but by proper self-training one can ensure that he does not lose this faculty. Versatility in working system and the challenges offered by environment are two very important factors that encourage people to retain, cultivate, culture and foster it.

Creative thinking is much more than using our imaginations to invent lots of new ideas. Creative thinking is a lifestyle, a personality trait, a way of looking at the world, a way of interacting with others and a way of living and growing. Living creatively means developing our talents, tapping our unused potentials and becoming what we are capable of becoming through self-discovery and self-discipline. Anytime we are faced with a problem or dilemma with no learned or practised solution, some creativity is required. Creativity is a vital ingredient in meeting the challenges of a continuous life cycle, a cycle in which growth and change are the norm from conception throughout life. A life filled with growth and change requires a conscious effort to think and practise creatively. To develop creativeness, the mind needs to be exercised as well as filled with materials out of which ideas can be formed and to form ideas, ideal thing is first hand experience. Creativity is the ability to see a situation in many ways and continue to question until satisfaction is reached. Satisfaction is a relative term. The creative process can involve tiny creative leaps or giant breakthroughs in thinking. Both require that an individual go beyond where he has gone before, embracing the unknown, the mysterious, the change, the puzzling, without fear. Creativity is well spelt with courage and risk-taking; the risk may be small or big. Creative potential is the ability to respond constructively and in non-habitual ways to change and stress.

If we focus on creativity as such, we will be able to discern many ingredients or constituent elements within. Creative thinking seeks to solve a problem on hand. Many alternative options are evolved, in some cases spontaneously and in some others slowly, depending upon the degree, quantum and quality of the faculty of creativity available with different individuals. On many a situation, it is surprising to see, there exist very simple solutions to complex problems, rejecting the general inkling that there shall be complex solutions to complex problems, and in this, people waste their creative energy by allowing the mind to run amuck, resulting in rendering the creative machinery over-worked and fatigued. If solutions are available ex-stock, there is no need of creativity; these pre-fabricated solutions are likely to be stale, without freshness and originality. It is like matching items of problems from one list with corresponding solutions appearing in the other list. Spontaneous flexibility and adaptability are considered integrated parts of a good creative thinking.

Hindrances to Creative Thinking

Willingness to take things for granted, accepting things as they are, hesitation to uncover hidden or overlooked opportunities, living with problems, satisfaction over the existing setups, refusal to accept latest innovative developments in technologies are all hindrances to creative thinking resulting from lack of applied curiosity.

There are some factors inhibiting or impeding the process of creative thinking. They relate mainly to cultural and environmental ethos. They are enumerated below:

(a) Social pressures to conform to rules, regulations, norms, stipulations of set patterns of behaviour in organizations, imposition of punishments or penalties on deviation and the like.

(b) Control-syndrome existing in organizations which prevents people from independent thinking and action kills creativity. All detailed specifications are laid down for strict compliance by all. There is no scope whatever for individuals to take any initiative and they 'switch off' whatever thinking capability they have. "Whatever I am told to do, I will do that only, right or wrong. I am the last man to opt for a self-inflicted injury," any one would say. They develop mental blocks. Authoritarian style of leadership demands such behaviour.

(c) Anxiety and fear too have a negative impact.

All these anomalies can be addressed and remedial action can be taken by those who get aware of their mental blocks. They can retrieve themselves by introspection and self-training. Even counselling is an additional method.

Fear causes either inactivity or curiousness, depending upon the extent of its content in a given stimulus. In some cases, fear takes over brain and stops its functioning; the victim gets unnerved and would not know what to do. If the fear-content in a particular stimulus is minimal, the victim is likely to recover and regain his thinking ability and might become curious and creative. Courage, on the other hand, makes a person active and curious. Anxiety is uneasiness with fear and desire regarding something doubtful. This uneasiness drives one to become curious to understand the nature and cause of fear with a view to seeking remedies for it. Anxiety is static, while curiosity is kinetic or dynamic. Anxiety *per se* is not problem-solving, but the discomfort it serves out is good enough to excite curiosity. The discomfort becomes a motivator for curiosity; curiosity does the job of probing; probing ends up with suggestions with regard to possible ways and means of solving a particular problem. Thus a scheme is followed; anxiety to curiosity, curiosity to creativity and their reverse order.

Curiosity is a virtue. It is an urge or desire to investigate and learn more about something. All members of the fauna exhibit curiosity. Human beings exercise selectivity and judgement in their choice of objects and situations for investigation and so also the type, amount, occasions, degree, extent and quality of investigation to be adopted; they concentrate on the rationale of investigation. Non-human animals do not exhibit this discretionary approach in response to the stimulus of curiosity. A striking difference is that a human is capable of being curious about his own self—self-reflectiveness and introspectiveness.

Curiosity is a great virtue, not always. It is to be employed in a judiciously way only. One should avoid extending it to encroach and eavesdrop into the private domain of others to extract confidential information pertaining to them in order to exploit or blackmail them or to reap sadistic pleasure. It is unethical and illegal. It invites discomfort besides embarrassments to such curious people as well as to those others. It is a trouble-shooting enterprise. We may have a duty to be curious, but there may also be occasions when we have a duty not to be curious. This is not merely to make the claim, more easily addressed by standard theories of moral obligation that sometimes we should not act on our curiosity. Acting on curiosity may harm other people or violate their rights to privacy. For example, one might be curious about exactly what Mr "X" and Ms "Y" did and how they felt when they engaged in "inappropriate intimate contact", but it would not be a proper or virtuous exercise of curiosity to be intensely curious or to dwell for long periods of time on this matter. The same will be true for many items featured in the tabloids. The popular expressions, "idle curiosity" and "morbid curiosity," reflect a reasonable judgement that curiosity can be a vice when it is exercised inappropriately.

"One who is too wise an observer of the business of others, like one who is too curious in observing the labour of bees, will often be stung for his curiosity." said Alexander Pope.

Curiosity can be a vice when it has inappropriate objects, and there are at least two ways that an object can be inappropriate, which roughly correlate with the notions of idle and morbid curiosity. An object might be unfit for curiosity because it is, in usual circumstances, trivial and uninteresting, like trying to ascertain the number of cement blocks on a sidewalk. Just as we regard some objects as more worthy of aesthetic appreciation than others, we reasonably consider some things more worthy of our interest and investigation than others. One may wonder how his neighbour's wife performs in bed; how human beings respond to experiments harmful to their bodies, or even to suffering; how the development of a fertilized egg could be stimulated to produce a monster rather than a normal human being; how to preserve a human being alive forever. One may wonder, but it would be wrong to seek to know, because he cannot possess such knowledge while willing what is good. To love the good and to possess what we love are, in this life, not always compatible. Curiosity of one should not be at the cost of creating animosity, ill-feeling, offence, anger, or vexation to others. One should not cause wounding of pride of someone. Curiosity may lead one to actions that promote human welfare, but the virtue of curiosity itself does not depend on its doing so. Curiosity often has other moral agents as its object, and when we express curiosity about other people, we often embarrass them in some way. "Be less curious about people and more curious about ideas" (Marie Curie).

Some people get obsessed with curiosity. A classic example of this trait is depicted in the famous cinema, *Rear Window* by Alfred Hitchcock, through Jeff, a professional photographer, obsessed with his profession. Despite his being confined to a wheelchair in his room for a period of six weeks due to a fracture on his leg occurred while attempting to take a picture of an accident involving a race car, he started watching his neighbours from the courtyard, through the rear window of his apartment, to relieve himself of boredom. Even the presence of his girl friend/secretary and the physiotherapist nurse could not deter him from doing so. One night he notices some strange movements of a person in the adjoining apartment. He keeps following the shady movements and alerts his secretary and physiotherapist nurse. Together, they keep a constant watch and witness the man murdering his ailing wife and trying to dispose her body. Though there were two other eyewitnesses, his secretary and the physiotherapist, he developed apprehension that he could not have helped the police in solving this murder mystery, because of the embarrassment he would have to face. But he does not bother; he undeterred goes ahead, taking help from his two companions, and ultimately succeeds in apprehending the murderer and hands him over to the police. As a classic twist, typical of Hitchcock, the end of the movie shows the hero's other leg also in plaster due to his adventure in his efforts trying to apprehend the murderer.

Spying

Spying is an art, skill and an adventure. It is motivated by curiosity. A spy is a secret agent employed to watch others and to collect information. Spying is what a spy does. It is the curiosity to know in detail of information that is maintained as secrets by someone else is the motive for spying. Most of such information is very useful for the person seeking them. The term 'spying' is generally associated with the military. Spying is a clandestine operation. "Everything is fair in love and war," and hence if any military organizations are engaging themselves in spying on their enemies, it is considered a justifiable demeanour. In this, there are no ethical, moral or legal grounds to be considered. The ends are more important than the means. History is witness to existence of such practices even in holy wars. Spying is being resorted to by corporate bodies, social groups and even by individuals. Corporate bodies engage themselves in spying to collect vital information on various strategies adopted by their competitors with a view to scuttle their efforts or to imitate them. In such cases, there are some moral or ethical restraints stipulated by responsible governments in order to curb or eliminate unhealthy trends and practices in the business world. It is a social requirement too. Some husbands suspecting fidelity of their wives resort to hiring the services of private professional secret service agents in order to spy and confirm or otherwise the basis of their suspicion. Even some wives too do the same in the case of their husbands; parents in case of their children. If the investigation reports of these agents do not confirm their suspicion, then their suspicion will be directed towards these agents. Unfounded suspicion is the symptom of some psychological disorder

There are some words like scooping, snooping, nosing, eavesdropping all of which are used in unethical, immoral or illegal contexts. These are, however, examples of the way in which curiosity works on people in the negative way. Of late, people use sophisticated electronic gadgets to do live audio-video recordings of people and situations wherein some offences are committed by some clever mischievous elements in our society. Such exposures are very useful for investigation by authorities. These are known as 'sting operations'. The morality or otherwise of such operations is debatable. Here too, the end is more important than means.

Eavesdropping

Eavesdropping is like spying, triggered by curiosity. This too is a clandestine operation to acquiring information about somebody, something or some situations for purposes of legal or illegal utilization, entertainment or sadistic pleasure. The word, 'eavesdrop' literally means 'drop of water dripping from the eaves of a house.' It is interesting listening in foil of stark silence all around to the musical notes that come out from the roof of one's own house when it rains. For some, it may be pleasant music while for some others displeasure, nuisance or cause of irritation. Drops and droplets of water keep dripping from the eaves even long after the rains stops. If it rains 'cats and dogs', then one can hear very vividly the rhythmic sound produced, as though, by heavy musical instruments like drums, among many a light one, especially, if the recipient roof has tin-top. It is one of the many types of Nature's orchestra made for the entertainment of all her animate objects. All imaginative people believe that even inanimate objects have most of the senses that the animate objects possess, and they too create music, the quantum of acoustic frequencies of which does not fall within the audible range of human beings. Let us at least imagine that such music is audible to inanimate objects or beings, especially in the absence of proof otherwise; granting them the 'benefit of doubt'. It is more interesting to listen to dripping noise of water-drops from the eaves of the roof of the house. The volume contained in each drop may be of the tune of half of a cubic centimetre, which is equal to nearly five hundred milligrams by weight. The falling is intermittent, with a gap of specific time-unit between two droppings. This gap as well as the weight will be good enough to make a perceivable impact of sound. It provides special effect of melody, because it is audible only when the rain stops, and when the eventual silence is allowed to prevail. It is most melodious in the dead of nights!

Anybody is free to imagine, seek and perceive the sense of enjoyment of this sound of music associated with or inherent in these droppings. It is left entirely to the choice of the listener. Aestheticism is one that can not be imposed on or inculcated in anyone; it can be fostered only if one has inherited it. The same kinds of droppings are used in mental conditioning and brainwashing or torturing of criminals and prisoners of war; it is not meant to entertain them anyway, obviously.

Each 'drop' figuratively represents in eavesdropping a unit of measurement of secret information. Each of them has a story to tell. All these stories are perceived as secrets by the listener because they are said in conditions seem ideally simulated for sharing secrets. Anyone enjoys secrets only if they are delivered to him in a manner befitting to secret-sharing system, that too in the solitude at nights. Secrets usually are shot into the ear at close range with clever acoustic modulations. Then alone their value as secrets is maintained sacred. A secret if it is loudly stated is likely to loose its strength and will not be as effective as the one stated with proper modulations incorporated in its delivery system.

'Eaves'-dropping' means figuratively, 'to stand under the eaves or near the windows of a house to listen for secrets'. Hence an eaves'-dropper is 'one who tries to overhear private conversations', and 'eaves'-dropping' denotes acts done by an eaves'-dropper. It is like crumbs or morsels of articles of food which crumb-crazy cockroaches, ants, rats and other insects and small animals eagerly await their 'fall' from dining-table tops. They stealthily move around the possible drop-sites, praying to God for crumb-rains. This is exactly the same case with eaves-droppers. These 'droppings' take place within or without one's own house. This business is flourishing very well these days, especially in urban areas where houses are 'flats' placed one over the other and these flat-columns are adjacent to each other. The occupiers of middle flats do not actually get 'enough quantity of drops' to carry on with this business, because of thick concrete slabs as floor-dividers and so also their thick walls. The business, however, is to carry on. They lend their ears to the conversations made by those on the upper floors, and extract the needed tidings. They analyse these tidings according to their perceptions that are usually based on jealousy, hatred, selfishness, hypocrisy, prejudices and other 'good' inherent qualities dearly fostered by them or imbibed from society. They then like to share the results of their analysis with like-minded friends in and around them. If they are not able to get hold of someone in the immediate neighbourhood, they do not mind seeking them elsewhere, even if they have to spend some money by way of expense on petrol for their vehicles. Luckily for them, there will be no dearth of such people in the society. It has the semblance of 'grapevine'. If they are unable to get desired data in sufficient quantum from those living in the flats above, they stretch their heads and plant their ears at the residences of those residing in the next column of flats. In some cases they take the help of powerful binoculars and audio-visual gadgets. Any effort in this direction will not be a waste; for, it will always be providing adequate rewards.

The information that the eavesdroppers clandestinely gather offers great sadistic satisfaction to them, especially if it pertains to some top secrets about their 'victims'. It is their hard-earned asset acquired painstakingly. Their satisfaction can be compared to that of a clever thief who manages to steal some precious possessions of others. Getting hold of such secrets of others is a very thrilling experience. They may exclaim "Eureka", like Archimedes did when he discovered the great principle, which was later named after him. It is also similar to the work of secret service agents who collect secrets and other vital information pertaining to their enemies by resorting to several methods. Secretly gaining access to confidential communications like listening to wireless or radio-telephony transmission or conversations taking place 'on the other side', or using laser interferometers to reconstitute conversations by terrorists 'outfits' is also eavesdropping. All the parties are very active and competitive in this respect; and all-out efforts are being undertaken by both national intelligent agencies and by the enemies, terrorists and other anti-national outfits. Ethicality or otherwise of this method is debatable; and here in this case, however, ends are more important than means. In eavesdropping too, 'agents' are sometimes employed. These agents are usually clever, mischievous and unsuspecting minors in the family who are compensated by small bribes or favours which they could have never received but for doing such clandestine operations. Such agents might resort, at times as the last resort, to blackmailing those who had employed them for such tasks, whenever they choose to avail such an option. Initially such agents get hold of a bit of information artificially or deliberately from the unsuspecting 'victims', they resort to blackmailing them in order to extract more information.

There is a positive side of eavesdropping. Some people who are inquisitive of knowing good things in life will be benefited by eavesdropping. They like to imitate the living style of the neighbours who are rich and considered modern and aristocratic, in order to get social recognition for them which is a psychological requirement. They have aspirations to improve the 'quality' of their lives. It may be thought of as an expression of their survival instincts. Others may name such initiatives as hypocrisy. It does not matter; so long as their efforts are not considered designed for malevolence or malice to anyone.

In olden days, people, especially women folk, were illiterate and not exposed to information on current affairs and development taking place in the society. The women folk would not come to the fore nor they were allowed to take any initiative in meeting 'others' in the society. The scarcity, non-availability or deprivation of information would make them restless and they become more inquisitive. This system is still being followed even in the present time by some crude social groups. Their shyness too is one of the reasons for this isolation and seclusion. But they used to get all information directly from the male members in the family like fathers, uncles, brothers, husbands or even grown-up male children, and indirectly through over-hearing or listening to conversations or discussions from their 'hide-outs' whenever visitors came. They used to make eavesdropping as the main source of information. Such information is very vital; no matter how it is collected. The information collected relates to various subjects, and thus they become more knowledgeable and hence confident of themselves. Some of them become efficient managers and administrators of household affairs. It is a matter of great surprise when one sees that these women used to hold more information with them than their male counterparts, because when opportunities are rare, one is inclined to make most of them efficiently. The use of their intelligence was required to be optimally stretched. They did. It is common sense to think that if anyone intelligent does anything in repetitive manner, he becomes expert in that field; and they thus have become experts in this field of eavesdropping. It does not mean that only women folk are in this business, some of the men folk, especially who are self-diffident and shy, too are proficient in this game of 'hide and seek'. There exist, however, inherent chances of the information thus collected could become corrupt, discrepant and distorted according to the levels of intelligence, education, experience and cognition, and so also characteristics of personality, culture and perceptibility of the eavesdropper.

> The important thing is not to stop questioning. Curiosity has its own reason for existing. One cannot help but be in awe when he contemplates the mysteries of eternity, of life, of the marvelous structure of reality.
>
> —Albert Einstein

> I keep six honest serving-men. They taught me all I knew. Their names are What and Why and When and How and Where and Who.
>
> —Rudyard Kipling

> The first and simplest emotion which we discover in the human mind is curiosity.
>
> —E. Burke

> The cure for boredom is curiosity. There is no cure for curiosity.
>
> —D. Parker

4 Propensities of Hypocrisy and Braggartism

> Man is the only animal that can remain on friendly terms with the victims he intends to eat until he eats them. —Samuel Butler

> Three things can not be long hidden: the sun, the moon and the truth. —The Buddha

> Hypocrisy can afford to be magnificent in its promises, for never intending to go beyond promise, it costs nothing. —Edmund Burke

A hypocrite is a person who pretends to have virtues, moral or religious beliefs and principles that he or she does not actually possess. His actions belie stated beliefs. He is a person who feigns some desirable or publicly approved attitude, but whose private life, opinions, or statements belie his or her performance in public. The degree of hypocrisy one possesses is equal to the absolute value of the difference between two variables, his beliefs and actions. It is this 'gap' that accounts for hypocrisy. Of course, it is not possible to measure these variables, but this formula does represent the relationship of these. Hypocrisy is the art of concealment of true character or belief. It is acting, feigning to be better than one is, or to be what one is not. A hypocrite is one who practices hypocrisy. It is one of the most commonly observed characteristics of human behaviour, the foundation of which is untruth and falsehood. False sense of pride and prejudices form the rudiments of hypocrisy. This is a specialized field earmarked only for human beings; entry of other animals in this domain is forbidden.

The practice of hypocrisy is rampant in urban society where people are 'modern' and 'educated'. The meaning of the word, 'modernity' is to be conceived in terms of ideas and convictions that a particular person or generation holds *vis-à-vis* their relevance to the present and future tenses, and not merely the changing living styles. It is a matter concerning mental outlook, not merely the looks, pretensions and fashions—the intrinsic and not the extrinsic. Vysa, Patanjali or Aryabhatta and Socrates or Plato of the ancient period are still modern, because their thoughts are relevantly alive even today and will ever remain so in the future. Similarly, our 'modern education' does not fall within the gamut of what Bhartruhari, a great scholar-sage of ancient India, had conceived and spoken of 'education'. According to him, we can call a person 'educated' only if he tells always the truth, and if he is the owner of a developed mind which is filled with lofty ideas and ideals. Only such an educated person would be entitled to be liberated from all sins. In that way, one can not consider most of the so-called 'modern educated' neither 'modern' nor 'educated' because majority of them do not fulfil the requirements of these criteria. They are rich and affluent. In our materialistic world, the rich are given special status and are respected. Respect is directly proportional to the extent of richness. The rich, because of possession of wealth, ill-or-well-gotten, wield great influence on the society. The less rich envy the more rich, and this gives rise to competition. The less rich or the poor blame or ascribe to God for their 'sad' predicament. There is unholy rivalry existing among the rich, they vie each other, and indulge themselves in rat-race in an effort to climb the economic ladder. In most cases this 'ladder' is imaginary or notional. They play the game of sort of 'the snake-and-the ladder'. The less rich too do not lag behind in their rivalry among themselves. Some of the less rich become members of a tribe called, 'neo-rich'; their rivalry now would be with the already rich. The rich develop contempt towards the less rich and the neo-rich and deride them. All these present a peculiar but interesting scenario. This is the realm of the wicked and the self-centered. There exists unhealthy and undesirable competition among all these people, motivated by jealousy. It has the semblance of a "Class War". During this process, whatever bit of the good and the noble elements present in their minds as 'original natives', brought with them on their birth, feel embarrassed, dejected and uncomfortable, and would electout to discontinue staying there, leaving behind only the bad and ignoble ones. In all these struggles of the rich and of the less rich, a major role is assigned to hypocrisy.

One envies another, if he must, by comparing quantum of misfortunes that has befallen on the latter is less than what has befallen on him. But, if the quantum of misfortune is more on the latter, the former will be feeling happy 'internally', but definitely sheds 'crocodile tears' on the other. Similarly, all persons do the same thing in their respective cases. The main criterion for one's feeling happy *vis-à-vis* another is that one should be equal or higher-up in cases of good things; equal or lower in case of bad things. Both jealousy and happiness move in opposite directions, and are keenly watching each other; and each waiting to snatch and occupy the only chair vacated by the other, in their 'musical chair game'. They also envy each other! Competition and frustration co-habit with each other. This combine usually leads to unhealthy and unethical envy, resulting in jealousy. Expressed or unexpressed jealousy provides the envying person with some sort of sadistic pleasure, a reward he earns as compensation for frustration. Jealousy does not occur between strangers. Self-diffidence is a cause for jealousy. Self-diffident people are more prone to being jealous. It is maximized when two people only are involved; if more people are involved at same time, it gets diluted. Jealousy frequents on people who obey their hearts more. Reason can eliminate it by proper analysis.

Hypocrisy is another indicative symptom of selfishness. People utter untruth or exaggerate or suppress truths in order to gain twin advantage of self-importance in the eyes of others on one side, and at the same time an opportunity to condemn others. Why should anyone lose this opportunity? This is an expression of sheer selfishness. Hypocrisy is thus the final finished product from the raw materials in the form of egoism, selfishness, jealousy and greed, and above all, inferiority complex.

Being 'formal' in one's behavioural transactions with others could mean a manifestation of hypocrisy. We usually term such behaviour as 'mere formality'. When someone says, "Please have it, it's all yours", "My pleasure", "Oh, don't bother", "Never-mind", "Thanks for accepting the present that I gave you", and the like, there could be some element of hypocrisy surreptitiously lurking beneath them. Bitter facts are often shrouded by a combination of good gestures, smiling faces and pleasant words. There is always a cause of worry when someone exhibits undue politeness and humility. There is a saying, "When an ox lifts its tail, everyone knows in advance what exactly it is for; when a cow does, none exactly knows what it is for, till her intensions are executed." Behaviour between two strangers is 'formal'; it is as though they are following certain laid down norms. In this case, certain level of hypocrisy is but natural and hence acceptable to both of those involved, unlike in the cases of familiar or friendly people. This sort of behaviour is noticed in the case of two young people of opposite sexes while meeting for the first time or even in the initial stages of their 'proclaimed' love-affair when they "I love you" and "I too love you".

Formal behavioural transactions occur under the influence of conditioning and the consequent copying. This all pertains especially to the domain of the educated, rich and aristocratic urban elites. The word 'diplomacy' is used in many situations. It is employed to help a person or situation. It acts like a sweet coating on a bitter pill. If one tells another that he is a fool, that 'foolish fellow' would resist vehemently and 'prove' that he is really foolish. If, on the other hand, the sayer opts to say, "My dear, please don't act like a fool". Another example could be to say, "Till I had met you, I was thinking that I am the most crooked, wicked and foolish fellow but after meeting you I had to change my opinion about me." The reactions of the latter would be sober and subtle and at times the one at the receiving end accepting those words even with a senile chuckle; he could even search, isolate and assimilate, for his own sake, the sayer's kind-hearted demeanour, sense of humour, love, care and considerations expressed in those words. The difference is brought about by diplomacy—a harmless but clever or skilful manipulation or manoeuvring. It could well seem at times to be a pre-designed mischievous perpetration of a fraud in terms of *suppressio veri* or *suggestio falsi.* If there is no malaise, it is a constructive and positive endeavour on the part of the diplomat. Process of conducting activities with another with tact is in order to bring about a good relationship. An executive who is diplomatic in dealings with clients, suppliers, and employees is careful to say the right things at the right time to avoid illwill, misunderstandings and confusion.

Pseudo-aristocracy is another nomenclature for hypocrisy. In urban settings, these 'pseudos' shamelessly boast of their family traditions openly in presence of other like-minded ones. There are different types of criteria being adopted for assessing and classifying aristocracy. Application of these yardsticks varies according to the societal characteristics such as general level of education, occupation, culture, race, geographical location and so on. In some societies, for example, yardstick adopted could be number of cattle and area of land each family holds, number of bungalows, cars, servants and animal pets, monitory assets, both in 'black' and 'white' category, and so on. Anyone who holds more of anything of these develops superiority complex and as a result such a person will start looking down upon those having less possessions. Here there is a vast playground available for these players to play around, and quarrel among themselves to decide and settle as to who among them are big or small aristocrats. Hypocrisy will have a field-day for expressing itself vehemently and openly, and, of course, shamelessly! Their quarrels might culminate with fatal injuries to someone amongst them. This is some sort of a perennial 'struggle for existence'. This is all the inter-play of intermix of their pride and prejudices that they fondly foster and hold as proud possessions.

Any perceived 'misdemeanour' on the part of any member of one family will be openly and vehemently criticized by members of another family, when they all meet in weekly congregation in their 'elite' club. Someone would say to the head of the 'guilty' family, "You see, our family is an old aristocratic one. It was established by our grandfather more than twenty years ago, (as though this period is good and long enough to establish aristocracy and family traditions!). We have some very good traditions. We condemn severely the misdemeanour of that member of your family. We can not accept this. All of you must have heard of the high reputation that our family carries. We can't accept you as one among us. Look at the way others too react." The old attendant in that congregation might muse, "Twenty years, my foot! No tradition worth the name can be built within twenty years. I have seen that fellow's grandfather when he was my colleague as an attendant. He was a humble man, but look at them; they are haughty, arrogant and egoistic. This probably might be the neo-rich culture. I am happy that I am not one among them. What a farce! What a fraud! What a non-sense!" This is all manifestation of sheer snobbishness.

Snobbery equates with hypocrisy. A snob is an 'ostentatious vulgarian; one who makes himself ridiculous or odious by the value he sets on social standing or rank, by his fear of being ranked too low, and by his different behaviour towards different classes' (*Chamber's Twentieth Century Dictionary*). Snowberry exists in societies that value class systems based on various norms of aristocracy, plutocracy, economic backwardness and casteism. There is rampant tendency on the part of the privileged ones to look down upon the underprivileged.

Hypocrites are posers and are connoisseurs in the field of 'show' business. They try to project themselves as honest, genuine, austere, gentle and good Samaritans. They have great marketing acumen. Most of the simple-hearted become victims of such misleading and mischievous propaganda, and purchase their projected version, like in the case of aggressive marketing strategies for consumables, good or bad, and the resultant succumbing of potential buyers. But sooner or later they might realize that it was all a mistake. It seems that there is an association formed by hypocrites, called World Hypocrites' Organization (WHO) for the promotion of this phenomenon. In fact there is hardly any requirement of 'promotional effort' in respect of very well-established products and services. WHO promotes welfare of its members. All are welcome to join this 'august' organization. Special incentive schemes are offered to new aspirants.

Hypocrisy is an all pervading universal phenomenon. The worst of all is what we see in case of worship of God. Love begets respect and the *vice versa*. Worship of God is an expression of both genuine love and respect for Him. All religious scripts pronounce loudly that those who worship God should have clean minds as a pre-requisite to prayers and worship of God. People flout all these norms. They do not know the exact meaning of what is called cleanliness of mind. All of them claim that their minds are clean. Why does man worship God? It is to get some favours from Him? He has plenty with Him to give; if He likes and wants, He gives. Why does man praise Him, sometimes alone and sometimes in congregations? The human being takes things for granted and thinks that He likes appreciation, admiration and extolment, sometimes even 'thanksgiving', and hence shower on Him all the good epithets available, in His praise. Man thinks, foolishly, that He is also like human beings who always enjoy flattery and adulations which blind them. When a man enjoys them he becomes willing to do anything that is asked for by the adulator or flatterer. One wonders if God succumbs to such tactics and strategies. He is not fallible and erratic like human beings!

Some people take to worshiping God only to show that they are divine. They want to score a point or two in the eyes of others. They do not hesitate to proclaim that they believe in universal love. There is a big gap between what they preach and what they practise. Such people visit the places of worship regularly; in most of the cases these visits stand for sheer formality. It is as though to record a "present, sir" in the Attendance Register, like in the case of school and its students. All the students attend classes *en masse* and earn the most important record of their presence, but only a few are really interested in studies. In some cases, when many of them visit the places of worship, they make most of it to discuss their individual as well as general social or political issues, thus converting the assemblage into a social or political gathering. There they even make marriage proposals for their wards, and, if possible fix dates for such marriages. "What a fall, my countrymen!" Where are the clean minds? Where are the much claimed love and reverence for God? It is hypocrisy galore!

Hypocritic behaviour is prevalent in most religions today. People belonging to one religious denomination arrogantly assume and assert that theirs is the only true perfect religion.

Sadly, they do not realize true perfection is unattainable, hence there is no perfect religion; There is no 'all-weather-proof' product available in the market. Religions, after all, are created by people to meet the social requirements of particular region. Krishna, for example, has addressed mainly problems of the social set-up prevalent in his time. Mohammed, again for example, has concentrated social problems prevalent in his time in the place where he was born and lived. In some respects they have all been social reformers. Though their utterances are of specific type addressing the immediate local problems, most of them have universal application cutting across the whole world. Hence somewhere along the way, most religions have forgotten the one thing that Krishna, Jesus, The Buddha or Mohammed, for example, came with the intent of teaching us to love all mankind. Religion is supposed to be about sharing one's love and respect for the Lord. The approach and methods enunciated by different religions may look different. That should not make anyone despise other religions.

The worst form of hypocrisy is expressed in the interpretations of religious tenets by those who foster extremistic views and perceptions. If anyone has to leave one religion and adopt another, the minimum requirement of qualification would be that he should have thorough knowledge of the one he leaves as well as that of the one he intends to be associated with. This rarely happens. Here, aggrandisement and fulfilment of egoistic satisfaction and some other temporary benefits form the main criteria. There are a lot of examples wherein persons leaving the fold of one faith and joining Islam for the sake of having more than one wife. Taking advantage in the cover of this 'provision' in the script was never intended. Some do go as far as shunning family members for leaving their religion. Nothing can be more devastating than being cut off from one's family simply because neither can he believe the way members of his family do nor can he force others to follow him. Everywhere we see a game of unfounded hollow self-elevation followed by deliberate downgrading of others. It is quite interesting to conceive that if the Lord judges us as harshly as our religious pandits do, then nobody is going to heaven. If one replaces his religion with another, he will be considered doomed in the eyes of the Lord, according to those in his previous denomination who try to replace God by themselves. Do they succeed in their efforts to becoming God? One will wonder as to where these beliefs come from; not definitely from the religious books. The subjects entailed in the books are misinterpreted with malise for reasons best known to the interpreters. It is up to God, if He desires so, to judge each and every one of us, and no one, but Him. It is all rampant hypocrisy flourishing in religions.

It is a fashion prevalent among the rich to take to charitable work in the society. They form trusts and build hospitals for charity, and credit huge sums of money, mostly ill-gotten, in the trust-accounts. Donations are made with full fanfare in full public view with full press coverage for wide publicity. They themselves become managing trustees of such trusts. They mismanage the funds therein in clandestine manner. The money they donate to the trusts is exempted from tax-levies. In many cases, this becomes the way to hoodwink the government. Thus it is a safe way to divert their excess money. In the eyes of the public, they become good social workers. It is crass dishonesty and deceit and hence hypocrisy.

Love *per se* is sacred and absolute. Man loves God, fellow beings, other members of the fauna and even flora. His love for materials is primary and paramount, making other love secondary. For him giving love is a business transaction, a *quid pro quo* arrangement, an investment. He always expects something in return. He does not provide any exception even to his love for God. He wants in return favours, in terms of boons that could enable him to get accommodated in heaven after his innings on earth whether he 'deserves' or not. His love for God is thus not unattached, and not devoid of self-interest. He feels jealous of one who gets 'more' from Him, feels happy if that person is given less than what he gets. This proves that his love for God is scant. What to talk about his love for others!

It is in the realm of love, perhaps, that hypocrisy is significantly rampant. If any sort of suspicion, mistrust or fear exists between two so-called 'lovers', their mutual conduct as well as behaviour will be of a cautious kind. They will have no choice other than becoming hypocrites. In fact, two hypocrites cannot really love each other. They only can become partners of some sort of unholy alliance, but due to situational pressures, they opt to act as lovers, as is done in cinemas with romantic themes. They compromise on the meaning of love. It is conditional love. It becomes a matter of convenience. And love can never be conditional, or a matter of convenience. It is neither negotiable nor barterable. It is 'lovocrisy', a coinage for describing the fusion or nexus between love and hypocrisy. It serves to tell love from hypocrisy.

Parents love their children in their infancy without any desire for something in return. At that stage, they are in a helpless predicament, and they need support and protection from those whom they can depend on. We name this 'Love'. The giver just gives it solely out of sympathy, and this sympathy is love. Thus they are given love in the form of care and sympathy which are the most essential requirements for their survival at that stage. The giver gives them happily and the receiver receives them gratefully. This love given at that stage is sacred. As they grow-up, they start returning love, but probably only the 'interest' of the 'capital' given to them. Capital is never returnable and not returned. Here there is no element of selfishness or hypocrisy. The love between a husband and his wife, in most of the cases, is negotiable, and there is a semblance of a business transaction. And in business there is *quid pro quo*. By and large, this contractual agreement is stable and permanent. This and all other types of love do have ingredients of hypocrisy, covert or overt.

When a death occurs in a house, all in the neighbourhood congregate there to offer their condolence. Some of them even shed tears of sorrow in an effort to lessen the sorrow of the nearest kith and kin of the deceased. Many times, some crocodiles too arrive there to shed their tears. They express their empathy. Even though the deceased was an ignominious rogue, someone among the crowd would say, activating his lachrymal glands, "He was always a misunderstood person. For me, he was good and quite likable. How sad he is no more." This is the ultimate in hypocrisy. Except the dead, everyone understands the system. By any reason, if the nearest neighbour forgets to utter such words, the predeceased spouse would adversely comment later on this unpardonable misdemeanour of that person, "Alright, I agree that he did not like my husband at all, but still he could have said a few good words about him. He is a heartless fellow." This is superlative hypocrisy.

Some people are in habit of keeping secrets for the sake of nothing. Women, for example, keep their age as a guarded secret. Married women hold back a lot of information about their physiological characteristics even from their husbands. The husbands will be made to struggle hard in extracting such information from them. Such struggles yield results that provide them with a lot of thrill. It is their shyness which does not allow them to be frank. The husbands enjoy all this. It is the Nature's game. One might link this secretive nature in them with some sort of interesting and inevitable hypocrisy, probably for want of other suitable terminology. It is all fun. People smile, laugh, weep, feeling shy and get angry, depending on the type of situation they are in. On many occasions, they smile or laugh, even when they are not happy, they weep even when they are not sorrowful, they pretend that they are shy even when they are not really feeling shy and they show their anger even when they are not really angry. This is all acting. Not only do these actors know as to why they behave that way, even the onlookers understand the reason behind such sorts of behaviour. It is all nothing but hypocrisy. An elephant has two sets of teeth, one set is for chewing food—the primary function—and the other set is just for showing to others. The second set seems to be more important, because, but for these impressive ones; many may not probably take an elephant seriously.

A hypocritical behaviour may not always be due to some deliberate or conscious planning by the mind. In the initial stages of one's life, every individual is born with all sorts of propensities, desirable as well as undesirable; but they are in dormant or in an undeveloped stage. They have the tendency to grow concurrently with all other organs and faculties. The growth of the undesirable ones is not to be left rampant, for it could prove very disastrous later on. Hence it becomes the primarily duty of those who are responsible to bringing up the younger ones, parents as well as society. The undesirable propensities are to be nipped in the bud-stage itself. There is many an undesirable trait included in the list. 'Hypocrisy' is one at the top of the list. Hypocrisy fosters egoism, disrespectfulness to others and sublime ideas, intellectual dishonesty, self-deceit, untruth and many other malicious traits.

Hypocrisy is seen in henpeckery. Women are fond of 'pecking' their husbands. But they flatly deny this reality. Even men both in rural and urban settings generally do not accept the fact that they are being 'pecked' by their wives. This is out of their shyness; and they are afraid of their being exposed. In rural settings, in the presence of other friendly couples, they agree for a meagre percentage, whereas rural women, up to about 20%. In urban settings, about 20% of men strike the deal generally, and in presence of friendly couples up to 60%. Women seem to admit privately up to 90% in presence of other women, to score a point or two there from, but they totally deny such a thing in presence of other men or couples or in public. There is a tendency to consider this word as a dirty and ignominious one. If we undertake to go for a confidential opinion-poll among, say, one thousand men, at random, in order to grab their 'confessions' or otherwise, and workout some statistical data, we are sure to get nearly nine hundred and fifty confessions *id est* 95%. The 5% less may have been caused, probably because, they were fast asleep or pretending to be so, or they could not understand the question, or they are so hen-pecked that they could not get permission from their wives to talk to public on such sensitive subjects. Let us first of all thank those 'brave' 95%, and 'excuse' the remainder 5%, as they are innocent, and 'they do not know what they are doing'. It is all gross hypocrisy.

Men and women do not like to be looking old, probably because they are afraid of losing their marketability. It is a highly infectious disease. Moreso, they feel that they will be left-out in the race, even become objects of ridicule. Because of this fear, they patronize and encourage the cosmetic industry. They periodically visit beauty parlours and buy beauty 'ex-shelf'. They manage to conceal their age as much and long as possible by getting their hair dyed and getting their faces 'face-lifted' by 'facials' and massages, at exorbitant costs. They take pride in getting these done and so also in using these technical terms liberally, while in discussions in their social get-togethers. Knowing these terms enhances their social stature and status. This is nothing but vanity. This vanity is synonomatic with hypocrisy, and nothing but hypocrisy.

There are discrepancies between the explicit or external and implicit or internal beliefs of persons and their actions. This is the criterion on the basis of which we can identify and classify the hypocrites. On the basis of this, we can broadly categorize them into mainly two, viz. the honest and the dishonest. The honest are the ones whose declared and the actual internal beliefs are the same, but their actions do not match them. Since their internal beliefs remain constant, though their actions contradict, they are honest with themselves, and strive to conform their beliefs around their own desires, actions or imperfections. In the case of the dishonest ones, their actions and the stated beliefs do not match each other, and they may remain non-hypocritical internally. While their stated beliefs and their actions are in conformity with each other, their internal convictions are different.

Uncertainty of beliefs and their impracticability in our societal set-up make people hypocrites. The inherent sensual desires drive them out into hypocrisy. Moreover, the lofty idealism that exists in our society prevents its members to behave in their own natural way. The society should condescend to a realistic situation if its members are to be unhypocrical. One should do his best to perceive reality, truth and morality objectively for what they are for. One should do everything humanly possible to keep the hypocrisy to a bare minimum. Conform one's actions to one's beliefs the best one can, but once he obtains a belief system in this manner, the perception of reality will be as close to actual reality as one can make it. If the beliefs are humanly impossible to be practised after this evaluation, then he will have to settle for being an honest hypocrite!

We are apt to exempt from being labelled as hypocrites some of those whose perceptions of reality conform to support their own desires and imperfections; they rationalize their actions, and are without objectivity. They conform their beliefs around. We are apt to exempt from the category of hypocrites some people whose beliefs and their actions to eliminate contradictions, rather than conforming their actions around their beliefs. Exempted further are those who never contradict their beliefs. They are completely devoted to what they believe in; they do not rationalize their own actions. Their beliefs and perceptions of reality are the result of either objective logic, blind faith or a combination of both. Regardless of the source of their beliefs, their beliefs and actions are without contradiction. It is best not to be hypocritical, but if one can not but become one, he should rather be an honest hypocrite than a person who tries to make truth conform around his or her own desires and imperfections. In other words, one should rather be an honest hypocrite than pretending, camouflaging or lying about one's imperfections.

Braggartism

Bragging is boasting, and a braggart is an empty or vain boaster, a braggadocio. It is a skill as well as an art which a braggart has mastery in. Braggarts are good psycho-analysts. They are capable of reading the minds of those around them. They take out an easily saleable variety of brag-stuff from among the many they have in their mental warehouse and serve for consumption and digestion to unsuspecting people. They impress people around them initially till the latter realize the hollowness of the bragging claims. The timing of realization is related to the levels of intelligence and imagination that each one among the 'audience' is bestowed with.

They can successfully shine and survive as braggarts in the company of relatively less intelligent people. They are intelligent enough to scan and measure the levels of intelligence and imagination together with the psychological propensities of those who offer themselves as potential audience. They, it seems, employ some devise for that. Depending on the reading on this measuring meter, they adjust their strategies, tactics and design of their bragging. They accomplish all this spontaneously; they ought to have very alert minds.

Name-dropping is the practice of mentioning names of important personalities or institutions into a conversation, story, song or any other type of communication with the sheer ulterior motive of impressing others. The event being described is usually a lie or a case of exaggeration or distortion. Name-droppers cleverly create a milieu where they could project themselves as the 'real ones'. This strategy is employed to position oneself within a social hierarchy. It is often used to create a sense of superiority by raising one's stature and status. They concentrate on their notional or imaginary accrescence. By implying (or directly asserting) a connection to people of high status, the name-dropper hopes to raise his or her own social status to a level closer to that of those whose names he or she has dropped, and thus elevate himself or herself above, or into, present company. Name-dropping can also be used to identify people with a common bond. By indicating the names of people one knows, one makes known his or her social circle, providing an opportunity for others with similar connections to relate. Names can be the ultimate status symbols, and as such, they should be collected and displayed—but one needs to be discreet. Dropped names are like donning false hair or a wig. Badly done, they are obvious and show poor taste. Carefully deployed, however, they work wonders for one's image-building temporarily at least. A big multi-coloured soap bubble, impressive and attractive, will burst and vanish in no time, without any fanfare or ceremony!

While studying at the university, I had a classmate of mine who had shown 'symptoms' of this disease of name dropping. Those were the days when motor cars themselves were a rare phenomenon. There could not have more than two or three scores of cars owned by that township then. As of now, after half of a century, the number could have swelled to two hundred scores. While we were walking back home after our classes, (and that was our daily routine), on one of such days, he shouted enlisting his ostensible agony and despair, when a luxurious car passed overtaking us, "Look, that is my uncle going in it. I do not know why he did not stop the car and gave us lift. Oh, he might not have noticed us." His shouting came out only when he was sure that the car would be at least twenty metres away from us; to a safe distance, 'out of range' or beyond 'striking distance', so to say. At the first instance, I was tempted to give him 'full marks' for this performance of his. After a while, I confronted him a bit cleverly and tactfully with a simple question, "Was that person in that car really your uncle? I know almost all of your relatives. I never before had seen him." He had to confess that he was not his uncle, and that he was trying to impress me by 'pulling a fast one'. He would have been tempted to 'bowl wild bouncers', 'wides' and 'no-balls' or the ignominious 'bodylines', (to borrow terms from the game of cricket), at me, if at all he could take me granted for a person having only a limited quantum of active cells in my brain. He did not dare equate my timidity to idiocy, and pass on any of that stuff to me for my consumption. My passive but positive stance would have given him enough inkling of my attitude and approach to life. Nice of him! None studies another just by only one interaction. One has to study holistically by analyzing him from different angles. I did all that to assess his propensities, attitudes and approaches to life in general. As he understood that I had understood him through and through; he stopped dropping names. He proved that he had sagacity too, besides cleverness. Later on, when I had come to know that he had joined a dramatic club, I had wished him great success when he would be a part of the cine world. I had my optimism in this; the optimism borne out of his otherwise excellent performance.

There are cases, for instance, wherein the act of inserting names of any famous persons, cultural organizations or institutions into a conversation in an effort to accelerating the building of rapport with someone, or to make one's self appear to be more important or larger than life. If someone says "Yesterday I met Mr. Gandhi at The Great Tagore Hall Show", he would have been expecting the listener to exclaim, "You attend such shows! Did you really meet Mr Gandhi? Great!" The statements like, "When I wanted to go to the Lion's Club, my Benz car did not start, I had to go by the other car, Pearl," "If the starter-key of 'Pearl' were misplaced, then I would have had to take my third car; thank God, I was lucky.", and so on are meant to mislead the listeners. The listeners are kept on 'hold' to count the number of cars he has had. The statement, "While I was getting down from the train the other day, my book, Golden Treasury, fell right out of my bag and fell on the track" too is designed with similar contents and intentions. Some people get one or two of their teeth capped with gold foil. It is considered to be sign of aristocracy. Such people prefer to pronounce some words like 'teeth', or 'cheat' as 'teeeth' or 'cheeet', stretching their mouths laterally to the maximum tensibility, only to make sure that their so-called 'aristocratic teeth' are shown clearly to the listeners who are made to 'watch' their conversations rather than to 'listen' to them. The reasons are obvious. Some people are habituated to employ their right hands for gesturing while talking about something. They invariably "decorate" fingers on their right hands with beautiful heavy rings. Some ladies use brightly coloured nail polish and do not forget to wear attractive bangles that make 'clang-cling' music notes. To add to the scheme of decorations, they wear expensive wrist watches on their right wrists, instead of the common trend of wearing on the left hand. With all these paraphernalia of decorations, they make hand gestures with these right hands, complementing their vocal exercises, in order just to impress onlookers or listeners. Such persons are more interested in 'showing off' this sort of vanity rather than concentrate on the subject-matter they deal with in their conversations. These are all expressions of bragging.

The slang usage of words, "windbags" and "gasbags" does denote bragging. By resorting to letting out their 'gas' or 'wind', they are trying to cover up their inferiority, inadequacies, lacunae, shortcomings, hollowness and vanity. It is nothing but crass hypocrisy. They presume that the listeners are captivated fools, and it is on this presumption that they thrive.

Braggartism is considered as an undesirable trait. It is very difficult to get correct information from or about the person who is said to be bragging, because bragging is often a clever concoction or admixture of truths, half-truths, untruths and lies, and hypocritical, hollow, exaggerated, manipulative and vane statements. It is difficult to separate chaff from corn. Initially at the first interaction, the braggart is not identified as one, even though the listener develops some sort of suspicion, but the person gets 'benefit of doubt'. He is considered a suspect case. It also depends on the level of intelligence and imagination of the listener. On subsequent encounters, the listener confirms the suspicion. Then onwards he will be able to remove the 'chaffs' and get hold of the elements of truth in whatever he states. He has to rack his brain for that. It is passive harassment. The listener increases the percentage of 'discount', and finally he takes the total statements to be expressions of total untruths; a sure case of bragging. In this process, the little bit of truth in the utterances gets into oblivion. He will be discredited. The moment he opens his mouth to speak something, the listener will be tempted to discourage him by telling, for the sake of an 'anticipatory bail', "...and you did that,...and you did not do that" and the like. He is sure to understand that the listener has gauged him correctly. It is total boredom to tolerate a braggadocio. Once a good friend, he will be dumped subsequently in the cold.

In some cases, some genuine self-confident achievers talk truly and genuinely about their unique achievements. They have probably no patience to give time for others to recognize, understand and appreciate their achievements which their listeners are not interested to listen. They harp on them in order to make them listen. Here such people underestimate, correctly or incorrectly, the levels of intelligence and imagination of the listeners. Probably, they are aware and conscious of the fact that this world is full of cynics. They are sceptical about the genuineness of their listeners. They are anxious as well as afraid if their case would be left unrecognized. They dislike taking chances. One might label this sort of behaviour as childishness; but it is certain that they have some minor curable psychological disorders. Such people are unfortunately declared as braggarts.

There is one fact that can not be undermined. Most of the humans are cynical, narrow-minded and self-centred; they have neither time nor willingness to listen to good things about others. They are apt to discount the veracity of what good is being stated about others, and at the same time swell, exaggerate or magnify their deficiencies or drawbacks. If the information emanates from very reliable sources, then the percentage of 'discount' will be diminished, but not to naught. Their manipulative thinking system even converts good points into bad ones. They might say, "You might be correct in the light of your experiences with him; but I do not subscribe to your views. My experiences are different. Anyway, be happy." There is also a morbid tendency to extract sadistic pleasure from unpleasant tidings with respect to others. "Seek, thou shalt get" is the doctrine they like to follow when they search for unpleasant tidings of others. Because of these dangerous traits, they do not see any truth in what others say about others, as their perceptions about others are, as such, myopic. It is convenient for them to rubbish even some truthful statements made by others. In this connection, the following elements may be of importance:

(a) In interpersonal transactions, people seldom pay adequate sincere attention to what others say. They prefer to switch off or disconnect the reception devices of the brain. They often pretend to be listening assiduously, but in fact they try to 'hear' only, and not 'listen'. Their intermittent, "Yes" or nodding their heads and donning or pasting a smile on their beautiful countenance would give an impression that they are really listening to all that intently. They accord a passive negligence.

(b) Because of the above impediment or handicap, the correct and complete truth in the information will not be registered in the mind.

(c) They fill up information readily available in their mental warehouse, preserved as precious assets, for completion, cohesion or cognition of this fractured information.

(d) Thereafter, a meaning will be supplied to the whole according to their learning, cognition, attitude and overall perception.

(e) The final output of information will be either distorted half-truths or untruths.

In our society, there is plenty of this tribe of braggadocios. Society is comprised of all types of people. To some extent, these braggarts with their art provide entertainment as well. They are very highly imaginative and intelligent, but their intelligence works often only in a tangential manner. It is interesting to listen to their bragging feats when one does not have anything else to do, but one should have to have lots of patience to tolerate such people. They are capable of spinning many a yarn.

Bragging is resorted to by both the young and the old alike. Children might brag for many reasons. First of all they might lack self-confidence and bragging makes themselves feel better. By bragging they try projecting indirectly faults on others and uplifting their own spirits; they begin to feel that they actually are something important in this world. It is an effort to know their place in school or at home. By bragging, they will get attention and will feel they belong somewhere. Children could brag about anything ranging from grades to sports and to wealth. If children are lonely, they might be under the wrong assumption that by bragging, people will like them better and they will make more friends. If a child brags he has to be helped gain his self-confidence. He has to be shown that everyone will like him more if he does not brag and he does not need to brag to get attention and feel wanted. Bragging is a disease and it is a vicious one. If a child does not brag, we have to make sure that he does not lose his self-confidence because of other children who do brag. He has to be convinced that he does not need to brag about his achievements in order to be appreciated. Also by praising him at home, he will feel less of a need to brag and will not be affected by children who do brag. Children are very vulnerable and they need love and encouragement. When a child brags, he is sometimes indirectly asking people to notice him and feel proud of him. The parents have to show what he means to them and how proud they really are. Bragging is something that children engage in. It should be stopped as soon as possible because as children get older, they might brag more and it will be harder to stop. Bragging is a very unsocial manner and can hurt your child in many ways.

To a great extent, society in which such people live is to blame. Society offers its several special brands of 'behavioural specimens' to its individual members to get themselves compared and contrasted with. As a result, some of them are rendered either diffident or over-confident. The diffident lot will suffer from inferiority complex and the over-confident superiority complex. Both of these traits are formed-up in individuals as perceptual cognitions and as they become conscious of them, some sort of psychological imbalance will be developed. Diffident ones search for something that can serve to compensate; and for this purpose they unconsciously choose the art of bragging out of a few available remedies. The diffident try to 'acquire' while the over-confident try to 'de-acquire'. Those who evaluate themselves as superior become over-confident. They under-estimate others and think that they would swallow their vane assertions as they are, without analyzing and ascertaining the truth-content of them. They start believing that they can get away with anything they utter. What a folly, my coutrymen!

There are a few important reasons why some people are prone to bragging. It all depends on their individual approaches to life, evolved while carrying on with the process of living in the world. Some of the factors may be brought out as follows:

(a) Genetic factors.

(b) Socio-psychological factors.

Genetic factors do influence human psychology and the consequent behavioural output. Individual life is perpetuated by genesis, the scheme of inheritance of various individual characteristics by one generation to the next one through genes. This process carries on perennially. The gene contains characteristic elements of personality of individuals. If the genes with bragging traits are passed on to successive generations, the inheritors also acquire the same characteristic traits.

Individuals live in society. Society inculcates in its members certain anomalous traits like hypocrisy and selfishness. There occurs a fusion of sociological factors with psychological ones of the individuals. Hypocrisy is the art of concealment of true character or belief. It is acting, feigning to be better than one is, or to be what one is not. A hypocrite is one who practises hypocrisy. It is one of the most commonly observed characteristics of human behaviour, the foundation of which is untruth and falsehood. False sense of pride and prejudices form the rudiments of hypocrisy. Hypocrisy and bragging cohabit harmoniously. Selfishness is another trait that brings about bragging. Selfish people perceive of everything that they possess as big, beautiful, best and the like—they confiscate and earmark all the epithets with positive meanings and ascribe all of them in their superlative forms to their possessions. In doing so, they compromise on many a thing. The ladies brag that their husbands are the most handsome and loving men in the world; the men, their wives are the most beautiful and loving. These assertions are meant for public consumption only. In private situations, they would be busy in searching for epithets with opposite meanings. Similarly their children are the best in every respect. These are all expressions of hypocrisy in relation to selfishness and in doing so they have to resort to bragging.

I happened to visit the family of one of my closest friends some time ago. It was the day that he had come to know that his only daughter had passed her graduation examination. Hardly had I entered the house, when his wife greeted me very cheerfully and conveyed to me the best item of news. My friend was not present there at that time. "Congratulations! What is the result like?" I enquired. "She has passed with First class with Distinction", was the reply. After a couple of minutes, their daughter came-in, and immediately I congratulated her for her passing the examination with Distinction. Her mother standing-by nodded her head cheerfully, absorbing the happiness that I had showered on her child. "Thank you, uncle. I didn't get Distinction, only a Second Division" said the daughter innocently. I helplessly watched the pale face of the mother. I could discern her hypocrisy. The mother is a simple person, but given to a bit of bragging at times, probably, for self-preservation and self-aggrandisement.

Braggarts thrive and live on their tongues which are unusually long and elastic and made of muscle tissues that are highly tensible, malleable and invulnerable to fatiguing. The size of their hearts is generally small and because of this they are capable of shifting them at will and ease and planting them anywhere within or even without their bodies according to what particular situations demand.

I happened inadvertently to be in the company of some braggarts. I did not mind being in the company especially of such people when I was looking for some relaxation in my idling times. One can get lots of fun. Anyone can imagine what would have happened. They engaged themselves in their usual business of bragging. They spin yarn after yarn. I sometimes wonder as to how they are able to sustain such behaviour of theirs without exhaustion and monotony. One is free to escape from their clutches or captivity at will when one is convinced that enough is enough. That is a great advantage. I heard one of them vociferously asserting that he never got beaten-up by anyone. One of them present there elected to contradict him, "I saw you the other day getting beaten-up by one Harry when both of you were standing near the Riverside Lodge." Promptly came the clarification that it was true and added that it was the only time such a thing happened. Then another member confronted him by asking as to what had happened on the previous Sunday near the Golden Theatre when a hefty person had kicked you very badly. "Yes, that was only time I could not prevent him from doing so. He was a stupid fellow. But these were the only two occasions where I could not avoid doing anything against." Then another member of the group narrated a third incident similar to the earlier ones. And a fourth one came out with another. He had to agree with all of them. Who can deny accounts narrated by eye-witnesses? He was thus cornered and brought to a situation that provided no escape routes. A pitiable scenario, indeed! I was convinced myself, "Enough is enough" and elected to escape from there. I do not want to imagine what would have happened to me if I had continued to be there with them for some more time. Monotony would have overtaken my intent of entertainment and relaxation.

In the *Encylopedia of Braggartism*, there is no mention of the words, 'shame' and 'shamelessness', and because of that braggarts are ignorant of their meanings. Ignorance is bliss and that is why they are shameless with respect to their patented trade. Shame is the 'humiliating feeling of having appeared to disadvantage in one's own eyes, or those of others: fear or scorn of incurring disgrace or dishonour.'

Shamelessness is immodesty or ignominy and insensibility to shame. The braggarts do not think of what others think of them when they eloquently express of their unreal exploits. It is like a smart and clever cat closing its eyes while drinking stolen milk. It deliberately thinks, for its convenience, that none is watching and going to catch it red-handed. Intelligent, alert and knowledgeable audience will understand that most of the yarns the braggarts spin have an ending like what happens when someone, curious to find out the size and other features of the 'seed' housed in an onion, trying to peel the different layers of the coverings of it. Onion gives an illusory impression to us that there could be some seed within, because of its beautiful and carefully arranged coverings. The act of peeling ultimately gives one only dismay and provides for the escape of a few drops from his lachrymal glands. An onion does not keep a seed within, and so is the yarn spun by the braggarts! The braggarts think that others are not watching or understanding their performance.

Even if they have some inkling that others are aware of their game-plan, they ignore it conveniently because it does not match with their scheme of things; it is inconvenient and 'sinful' for them to take note of such 'anomalies'. They deserve and earn effortlessly the label, 'shameless'.

It seems that they have 'thick skin' covering their entire body and even mind. Let us not be anxious or optimistic that one day the medical research would come up with some magical medicines to melt away the 'extra thickness of their skin' and the consequent weeding out of the entire species from the face of the earth. Others would have to learn to live without these entertainers, if on one fine day the world would be without them! Let us pray to God to render these medical researches futile. Let us have faith in Him, and He will not let us down! Let us 'knock the door, and the door will be opened'.

These braggarts would not have been braggarts, had they ever realized that they are suffering from some disorder or sickness. If aunty had a mustache, she would have been an uncle, but aunty can not sport a natural mustache and become an uncle. The braggarts can not change their identity very easily. Bragging is a weakness or a psychological disorder similar to that of drug-addiction, but not as serious as the latter. They can be salvaged by counselling, the main thrust being instilling sense of shame by involving them in situations, real or simulated, where they have to look at life seriously. They have to be brought back to realities of life by cutting them to size; the artificial ill-gotten 'tallness' has to be subjected to 'hedge-cutting'. Even though they contribute to fun and entertainment of people, most of times they prove themselves to be menace, especially when they indulge themselves in anti-social pursuits of cheating innocent unsuspecting people who take their bragging on its face-value. Insurance companies do not have provisions to offer compensations to damages caused by these unscrupulous elements. All braggarts are hypocrites and all hypocrites are not necessarily braggarts; both of them are undoubtedly shameless. The hypocrites and braggarts manifest their characteristic behaviour not only through their words but in physical demeanour as well. Often both their words and behaviour complement each other. Even some ambitious dumb people are observed to be practitioners of these forms of art; the blind, however, are unable to practise it in the absence of vision. These hypocrites and braggarts try to overdo their performance in order to preventing their 'victims' from having any 'breathing' or thinking time, for, that might upset their game plan. In most cases there might not be any deliberate design on their part to resort either to hypocrisy or bragging; it is a case of force of habit. These hypocrites and braggarts are often not 'natural elements or products'. They are produced by the process of mutation and synthesis, the main agent of which is society. They themselves, probably, more often than not, might be victims of an automatic programming in their minds. They are a helpless lot, suffering from psychological disorder. They are captivated slaves and despite their sincere efforts in terms of introspection, accidental or otherwise, they seldom succeed in retrieving themselves from the clutches of these cursed diseases; even a divine intervention might not help them. Others should have sympathy for them. Let us forgive them. *Sic transit Gloria mundane.*

Braggartism is the game that hypocrites play. It is the cover they don to keep away their deficiencies, inadequacies, inferiority complexes and the general diffidence from public view. They pretend to be what they are not, and probably they try to express as to what they might be intending to become.

> "Every ass loves to hear himself bray." (An English proverb)
>
> "Where boasting ends, dignity begins." (Young)
>
> "It is important that you recognize your progress and take pride in your accomplishments. Share your achievements with others. Brag a little. The recognition and support of those around you is nurturing. It is not bragging if you can back it up." (Mohammad Ali)
>
> "If you done it, it ain't bragging." (Walt Whitman)

Anger as a Behaviour

5

Anger is "hot displeasure, wrath, often involving a desire for retaliation". Anger is generated in the heart of a person. It is the opposite of love. Hatred and love are separated by a thin wall. Anger is the obverse side of the coin of love. In most cases, the intensity of anger of a person on another is directly proportional to that of his love for that person. It is also an expression of sublimated love for someone or something *vis-à-vis* his or its enemy. It is the response to stimulus of an internal or external irritation. One could be angry at a specific person, such as a co-worker or supervisor, or event, a traffic jam or a cancelled flight, or it could be caused by worrying or brooding about one's own personal problems. Memories of traumatic or enraging events can also trigger angry feelings. Anger is often disproportionate to the cause; it depends largely on the inherent belief system, past experience and the perception of the present situation. It is the nexus between personality characteristics of persons getting angry and situations in which these characteristics operate, that determines the resultant ways of behavioural output.

Most commonly, those who experience anger explain its arousal as a result of "what has happened to them" and in most cases the described provocations occur immediately before they experience anger. Such explanations confirm the illusion that anger has a discrete external cause. The angry person usually finds the cause of his anger in an intentional, personal, and controllable aspect of another person's behaviour. This explanation is however based on the intuitions of the angry person who experiences a loss in self-monitoring capacity and objective observability as a result of their emotion. Anger can be of multicausal origin, some of which may be remote events, but people rarely find more than one cause for their anger. Experiences of anger are embedded or nested within an environmental-temporal context. Disturbances that may not have involved anger at the outset leave residues that are not readily recognized but that operate as a lingering backdrop for focal provocations (of anger). According to *Britannica Encyclopedia*, an internal infection can cause pain which in turn can activate anger.

Anger is not a matter of chance, but more often than not a matter of choice. There could be an 'affordability' factor in many cases of angry demeanour. If one can 'afford' to be angry with a person irrespective of the strength of the impinging stimulus caused by him, he elects to be angry; the intensity of anger also varies according to his convenience. If one does not like or hate the countenance of a person, due to any reason, real or imaginary, he chooses to 'blast' him on some pretext or other; he, in fact, should have been waiting for such a chance. Such persons get chances too! Anger is an emotional state that may range from minor irritation to intense rage. The physiological effects of anger include increased heart rate and blood pressure. Anger becomes the predominant feeling behaviourally, cognitively and physiologically when a person makes the conscious choice to take action to stop immediately the threatening behaviour of another outside force. As with any emotion, the display of anger can be feigned, pseudological or exaggerated.

A belligerent behaviour may prove to be a successful strategy and mechanism for achievement of goal. A certain amount of anger, therefore, is necessary to our survival. It is a natural, adaptive response to threats; it inspires powerful, often aggressive, feelings and behaviours, which allow us to fight and to defend ourselves when we are attacked. Anger is viewed as a natural and healthy response that has evolved to enable us to deal with threats. Modern psychologists view anger as a primary, natural, and mature emotion experienced by all humans at times, and as something that has functional value for survival. Anger can mobilize psychological resources for corrective action. Uncontrolled anger can however negatively affect personal or social well-being. It has also been shown that the display of anger can be used as an effective manipulation of strategy for social influence. While many philosophers and writers have warned against the spontaneous and uncontrolled fits of anger, there has been disagreement over the intrinsic value of anger. Dealing with anger has been addressed in the writings of earliest philosophers up to modern times. Modern psychologists, in contrast to the earlier writers, have also pointed out the possible harmful effects of suppression of anger. Anger can potentially mobilize psychological resources and boost determination toward correction of wrong behaviours, promotion of social justice, communication of negative sentiment and redress of grievances. It can also facilitate patience. After a storm the atmosphere gets calmer and cooler.

Anger is fairly high with people who have high expectations of themselves. Highly egoistic and perfectionist people are more prone to getting frustrated when things do not follow a particular plan, and thereby feeling angry easily, because they are apt to feel and believe that they "deserve better than this". The instinctive and natural way to express anger is to respond aggressively on the other hand, we can't physically lash out at every person or object that irritates or annoys us; laws, social norms, and common sense place limits on how far our anger can take us.

Three types of anger are recognized by psychologists. The first form of anger named "hasty and sudden" is connected to the impulse for self-preservation. It is shared between humans and animals and occurs when tormented or trapped. The second type of anger is named "settled and deliberate" and is a reaction to perceived deliberate harm or unfair treatment by others. These two forms of anger are 'episodic'. The third type of anger is however 'dispositional' and is related more to traits of character than to instincts or cognitions. Irritability, sullenness and churlishness in postures are examples of the last form of anger.

Anger can be destructive when it does not find its appropriate outlet in expression. Anger in its strong form, impairs one's ability to process information and to exert cognitive control over his behaviour. An angry person may lose his objectivity, empathy, prudence or thoughtfulness and may cause harm to others. Unexpressed anger can create other problems. It can lead to pathological expressions of anger, such as passive aggressive behaviour, getting back at people indirectly, without telling them why, rather than confronting them head-on or a personality that seems perpetually cynical and hostile. People who are constantly putting others down, criticizing everything, and making cynical comments haven't learned how to express constructively their anger. Not surprisingly, they aren't likely to have many successful relationships. Finally, one can calm down inside. This means not just controlling his outward behaviour, but also controlling his internal responses, taking steps to lower his heart rate, calm oneself down, and let the feelings subside. It is better to control it before it starts controlling oneself. One should have some built-in mechanism to anticipate or project his likely behaviour in case of his getting angry on persons or situations.

There is an interesting behaviour discernible in some people. They tend to surrogate or transplant their anger contracted earlier somewhere into a present situation that is totally unrelated with the earlier one. It is often viewed by students who are awarded punishments by their teacher disproportionate to the seriousness of the 'offence' perpetrated by them while at school as surrogated dispensations of the residual effects of irritation, anger or disillusionment that such a teacher might have contracted at his home and had brought with him to the classroom. It is often the case that in situations where a person is very furious with one and he transfers a part of his anger to another who comes in as an innocent peace-maker or negotiator. The negotiator might get the ire and even a slap or two from that person who is angry. May God save all such unfortunate ones, I mean the negotiators!

Buddhism in general teaches that anger is a destructive emotion; nonetheless it might have some positive effects in terms of survival or moral outrage. Anger of any kind is not considered as a virtuous emotion, nor aggression as constructive behaviour. The Buddha has taught that there are three basic *kleshas* (negative vibrations) at the root of *samsara* (worldly existence of bondage, illusion and the vicious cycle of rebirth). These are greed, hatred, and delusion (attachment, anger, and ignorance). They bring us confusion and misery rather than peace, happiness, and fulfilment. It is in our own self-interest to purify and transform them into positive vibrations.

Similarly, all other denominations of religious faiths, Hinduism, Christianity, Islam, Judaism, Sikhism, Jainism and Zoroastrianism preach same or similar views on anger. In many religions, anger is frequently attributed to God or gods. Primitive people held that gods were subject to anger and revenge. Many believe that opposition to His Will results in His anger. It was a belief (or superstition) among certain aborigines and tribals that whenever they had to face challenges from Nature, like devastating floods and droughts and epidemics, they used to attribute all these to God's fury. They used to resort to 'remedial measures' to appeasing God and thereby seeking His pardon for the alleged causes of His anger.

Management of Anger

Anger can cause distortion, damage or destruction to one's mind and thoughts. Hence it is imperative that it is managed. It is a fire that needs to be doused. The goal of management of anger is thus to reduce both one's emotional feelings and the physiological arousal that anger causes. One can't get rid of, or avoid, the things or the people that enrage him, nor can he change them, but he can learn to control his reactions. It is better that one changes his attitudes rather than trying to change others. There are psychological tests that measure the intensity of angry feelings, how prone to anger one is, and how well he handles it. But chances are good that if one does have a problem with anger, he is already aware of it. If anyone finds himself acting in ways that seem out of control and frightening, he might need help finding better ways to deal with this emotion. It is observed that some people really are more "hot-headed" than others are; they get angry more easily and more intensely than the average person does. There are also those who don't show their anger in loud spectacular ways but are chronically irritable and grumpy. Easily angered people don't always curse and throw things; sometimes they withdraw socially, sulk, or get physically ill. People who are easily angered generally have what some psychologists call a low tolerance for frustration, inconvenience, or annoyance. They can't take things in stride, and they're particularly infuriated if the situation seems somehow unjust: for example, being corrected for a minor mistake. "You too make such mistakes, why me only" would be his retaliation—an effort to redeem themselves by some such sort of self-defence.

What makes these people behave this way? A number of things. One cause may be genetic or physiological. There is evidence that some children are born irritable, touchy, and easily angered; and that these signs are present from a very early age. Another may be socio-cultural. Anger is often regarded as negative; we're taught that it's all right to express anxiety, depression, or other emotions but not to express anger. As a result, we don't learn how to handle it or channel it constructively. Research has also found that family background plays a role. Typically, people who are easily angered come from families that are disruptive, chaotic, and not skilled at emotional communications. Psychologists now say that this is a dangerous myth. Some people use this theory as a license to hurt others. Research has found that "letting it rip" with anger actually escalates anger and aggression, and does nothing to help someone or the person he is angry with, resolve the situation. It is best to find out what is it that triggers his anger, and then to develop strategies to keep those triggers from tipping.

People use a variety of both conscious and unconscious processes to deal with their angry feelings. The three main approaches are expressing, suppressing, and calming. Expressing your angry feelings in an assertive, not aggressive, manner is the healthiest way to express anger. To do this, one has to learn how to make clear what one's needs are, and how to get them met, without hurting others. Being assertive doesn't mean being pushy or demanding; it means being respectful to oneself and others. Anger can be suppressed, and then converted or redirected. This happens when one holds in one's anger, stop thinking about it, and focus on something positive. The aim is to inhibit or suppress one's anger and convert it into more constructive behaviour. The danger in this type of response is that if it isn't allowed outward expression, one's anger can turn inward, on oneself. Anger turned inward may cause hypertension, high blood pressure, or depression. When none of these three techniques work, that's when someone or something is going to get hurt.

Simple relaxation tools, such as deep breathing and relaxing imagery, can help calm down angry feelings. There are books and courses entailing various relaxation techniques; and once they are learnt, the techniques will be offering great help to anyone in any situation.

Some simple steps one can try:

- Breathe deeply in and out from the diaphragm; and not from the chest. Follow *Pranayaama* techniques.
- Slowly repeat a calm word or phrase such as "relax," "take it easy." Repeat it to oneself while breathing deeply.
- Use imagery; visualize a relaxing experience, from either memory or imagination.
- Non-strenuous, slow yoga-like exercises can relax muscles and make one feel much calmer.
- Count up to 100.
- Drink a glass of water.
- Divert attention through music.
- Go for a brisk walk.
- Change the subject of discussion that causes anger.
- Try to relax by meditation.
- Try to analyse oneself honestly and unbiasedly and prove that he himself is only wrong and that the other person is indeed correct. This is the ultimate.

- A cognitive restructuring to change the way one thinks is what is required. Angry people tend to curse, swear, or speak in highly colourful terms that reflect their inner thoughts. When one is angry, his thinking can get exaggerated and overly dramatic. It is good trying replacing these thoughts with more rational ones. For instance, instead of telling oneself, "oh, it's awful, it's terrible, everything is ruined," tell the self, "it is frustrating, and it is understandable that I am upset about it, but it is not the end of the world and getting angry is not going to fix it anyhow." Be careful of words like "never" or "always" when talking about oneself or someone else; they serve to make you feel that the anger is justified and that there's no way to solve the problem. They also alienate and humiliate people who might otherwise be willing to work with him on a solution. Remind that getting angry is not going to fix anything. It won't make one feel better, but instead, it may actually make him feel worse.

Logic defeats anger, because anger, even when it's justified, can quickly become irrational. One must use cold hard logic on oneself. Remind oneself that the world is "not out to get me"; he is just experiencing some of the rough spots of daily life. Do this each time one feels anger getting the best of him, and it'll help one get a more balanced perspective. Angry people tend to demand things: fairness, appreciation, agreement and willingness to do things their way. Everyone wants these things, and we are all hurt and disappointed when we don't get them, but angry people demand them, and when their demands aren't met, their disappointment becomes anger. As part of their cognitive restructuring, angry people need to become aware of their demanding nature and translate their expectations into desires. In other words, saying, "I would like" something is healthier than saying, "I demand" or "I must have" something. When one is unable to get what one wants, he will experience the normal reactions; frustration, disappointment, hurt but not anger. Some angry people use this anger as a way to avoid feeling hurt, but that doesn't mean the hurt goes away.

Sometimes, our anger and frustration are caused by very real and inescapable problems in our lives. Not all anger is misplaced, and often it is a healthy, natural response to these difficulties. There is also a cultural belief that every problem has a solution, and it adds to our frustration to find out that this is not always the case. The best attitude to bring to such a situation, then, is not to focus on finding the solution, but rather on how one handles and faces the problem.

Make a plan, and check the progress along the way. Resolve to give it one's best, but also not to punish oneself if an answer doesn't come right away. If one can approach it with his best intentions and efforts and make a serious attempt to face it head-on, he will be less likely to lose patience and fall into all-or-nothing thinking, even if the problem does not get solved right away.

Communication skills is to be employed. Angry people tend to jump to and act on conclusions, and some of those conclusions can be very inaccurate. The first thing to do if one is in a heated discussion is to slow down and think through his responses. He should not say the first thing that comes to his mind, but slow down and think carefully about what one wants to say. At the same time, listen carefully to what the other person is saying and he should take his time before answering.

It's natural for anyone to get defensive when he is criticized, but he should not fight back. Instead, listen to what is underlying the words spoken by the other. It may be that this person might be feeling neglected and unloved. It may take a lot of patient questioning, but anger of either of the participants should not be let to spin the discussion out of control, rendering the situation a disastrous one.

People who are bestowed with a great sense of humour are generally less prone to losing temper. They are capable of viewing any persons or situations 'with a funny side up'. Building-up of temper can be compared to accumulation of electric charge of high voltage which demands an early discharge, in search of equilibrium. Humorous people do not allow any accumulation or brewing-up of irritations; they have in them built-in ventilators. Despite provocations from people susceptible to contracting anger, such people manipulate situations to suit to their philosophy, thereby diffusing or rarefying tensions. A 'silly humour' can help rarefy rage in a number of ways. For one thing, it can help one get a more balanced perspective. When a person gets angry and calls someone a 'dog', for example, he should stop and picture what that word would literally look like. A dog in fact is the symbol of friendliness, loyalty and many other most desirable virtues which even the addresser may not possess. Then it can not be an abuse, but a 'misplaced or inadvertent compliment'! The more detail one can get into his imaginary scenes, the more chances he has to realize that he is being unreasonable; he will also realize how unimportant the things he was angry about really are. If he practises this technique whenever an 'abusive' name or epithet comes about in his mind for ascription to another, the anger will be driven away. Humour can always serve to relieve tension *vis-à-vis* persons or situations.

There are two cautions in employing humour. First, one should just not to "laugh off" his problems; rather, use humour to help himself face them more constructively. Second, one should not resort to give in to harsh, sarcastic humour, for that is just another form of unhealthy expression of anger. What these techniques have in common is a refusal to take oneself too seriously. Anger is a serious emotion, but it is often accompanied by ideas that can make one laugh. One has to sniff, scan and search for this accompanying humour. One is sure to locate it. One should be apolaustic in his approach to life.

It is natural for anyone to get monotonous with his immediate surroundings, which include persons, objects and situations, if he has to interact, view and deal with them perennially without any change. This monotony can cause irritation and the inevitable consequential anger. One should try to change one, a few or all the components of environment in order to avoid getting angry. One should give oneself a break. It is very necessary to earmark the most appropriate time for negotiations or for discussions on serious matters so that these do not get into rough weather with the inevitable culmination into sheer angry arguments benefiting none. Whenever one option brings about confusion or irritation, it is better to switch to alternatives, rather than fastidiously clinging to that particular option. One should be versatile.

One can not eliminate anger and it wouldn't be a good idea if one could. In spite of best efforts, things that cause anger will happen; sometimes it will be justifiable anger. Life will be filled with frustration, pain, loss, and the irrational and unpredictable actions of others. One can not change that; but he can change the way he lets such events affect him. One has to prevent his angry responses from making him even unhappier in the long run by controlling them.

The Universe can be argued as all coincidental chaos. We do not know what will happen next. We can assume, but we cannot guarantee. So let us not take it so personally when things do not go our way. There is a positive lesson to be taken from any situation; one just has to look for the positive, instead of focusing on the negative. Anger bottled up inside or bursting out is hazardous to health. Every time one loses one's cool, one is probably shaving off a few minutes off his life. Imagine if one is frequently getting mad. These minutes add to hours and days and eventually years. And shortening his lifespan, think of the effect it has on his health in the remaining years! One should simply be ready to accept any situation. He should accept the fact that nothing, he can do, will affect the outcome. The only thing he has control over is how he reacts to it. React to it in the most beneficial, productive way one possibly can. Anger, better control it before it controls you.

Love and Loving— An Obscure Notion

6

We seldom talk about 'love' *per se* in our day-to-day life. It is a presumed perception. It is a concept cultured and warehoused in the subconscious mind. It is available therein in the form of preserved frozen feelings. Feelings are the patented product of the hearts of people.

One can not rely on feelings, because they manipulate and change their colour at random like chameleons do, adapting to the changing situational factors. These feelings have low freezing as well as melting points, and at times they are highly volatile like ether, depending upon the 'atmospheric conditions' prevalent at points of time. They are like creeper plants that grow very well with some support. Likewise, in order to stabilize them, support has to be provided to them jointly by intelligence and imagination. Once they become stable, they prove themselves to be very strong and dependable; otherwise they could become highly dangerous. This is how love works.

Love is one of the most misunderstood concepts. Love has many facets and connotations. Love can be love for God, love for Nature and its manifestations, love for the world, love for the humanity, love for one's country, love for one's society, love for parents, love for one's family and finally love for the self. Then there can be love for music, art, literature, sports and aesthetics, and many other things. These are all different types or shades, and to be seen as such for easy perceptual handling. Our main problem is that we loosely employ this word, love, to describe love with a universal, all-inclusive and absolute meaning and connotation. Here we go wrong. And the result is confusion. If one wants to view the Earth wholly, one has to go a few hundred kilometres out into the Space. If one stands on it and tries to comprehend its shape, he will only fail in his endeavour. There was a time when we used to believe that the Earth was flat. Reason is the same. Similarly, it will be difficult for one to comprehend love in its entirety or wholesomeness, when one is oriented to experience it in segmented and parochial manner. This is the situation where we are in. What is needed is a circumspective approach. It is next to the impossible.

It is impossible to provide a direct definition to this word, love. Love is hardly perceptible to our five senses, viz. seeing, hearing, touching, smelling and tasting. It can probably be expressed indirectly in terms of an effect, experience, notion, feeling, or reaction, either collectively or severally. It has no physical existence; it is metaphysical or abstract. I am apt to equate effectively love with 'care'. Genuine and unconditional care is the expression as well as manifestation of love. Degree of caring indicates presence of love, and it functions as measuring device for love. Love is absolute truth, it is uni-shaded. When someone says, "I truly love you", it only means he or she does not love the other person; it is sheer hypocrisy and hoodwinking. It is like someone saying stressfully, "I have heard with my both the ears", as though he has some other audio reception system too installed and available with him for the purpose of hearing! One should reject outright such statements as they are devoid of credibility. Love can not be expressed through any spoken medium; sometimes it can be detected through 'the language' of the eyes; no other human organs are equipped with such sensitivity. The heart is highly irrational, super-sensitive, volatile and untrustworthy while the head is highly logical, rational and insensitive; but trustworthy otherwise. There is often a tendency on the part of the heart, unlike that of the head, to cheat its owner. The interpretation and appreciation of love by such an imperfect apparatus called heart alone would be disastrous. Similarly, head, an insensitive system, will not be able to perceive and appreciate it. We can not leave this subject of love entirely to the perception of heart, nor can we leave it to the head. Hence the combination of both these, called mind, can only be entrusted with the job of detection, appreciation and experiencing of love. Love, therefore, is a thing to be experienced only by one's mind.

Love is an ocean which has depth, width and vastness. Even oceans have different names artificially assigned by us in order to differentiate and conceive their existence in a palpable sense. If one does not want to get mad, it is better for him to conceive that the whole of universe is only what we see as the solar system, and nothing beyond. We can very well imagine that the frog living in a deep well to be very happy and contended with the 'universe he has created for himself' within the circular wall of the well. He refuses to believe that there could be any other area or space beyond his well-space that the universe of his is occupying. For him the universe starts and ends there in his well. If he ventures to conceive that there could be something beyond that, he would be risking his mental balance. And why should he? Now he is able to hum or whistle his favourite notes unperturbed, and to dance merrily. The human beings have their own limitations. In a sense these differentiations are imaginary. If one believes in God and loves Him, one is left with no choice except accepting the concept of universal love. One has to love everything. It is too difficult a proposition for ordinary human beings to imbibe and practise. This is a concept incomprehensible and untenable to them. Because of this, initially, they have to conceive and understand love in parts, and step-by-step, and they should add-up these parts to make it a whole. One can not devour a large quantity of food in one go. He will be able to eat large quantities, as much as he wants, if he goes forward slowly and steadily. This is the way he can grapple universal love.

Why should we love God? Is it because we are afraid of Him? Is it because He is the giver? Is it because He loves us? Why does man worship God? Is it to get some favours from him? He has plenty with him to give; if He likes and wants, He gives. Why does man praise Him, sometimes alone and sometimes in congregations? He takes things for granted and thinks that He likes appreciation, admiration and extolment, sometimes even 'thanks giving', and shower on Him all the good epithets available, in His praise. Man thinks, foolishly, that He is also like human beings who always enjoy flattery and adulations which blind them. When a man enjoys them he becomes willing to do anything that is asked for by the adulator or flatterer. One wonders if God succumbs to such tactics and strategies. He is not fallible and erratic like human beings. We ask ourselves these and several other similar questions as above, and search satisfactory answers for all of them. These are probing questions serving to help a thorough analysis of our minds, and so also to identify the various elements constituting what we call love. The total picture will be brought to focus. This leads us to understanding of the meaning of love in its entirety. We would start loving Him, only for love's sake. It is the most special type, and is different from other types. Here, the love is tantamount to unconditional surrender, and it is total. Unlike other types of love, it is devoid of any hypocrisy, scepticism, dilution, reservation or attachment. As a prerequisite, our minds are required to be kept clean and vulnerable. True Love generates utmost respect and devotion. It lightens our minds so much so that they would be ready to float and takeoff to realms of a different kind; that is the realm of bliss. This is what we call love for God. The equation, 'God is equal to love', can be understood only in this manner. The essence and spirit of this equation should be imbibed, and permanently stored in the whole of body-and-mind systems of individuals. Simple parrot-like reiterations of this equation is of no use. Reiterations, as a rule, are done only in cases of borrowed ideas in order to remind oneself of their availability for ready use, if and when they would be required. But reiterations are not required in cases of imbibed ideas, for they now belong to the individuals themselves, their rightful property.

Nature is manifestation of God. So, logically, loving and respecting Nature is equivalent to loving and respecting God. But unconsciously the love for Nature gets diluted *vis-à-vis* for God. It is not possible, for example, for an employee of a business enterprise to pay respects in equal measures to the proprietor as well as to his immediate supervisor. Nature manifests itself in many forms. The fauna, the flora, the rivers, the mountains and the hills are the main manifestations. It is this Nature that nurtures each one of us. Our very existence solely depends on her. Watching as well as knowing of this Nature offers one of the greatest and the most exciting experiences that one would have. What is required is keen intelligent observation of some of the simple manifestations that it naturally emits and offers. We have only to watch them as they occur. Nature tells tigers to hunt, kill, and eat deer; deer to eat grass; elephants to eat vegetation; ants to enjoy sweets; bees to collect honey from flowers and live on it; cows to live on grass and young calf on its mother's milk; birds on fruits; giraffe to stretch its long neck to reach its food, kept above, on tall bushes and trees; plants to draw their food from inside the earth; flowers to look at sun and blossom; micro-organisms to our development as well as destruction, grass to grow on the surface of the earth; rivers meet water requirements of everybody and everything; and above all, most importantly, air is supplied to all under Nature's own personal supervision and control in order to avoid any breakdown in supplies of this vital ingredient. What a flawless organizational set-up our Nature has made!

Can anyone be ungrateful to this Nature, which is rudimental as well as fundamental to the very sustenance as well as existence of life itself? None can afford to ignore this fact. Genuine gratitude begets respect, and both of them together confluent into love. We have to love her with the same intensity and fervour as we do in the case of God. This love has to be undiluted and absolute. Keeping the total quantum of love earmarked for the Nature intact, we are apt to apportion our love to the individual members of the various manifestations, the human beings, the other members of the fauna, plants and trees, the mountains and the hills and their valleys, oceans, lakes and the rivers. Indian religion, the Hinduism which represents ancient civilization of the world, considers each of these as demi-Gods: They thus have animals such as elephants, lions, tigers, monkeys, buffalos, cows and even rats; reptiles like snakes trees like banyan; plants like basil; mountains like the Himalayas; rivers like The Ganges, Kaveri, Godavari and Krishna; and are all respected, loved and even worshipped in some way or other by all Hindus.

They have given god-status to all the known and even unknown stars in the cosmos, including the Sun and all of the members of his family called the Solar System. They all are worshipped. They believe that all these celestial objects exercise great influence on individuals. They have devised a 'science' called Astrology, the practical Astronomy, to reckon the influence of these celestial bodies on human and terrestrial affairs. The Hindus believe that most of the demi-gods have adopted and converted some of the animals into their *carriers or* vehicles, and are seated on them, the elephant-faced demi-god, *Ganapati* has a mouse, the time-god, *Kaal,* a buffalo, goddess of female energy, *Mahakaali,* a lioness, Lord *Shiva,* an ox and so on. Most of the fragrant flowers are considered sacred and revered, and are offered while praying to God. They have some abstract demi-goddesses too like Sleep, Love, Art and the like whom they revere.

Similar concepts were prevalent in ancient Greece. The Greek could conceive of many gods connecting to various activities of man as well as things and objects available in Nature. They had, for example, Venus (cupids), Eros (love), Hera (marriage), Zeus (weather) and hundreds of gods like these. They ascribed conceptual divinity and reverence to them, for that was the way that could enable them to lead dignified lives which is the ultimate objective. The Zoroastrianism, an ancient religion, considers Fire as god and believers of that religion worship Fire. All these mean love and worship of Nature.

In fact, everything around them is seen as part of God. When the Hindus name a thing as God, they do not mean to give them status equivalent to what we give to the 'only' almighty God, as conceived by Islam, Christianity or any other denominations. There could be no wonder if people who subscribe to faiths other than the Hinduism do not agree with this sort of ideology that contemplates on 'many mini- and demi-gods'. It is difficult for them to conceive this philosophic approach. This philosophy desires to convey that divineness is all-pervading, and as such it should serve as deterrent against doing wrongs against any objects, animate or inanimate, existing on this earth. The logic behind their giving this special status as mini- or demi-gods to all of them could be that, in the earlier days, it was believed that if any object is given such status by providing a religious colour, people would love and respect them and thereby take care of them. In the olden days, people used to live in forests, at that time the forests used to be their parents who used to feed and protect them. They had learnt, in natural course, to respect all the members of fauna and flora. In effect, in order to comprehend this philosophy, this aspect of worshipping each and everything is to be perceived in a larger perspective as an expression of sincere desire and earnestness to love and respect the great Nature. This great philosophical approach is the ideal one for protecting our environment. Vegetarianism among Hindus, Buddhists and Jains is as a result of this philosophy.

The Hindus believe that all living beings other than plants have 'spirits', the divine presence, in them, and that is why killing and eating of other animals are prohibited, and hence they are practising protagonists of vegetarianism. This is a naturalistic eco-friendly dogma. The Hindus believe in two very important tenets, *vasudhaiva kutumbakam* (the entire fauna as well as flora is to be conceived and considered as members of one family, the concept of a world family), and *loka samastha sukhino bhavantu* (let the whole world become happy). The meaning and the spirit of these phrases speak volumes. These are great ideals that are very vital for sustenance and survival of life on this Earth. These are all in effect expressions of love and loving. Included therein are love for humanity, love for society, love for parents and love for one's own nuclear family.

Love for the self is totally different from being merely selfish and self-centered, unlike what we usually are prone to connote and understand. One has to identify and understand this 'self' of his, and feel and recognize the divineness within. In fact, this is the most difficult but important thing, but once this is achieved, all other things will naturally fall in line. For this, one has to repeat several times in his mind, "I am good", and "all others are divine", and earnestly believe in them; attach oneself with such thinking, and follow the three ideals enunciated in the saying, "See no evil. Hear no evil. Speak no evil". By this method, one will be able to cast off the cursed disease called egoism. This is the short-cut method for realizing the self. There are several ways other than this like total abnegation or renunciation of the 'earthlies', practising mind-controlling techniques of yoga and meditation, as prescribed in the various religious scriptures. There will nothing be left with him except the ultimate, the love for God.

The term 'love' has different meanings and connotations in the various stages of life of every individual. In one's infancy, one needs love from his parents. At that stage, he is in a helpless predicament, and he needs support and protection from those whom he can depend on. We name this 'Love'. The giver just gives it solely out of sympathy, and this sympathy we call love. The child did not 'ask' for its birth as a favour from its parents. Logically it has no obligation to anyone. There is every reason why its parents should feel 'guilty', at least notionally, for bringing it to this earth. The feelings of sympathy and the notional 'guilt' together with its atonement become unconscious motivators for the parents, the mother in particular, for caring it. There is no need for obligation or gratitude on the part of the child towards its parents; albeit the latter ought to have them for the child. Thus he is given love in the form of care and sympathy which are the most essential requirements for his survival at that stage. The giver gives them happily and the receiver receives them, probably, gratefully, without even any implied *quid pro quo* arrangements. This could turnout to be an implied unconscious long term investment by the giver, as a deal for deferred pay-back, in the same coin, if and when required by the giver. Nothing in this is considered wrong as it is neither deliberate, and conscious nor designed. At best, it may be considered as a transaction in love. This process of giving and taking continues till the child reaches his adulthood. Here, the love is devoid of any hypocrisy, jealousy and selfishness. It is all in tune with the game-plan of the Nature.

It is well recognized that a mother's love for her children is most sacred. A mother may be natural, surrogated, commercially or otherwise or accidental. In case of commercial surrogation, a lady gives out her womb on rent to someone sterile on certain specified considerations in accordance with a contract. As soon as the child is born, the contract will be discharged with the fulfilment of contractual obligations on either side. Here, love is secondary. The second type of surrogation relates to humanitarian or philanthropic nature. Here, the consideration for surrogation is due to sympathy or love. Recently, a case has come up wherein a lady had volunteered to become a surrogated mother to beget a child for her own sterile daughter. A grandmother becomes the mother of her own grandchild! She had agreed only to alleviate her sterile daughter's frustration, and so also in saving the latter's marriage. In certain cases, children are born through rape of women by some unscrupulous men. This is what is meant by 'accidental' surrogation. Here too, there is no consideration of love. A mother will have all the love for a child born in the natural way. Similar is the case with surrogation out of sympathy and love. Here in all the cases, love as well as loving for a child is only a matter of situations and conditions in which the child is born. There can not be any absolutism in love; conditions are attached.

When the child reaches adulthood, his requirement of love expands and gets diversified. He requires love from a person of the opposite sex. It is physiological and psychological at that stage. This is also love but it has a different face and shade compared to that of what he has been bestowed with hitherto. "It is a call of flesh to flesh", as Bernard Shaw calls it. It is essentially an expression of sensuality which is a gift from Nature. Nature wants procreation in order to perpetuate life and thereby, herself. Here in this case, the love is being transacted and it has the semblance of a *quid pro quo* deal, a give-and-take system. Here, the love may not be pure and absolute, and may have elements of latent hypocrisy, jealousy and selfishness. Here, there is no surrender possible because any surrender would be mistaken by the other person for weakness, and hence there is a chance of exploitation by the other person. Both will, therefore, resort to a 'hide and seek' game, a sign of mistrust and hypocrisy.

It is in the realm of love, perhaps, that hypocrisy is significantly rampant. If any sort of suspicion, mistrust or fear exists between two so-called 'lovers', their mutual conduct as well as behaviour will be of a cautious kind. They will have no choice other than becoming hypocrites. In fact, two hypocrites cannot really love each other. They only can become partners of some sort of an unholy alliance, but due to situational pressures, they opt to act as lovers, as is done in cinemas with romantic themes. They compromise on the meaning of love. It is conditional love. It becomes a matter of convenience. And love can never be conditional, or a matter of convenience. It is neither negotiable nor barterable. It is 'lovocrisy', a coinage for describing the fusion or nexus between love and hypocrisy. It serves to tell love from hypocrisy.

A glaring example is seen in case of young lovers before their marriage. "I love you", tells one to the other, and the other replies, "I too love you." Then both of them look at each other to measure the depth of love each of them is claiming to have for each other. There is an element of suspicion and fear lurking somewhere. There is no need for expressing love openly through words. When someone says, "Yes", it may as well mean, "No." In an effort to impressing one partner, the other may resort to pretending, posing and telling lies to the other. Love cannot have fear and lies as its base. This type of love is transient and conditional, whereas the one that he had experienced till his adulthood was more real, permanent, tenable and tenacious. When he becomes a parent, the spectrum undergoes a change. The initial 'flesh-to-flesh' love gets transformed into a sense of belongingness, a sign of true love. He is to start giving to his child the same type of love which he was getting when he was a child. It is a fact that none returns love either qualitatively or quantitatively to his parents. The 'capital' of the investment is forfeited, and probably only 'interest' accrued thereon on that capital is paid to the depositor. The capital is paid to his children, as though the depositors had authorized him to pay the capital to their grandchildren. The cycle thus continues.

In fact, love is like pickles which taste good when it is matured. The initial love based on sensuality gradually turns into such a 'pickle', as a married life happily advances. They get into a dependency syndrome and the old couple experiences a true sense of belongingness and true love then. In fact, loving companionship is really required at two stages of one's life, *viz,* one in youth and the other in old age. In the first, it is for satisfying the sensual and affiliated psychological needs leading to procreation, and in the second, it is for mutual help for their infirm physical conditions, and to surmount monotony and loneliness, both characteristic of old age. In the first case, love is raw, *ad hoc,* conditional, tender, tentative and transient, whereas in the second, love is matured, enduring, tenable and tenacious. The equation sets itself balanced. One would say ultimately, *Sic transit gloria mundane.*

Intuition reflects power of the mind by which it immediately perceives the truth of things without reasoning or analysis. The incidence of this phenomenon, it appears, is the result of some unknown or imperceptible programming in the brain brought-in by some unknown agency or indelible inherited impressions imprinted on the brain. Incredible it is. Intuition comes about impulsively, leaving behind no overt evidence of pre-meditation or deliberate design. Intuition and instinct are 'born twins' with identical features. Instincts are involuntary prompting actions; the mental aspects of theirs take rank between unconscious reflex activities and intelligent conduct. The natural impulse is independent of reason or experience. Intuition springs out from accumulated effects or impressions from past experiences kept 'saved' in one's brain-computer. The moment an individual faces a problematic situation, a matching solution is served out to him readily available 'ex-stock' from his already 'saved' assets in his brain. This we call instinct or intuition. Intuitionalism is a doctrine that envisages that perception of truth is by intuition. There is apparently no room for exercising sense of reasoning or analysis. Everything happens unconsciously and instantaneously and that is why we reckon it as a semblance of an automatic programming of some sort in the brain. The incidence of love and loving may be thought of as the handiwork of one of instinct, intuition or imagination of persons involved. Love thus felt generated may be notional, virtual or hallucinate, and hence impalpable. Such love may be abstract and transient. Its arrival could be as spontaneous as its exit. It could evaporate like ether. It will be like a dream. In short, it will not be anything beyond a pleasant piece of expression, like someone claiming 'love at first sight'. People attach supernatural or superstitious beliefs to such a 'love'. Hence instinctive, intuitive or imaginative love may be kept in realm of poetic insights, and understood as such.

'Love' has been ascribed a divine dimension too. They say that marriages are held in heaven. Some people believe that whenever an individual is created by the creator, another individual of the opposite sex is too created as the former's spouse, whether some others believe this or not. Some categorize this as superstition. In any case, it seems that there is hardly any corporeality in that statement. At best, we can call it a figurative expression coined by some imaginative persons. Such statements have a positive effect when meant to cement relationships between husband and wife, because they are probably conscious of the existence of God and the conceptual existence of hell and heaven. They are afraid of the 'Damoclean Sword' hanging overhead, should they flout the rules of the 'game'. Let us be positive for His sake!

The members of the fauna too love each other. Their love is of a limited and encompassing variety, but genuine and devoid of any hypocrisy, unlike in the case of the humans. Behind the love expressed by the latter, there is usually an agenda of self interest which they cleverly camouflage and hide. To help them in this, they have their intelligence and imaginative power. The animals other than humans practise and exhibit love as well as loving in an open and overt manner because of the absence of pronounced intelligence and imagination. Their behaviour is based on sensuous feelings which ultimately lead to procreation and perpetuation of their species. It is the Nature that has bestowed these feelings upon them in order to impose its will upon them.

Apart from loving members of their own species, they exhibit friendliness and love for others too, though the purpose of this behaviour is naturally different. Some of them like the ones in the feline clan, for example, have set rules, regulating their behaviour among themselves. They have great regards of love and feelings of belongingness among themselves. They do not hunt or kill each other. They, like many other members of the fauna, are not cannibals. They fight collectively against their common enemies. Sometimes they hunt collectively if their prey is found to be stronger and unmanageable singly. The males fight among themselves only in cases of theft of love of their females. But, for reasons best known to them, they hesitate to cultivate friendship with those of other species or clans. Some of them like cats are domesticated by humans. Lions and tigers, though rarely, too are made pets by humans, but their loyalty is questionable many a time.

The domesticated animals, like cows, buffalos, monkeys, dogs and even cats cohabiting in the same household develop understanding and friendship among themselves, owing to the absence of fear of any sort. Animals are known to behave instinctively. The other day, as was reported, a mother bitch was seen lending her breasts to a needy orphan monkey-baby forsaken by its mother. The innocent baby, probably without recognizing the benevolent donor, was enjoying itself to be part of this philanthropic 'milk donation' scheme where it was the lone beneficiary. The new-found 'mother' was seen enjoying herself even more than the beneficiary. All her typical canine mode of expressions clearly depicted her feeling of pride. It seemed that she had boldly overruled the protests and resentment 'vociferously expressed' by her own pups in order to dissuading her from taking-up this venture. The canine pups, more than the loss of some quantity of milk that is solely meant for them, did not like the idea of sharing their mother's love with an 'intruder'. There might have been sonant exchanges like, "No mummy, no", "No children, no" preceding her final verdict. Their love is devoid of any sort of pretensions.

In another case, as reported, a monkey and a dog are both members of a human family. The elders in the family go outdoors for work for long hours, leaving an infant son at the care of these two members. Both of them jointly look after the child very well by feeding him with the food that his mother has earmarked for him and kept in the custody of these two. They were his security guards. They seemed to be more devoted to their duties than human guards on employment. The monkey prefers sweet lemon juice to milk. By any chance if the elders forgot to add sugar the monkey would throw it away. They all play the game of love. We can not say that it is instinctive behaviour and leave it at that. It is a suspect case of evidence of intuition and reason coming into play. It seems that there is no direct evidence to conclude about the role of intuition as well as reasoning *vis-à-vis* their actions and reactions. Whatever may be the case, it is sure that they are all players in love-game.

One can see in forests, some trees of the same species live together. Reasons could be many. Nature probably wants them to be together, in order to facilitate their procreation and propagation. There is some evidence to suggest that even plants too love each other. They are pained if anyone of them is 'murdered' in their presence by the unscrupulous human beings to meet their selfish ends. Only imaginative people can see their agony and 'tears'. It seems that they love each other and are happy to live together, as a 'society'. Since they do not move about like members of the fauna, they await breeze and winds to help them dance with the whistling music that they bring with them. Human beings with imagination and romantic minds might be able to observe this. Such people might also be able to listen to the chorus of happiness they sing! These are all expressions of love and sense of belongingness.

Expression of Humour— A Peculiar Interaction

7

Manifestation of sense of humour by the human beings in their interacting realms provides one with an inkling of one of their communicative behaviours. It is peculiar and special type of communication. It provides one with an insight into the working of their minds. Its employment is peculiar to humans; other members of the fauna do not possess this faculty. Communication of ideas can be done most effectively if it is done humorously, for, humour is as sweet as sugar. Everyone including those who are afflicted by the disease of diabetes likes and enjoys sweetness, even though overdose might induce monotony, sedation or even death to some people, depending upon their levels of acceptance and absorption of sweetness. Similar is the case with humour. A few cases of 'indigestion' due to overdose of it too are reported. Cynics do not enjoy humour; they do not know the art of smiling or laughing, except probably when two cynics share their cynical pursuits. A 'test dose' of humour can be administered to persons to confirm if they are cynics or not. Even though it is a Herculean task to 'convert' such persons, there have been some success stories. The results may not be commensurable with the efforts.

Human beings are endowed with abundant intelligence. It is this intelligence that makes them different as well as superior to all other beings on this Earth. Intelligence has its many facets and dimensions when it expresses itself. Whatever we humans conceive, create or construct everyday forms nothing but evidence of its presence in us, though of course, ostensible in different individuals in varying degrees of both quality and quantity. It is, in fact, this element of variance that renders the study of the human minds by humans themselves very challenging and difficult, even though, at times, rewarding and thrilling.

Thus, it offers great realms, avenues and opportunities for research scholars. Intelligence manifests itself in human beings in many ways. Sense of humour is one such manifestation. The presence of sense of humour, therefore, provides direct proof of the existence of a good deal of sagacity in persons, while its absence may not mean lack of it. A good joke passed on by an initiator to a target person or group of persons causes a boisterous laughter. But it is not the case always. Sometimes it may produce only a chuckle, a grin or even no reaction at all, despite the fact that the initiator, the target and the humour-content, intensity and other characteristics of the joke are the same. This phenomenon is mainly due to varying perceptibility levels at different times and situations, and mood, primarily, of the target group/lot, and, secondarily, of the initiator and situational peculiarities. An initiator may be any of the following types:

- Stranger Initiator
- Familiar Initiator
- Friend Initiator
- Comedian Initiator

Stranger Initiator

Assuming that the humour-content, quality and other characteristics to be constant, we will see that the reaction or response by the target people to joke initiated by any of the four categories of initiators will be of different types and degrees. A 'stranger' initiator, may not excite the minds of people to whom the joke is directed, and bring about humour-sensation in them. The reason for this could be that they are not able to perceive or digest the humour. Most people, while in direct conversation with proper eye-contact, fail to listen to what exactly is being spoken, as at the outset, instead, they spend time mainly only in understanding the 'stranger'. Hence, the resultant response will have to fall short of the desired level. This approach is more noticeable when the persons involved are of opposite sexes.

Familiar Initiator

A 'familiar' initiator is one who is a less 'stranger'. He obviously had more outings with the target lot on a few occasions earlier. Here the humour-generation response by the target would be much higher than that in the case of the 'stranger' initiator for the same intensity or quality of humour.

Friend Initiator

A 'friend' initiator is similar to the 'familiar' type, but the understanding between both the parties is very great, thereby humour-generation response is also immense. The target is 'conditioned' by the possibility of reasonably accurately anticipating the intensity of humour-content in a joke which is yet to be sent out by the 'friend'. Here the response is normally positive as well as adequate. The only problem is that there is a chance that the type of initiation and the type of humour could fairly be the same, and that the target might perceive them to be monotonous reiterations. There is an element of mutual inductance or conditioning between the involved parties. This could cause communication barriers. A careful intelligent and alert initiator will take guard against such anomalous results, well in time.

Comedian Initiator

A 'comedian' initiator is a person who is recognized in the world over as a professional comedian. The mere mention of his name or showing his photograph to the target audience would condition them. For example, if one announces before an audience that a famous comedian would be amid them shortly, each member of the audience would start 'salivating'. They would have fully got themselves set to laugh, awaiting the emergence of the comedian on the stage. They even start laughing; sometimes even before realizing as to what the joke is about. There is a 'hypnotizing' effect, so to say. There can be variations and exceptions to this behavioural pattern.

The physical appearance and demeanour of the initiator also have their say in the matter of effectiveness, while administering a joke. If the initiator has a 'not-so-handsome' or nearly ugly countenance, his humour will interest the target group more. It is because of the fact that the humour-provocation initiated by such a person could have been much above the expectation-level of the target group. This is a surprise treatment, a mild shock, all the same, helping the initiator's cause or mission.

In order to avail desired effect, in most cases, a bit of conditioning of the target-minds would be required. The person who initiates a joke or a humorous situation should understand, well before his initiating it, the perceptibility level of the target person/persons. Even a good joke or a humorous situation might get undermined or uncared for, if it is fed to a listener at his imperceptible state of mind. The initiator has to be intelligent as well as alert to make the most of the opportunities or situations in order to attain the effect desired and designed. It is like the 'bowling' in game of cricket. The bowler has to understand the weakness of the batsman facing him to get the latter to the former's trap. The level of satisfaction which the bowler attains when his opposing batsman gets 'back-to-the-pavilion' is almost the same kind as the initiator of joke gets when his 'victim', I mean, the target subject demonstrates his pleasant acceptance as well as enjoyment of humour. A boisterous laughter or chuckle thrown out by the subject is the ostensible expression of such feelings. But, unlike in the game of cricket, here both the parties to this 'game' enjoy and cherish, though, probably, the initiator gets the lion's share.

Sense of humour is an asset in the hands of anyone who has to interact with others. It can be profitably employed by a leader or manager to enhance his effectiveness. A manager gets his work done through his subordinates. The work can be got done by two ways, namely, by force, coercion or threat, or by persuasion and participation. Both are probably effective, but the latter enables the manager to deal with human beings as human beings and not as 'two-legged machines'. Let them work and live happily. This is a philosophic approach.

All living things are allergic or the least resentful to any sort of sorrow, pain or discomfort. These form strong stimuli to which they react adversely. These reactions may manifest in different ways, depending upon various other influencing factors.

One case of expression may be overt belligerence, while the other, covert dissatisfaction. Others assume their positions on the continuum of these extremes. Most of human beings have affinity for comfort and pleasure. Hence, they have inherent and natural proneness to light-heartedness. Human beings crave to be comfortable at all times, as far as possible this ardent propensity forms an integral part of their psyche-system and it evolves determinants of modes and trends of their behaviour. The man's affinity for comfort, pleasure and happiness is such that any deprivation or even potential threat to its continued enjoyment will render him frustrated. Like in the case of a weighing balance trying to regain its equilibrium after its having been disturbed, the human mind tends to reach back to its previous state, at the earliest opportunity. This effort may be voluntary or deliberate. Men have, thus, inherent and natural proneness to light-heartedness in varying degrees. In some, it may be minimal and underdeveloped, while in some others it may be in abundance and fully developed. All other cases find their places in between these two extremes.

A manager must have a keen sense to sense, discern and reckon this light-heartedness. Having done so, he should be able to manipulate these propensities in such a way that he will be able to get them perform adequately. They like to obey a manager willingly who is genial and light-hearted in nature, and who is considered one among them. A manager should become a 'familiar' or 'friendly' initiator, as and when situation arises, but definitely not a 'stranger' or 'comedian' initiator. He is sure to achieve his goals in the most economical, efficient and effective manner.

"A leader is a person who influences a group to follow the course of action he advocates." A leader is always identified with the group of which he forms a part. A person who is the leader of an intellectual group concerned with abstract ideas must be different from the person who leads, say, an athletic club. To get a picture of leaders and leadership, we consider the group situation in which the leader operates. This is not to say that leaders of different groups will have no traits in common or that the person who emerges as the leader of one group is unlikely to become one of any other group. It is, indeed, possible to list some general qualities that often distinguish people who emerge as leaders—they are all active participators in their groups, they are dependable, persistent, self-confident and socially popular. Having these qualities, however, does not ensure leadership in every group, but in many situations, the person who possesses such a combination of traits will probably be prominent contender for the leader's slot. A leader has to be a manager and vice versa. Hence, these two words are synonymatic, and used, as such, in this treatise.

Effective leaders seem to be sensitive and thereby pay enough attention to people, their morale, organizational culture, fostering right kinds of values and attitudes in them, providing avenues for development of their competence, and channelling their energies in the right directions. The manager or leader must ascertain for himself if his philosophy and style percolate down the line. He should devise means to know if he is paying adequate attention to 'softer dimensions' or the leadership he provides results in the optimum utilization of human potential and thereby ensuring organizational effectiveness. He should constantly introspect and evaluate his own performance. He is to form-up a second nature in him to look into a mirror often.

Management is what a leader or manager does, and what does he or she do? He or she 'gets things done through others'. That would mean that a leader's main task is getting things done through his subordinates in such a way that he is able to accomplish adequately the responsibilities entrusted to him by his organization. The method and manner in which he does this entirely depend upon him. To aid him in this, he must have adequate professional knowledge and practical experience. Further, he should have mature and pragmatic knowledge of how human minds work, or the least, of how do the minds of his followers work. Thus a leader should become a perpetual student as well as practitioner of practical human psychology. This includes psychology of man as an individual as well as a member of a social group. Management is a 'social process' being carried on in an organization that is viewed as a 'social system'. We are apt not to perceive a person as an individual, instead, a part of a social group, and his being managed is a social process.

A leader who has to get things done by his people must have a keen sense to sense, discern and reckon his men's inherent and natural proneness to light-heartedness. A bit of introspection, on his part, enables him to empathise and understand as to what goes on in their minds under various stimulating conditions and situations. A leader has to manipulate or manoeuvre these inherent and natural propensities in such a way that he is able to achieve the behavioural pattern from his men according to his designs. Men have to be brought to do work willingly and a good sense of humour at the disposal of the manager makes the led 'hypnotized' so to say, and obeying his commands. These commands will appear to them as pleasant persuasion from their leader, and they are obeyed most willingly.

A leader should become a 'pied piper' with respect to his men. For this, apart from other motivating factors, his sense of humour has a quintessential role to play. He should don a genial air which is nothing but an indirect expression of his pleasant and other positive ways of thinking, as 'countenance reflects the mind'. This may, at times, be wrongly interpreted by his men unless they have full faith and confidence in their leader's intelligence, knowledge and wisdom. Hence the leader, by his demeanour both on and off the working environment, should establish the fact that their leader is really superior to them in most of the fields, if not all. Once this is done, his genial air and demeanour mean all well to them and he will be loved and followed.

A leader should have good sense of humour, both assimilative and disseminative, which he should employ and exploit to the fullest advantage. This is an invaluable resource and asset bestowed with him. He can benefit from it immensely. He is sure to achieve his goals in the most economical, efficient and effective manner. If a manager does not possess this sense and most importantly if he is aware and conscious of this fact, he can inculcate it with full determination and purposive self-training. This, of course, is to be preceded by a change in his attitude and philosophy. It is difficult, but not impossible for an alert, intelligent, versatile person, so is any leader. One should cooperate with oneself in this. That is the minimum requirement. In order to perform his job as a manager or as a leader, he has to be a good communicator but for which he would fail in achieving his goals. Leading or guiding can be accomplished only by communicating to his followers what his ideas are and what he intends to accomplish. Hence communication is of paramount importance and a good sense of humour in him makes things easier.

8

Sportsmanship—"Love All"

According to *Chamber's Dictionary*, the word 'sport' means to play, to amuse or to make merry; sport is recreation, pastime or game; and sportsman is one who practises, or is skilled in sports: one who shows a good spirit in sports. It means that a sports-field is not battle field, where two warring parties meet and settle their disputes by resorting to any means. The saying that everything is fair in war and love is not to be applied in the sports field, because sport fields are not battle fields nor the players are involved in war games, nor are they playing the game of love. The means to achieve ends, therefore, must be just, moral, ethical, benevolent and transparent. Here in the case of sports, the means is more important than the end. "Love all" is the starting and ending points of any game. This phrase is to provide a caution, reminding especially the participants, among others, to uphold good traditions of sports and sportsmanship always.

Sportsmanship is behaviour of sportsmen in conformity with the laid down or conventionally accepted rules, spirit, and etiquette of sports. More grandly, it may be considered the ethos of sport. It is interesting to conceive that the motivation for sport is often an elusive element. Sportsmanship expresses an aspiration or ethos that the activity will be enjoyed for its own sake, with proper consideration for fairness, ethics, respect, and sense of fellowship with one's competitors. Being a "good sport" involves being a "good winner" as well as being a "good loser". Often the pressures of competition and aggrandisement of individual achievement seem to work to deny enjoyment and thrill to participants. As a result, sportsmanship may be contrasted with gamesmanship. Unfortunately many role models nowadays are planting the idea of gamesmanship, instead of sportsmanship, into the heads of young athletes. Gamesmanship is commonly known as the art of winning games. In order to gain advantage over their opponents, they do not mind pushing the rules to the limit, and using whatever means, already available or invented. Coaches advocating gamesmanship are enemies of good sportsmanship. As a result, they create bad sportsmen. "If I win, I gain. If you lose, then too I gain. If you win, nay, that's not going to happen, I will scuttle even your remote chances of winning by adopting any means—so you can not win, win I must." This is the theme of bad sportsmanship.

A competitor who exhibits poor sportsmanship after losing a game or contest is called a 'sore loser'. Behaviour includes reacting immaturely or improperly, making excuses for their loss, referring to unfavourable conditions or other petty issues. Examples of poor sportsmanship are winners "rubbing salt in the wounds" of the losers, or the losers expressing frustration at not winning, perhaps to the point of holding a grudge, booing the winner's national anthem or failing to congratulate the winners.

> The most important lesson I've learned from sports is how to be not only a gracious winner, but a good loser as well. Not everyone wins all the time, as a matter of fact, no one wins all the time. Winning is the easy part, losing is really tough. But, you learn more from one loss than you do from a million wins. You learn a lot about sportsmanship. I mean, it's really tough to shake the hand of someone who just beat you, and it's even harder to do it with a smile. If you can learn to do this and push through that pain, you will remember what that moment is like the next time you win and have a better sense of how those competitors around you feel. This experience will teach you a lot on and off the field!
>
> —Amy Van Dyken

> In the end, it's extra effort that separates a winner from second place. But winning takes a lot more that

> that, too. It starts with complete command of the fundamentals. Then it takes desire, determination, discipline, and self-sacrifice. And finally, it takes a great deal of love, fairness and respect for your fellow man. Put all these together, and even if you don't win, how can you lose?
>
> —Jesse Owens

Sportsmanship typically is regarded as a component of morality in sport, composed of three related and perhaps overlapping concepts—fair play, sportsmanship, and character. Fair play refers to all participants having an equitable chance to pursue victory and acting toward others in an honest, straightforward, and a firm and dignified manner even when others do not play fairly. It includes respect for others including team members, opponents, and officials. Character refers to dispositions, values and habits that determine the way that person normally responds to desires, fears, challenges, opportunities, failures and successes and is typically seen in polite behaviours toward others such as helping an opponent up or shaking hands after a match. An individual is believed to have a "good character" when those dispositions and habits reflect core ethical values.

Good sportsmanship encompasses respect for the game or sport they play and practise, respect for coaches and guides who help them and all players, seniors or juniors. In short, they must develop a high sense of discipline which will only carry them along. They should become broad-minded. This is possible only if they are brought up with lofty ideals which their idols or seniors were proud to hold. They expect their role models or idols to behave in real sportsmanlike manner. They go through the life stories of great sports personalities, obtained through books, printed and visual media and success stories narrated by their mentors. They then understand that the real winners in sports and games are those who know how to preserve dignity at all times irrespective of what the outcome of the activity is. Shaking hands genially with opponents before the sporting activity begins, appreciating and acknowledging for good performance by the opponents, heartily congratulating them if they get the ultimate result in their favour and considering the opportunity to participate in the activity is more important than the actual winning or losing.

Let me cite some examples of truthful and dignified behaviour in the game of cricket. In the game of cricket, a fielding player truthfully acknowledges that the 'catch' that he has held was not in order, because the ball had touched the ground before it came into his hands, even when all other fielders and the umpire had thought otherwise. He could easily have taken advantage of the situation, but he opted for the truthful path—denial of catch. In another case, when the umpire had declared a batsman "not out", because the former was 'sure' that the ball had not come in contact with the bat, the batsman knew the truth and confirmed to the umpire that it was a case of misjudgement on the part of the umpire; and he walked-out of the crease, declaring himself "out". His demeanour was truthful and dignified. In yet another case, a fielding cricketer positioned near the 'boundary rope' at the square area, has stopped a ball, a well-steered 'square-cut' from the batsman, about a metre from the boundary rope. By the time the ball was stopped, the batsman could run twice across, availing 'two runs'. But the umpire was apprised by the fielder that his left foot had touched the rope at the same time as he had held the ball in his hand, and that the batsman deserved four runs instead of two. The umpire acted accordingly. Here too, the behaviour of the fielder has been exemplary, truthful and truly sportsmanlike. In all these cases, outcome of the particular game could have been altered depending on the stands these cricketers would have taken. There has been many a case in every other type of sports and games, like football, hockey and athletics. In all these too, sportsmen face such challenges, and they respond to such situations according to the level of their inherent or imbibed characteristics of honesty and sportsmanlike qualities.

Playing a sport fairly, winning with all humility and losing gracefully are all about good sportsmanship. In today's society, winning comes before everything, but if winning requires neglect of good sportsmanship, then nothing is gained in the long run. Sportsmanship matters not only in sports, but also in the rest of every activity in our everyday lives. In any competition, whether a job interview, a school science fair, or even a friendly game of cards with some friends or in politics sportsmanship teaches you to win humbly and lose gracefully. Sportsmanship also helps us to understand each other better, because when we get along, we can listen to the other person's perspective, and see where they are coming from, and avoid a bad, possibly violent situation. Almost everyday on the news violence is reported at a sporting event, evidence of bad sportsmanship. Without sportsmanship there would be no sports, because no one would want to compete with a person who when lost, would throw a fit, cry, and whine. Young athletes usually learn sportsmanship from an older person, like a parent or probably the most influential role model, a professional athlete.

To be good sportsmanlike is easier said than done. Let us understand the psychological aspect of human behaviour. Often our responses to stimuli get disproportionate to the stimuli factors. There is an inherent propensity in all human beings to behave impolitely, unkindly and rudely with fellow beings on the slightest of pretexts. In adverse situations this propensity gets to the worse and uncontrollable. They lose their mental equilibrium. If a team loses a very 'prestigious' and keenly contested competition, that too by a thin margin, it is rather very difficult for the losing team to ignore the loss and 'humiliation' that its members have to bear, and to congratulate the winning team, that too at the very moment on the spot in the play-field. The natural tendency is to react negatively. To congratulate the winning team at that time is a daunting task. It requires lot of large heartedness, courage, training and discipline in doing so. It is all possible only with inculcation of true sportsmanlike qualities that could enable him to take everything in its stride.

Barring a few, most of the sports are for the young men and women. Hence it is imperative that young children before they enter into adolescence are to be encouraged to take part in all sporting activities. We have to catch them young. They need to be trained at that stage. The parents, teachers and older players have a responsibility in identifying each child's aptitude for a particular sport, and provide him with infrastructural facilities as well as training and the needed guidance. The children should be encouraged to adopt role models too, so that they could emulate and imbibe the sterling qualities of their idols or role models. That is how their sporting career should commence.

"Catch them young". All training, therefore, should be imparted to the young children so that they become true sports persons when they grow up. Good sportsmanship is an asset. They display these essential qualities everywhere, in classrooms, at home and in social life. They will become capable of tackling many problems in their lives as they grow-up. They will become good citizens. Good sportsman spirit does not mean behaviour in the sports field only. It is a total package of orderly behaviour in public too. The coaches should provide emphasis on the great fun attached to playing a game, not necessarily only the winning part. They should not encourage, orient or condition the children only about being in first place and say that anything goes as long as they win. They pick up the message that it is justified to be ruthless on the field. If parents constantly pressurise them by applying undue influence to improve their performance every time, the children will be forced to resort to any means to achieve the desired results; they get the wrong message that end is more important than means. It is an undesirable trend. Adults should emphasize on good sportsmanship, and make them understand that winning as just one of several goals they would like them to achieve. They help young athletes take pride in their accomplishments and in their improving skills, so that the children see themselves as winners, even if the scoreboard does not show the numbers going in their favour. The best coaches, parents, elders and senior athletes must encourage their wards to play fair, to have fun, and to concentrate on helping the team while polishing their own skills. Lessons to good sportsmanship can be taught to young children as and when they start playing. The best way probably would be through a system of situational analysis. It will be advantageous to consider real life situations in the sports field wherein the children play and interact together and analyse, in their presence, the various behavioural aspects of their actions and reactions in the field; a practical workshop. Video footage focused on specific actions will be of immense help for such analyses. A 'brain storming' session involving all concerned can also be conducted. The results of such 'exercises' will be highly rewarding.

"Handle with care". Ramesh, eleven years of age, is a member of junior football team. The team has lost a crucial match by a solitary goal despite good showing by the team. Ramesh, playing in the 'forwards' position had had two golden chances to score, but he missed both of them. Had he not missed those chances, obviously, the team would have won the match. At the end of the match his ambitious and anxious father scolded him for the 'misses', in front of many others. Upset by the inappropriate behaviour on the part of his father he started crying. These parents get so wrapped up in winning and losing or how well their own kids perform that they lose sight of what is really important—promoting a sense of good sportsmanship. As a part of inculcation of sportsmanship in young children, parents, teachers and elders have to be very careful in handling their ward in such situations.

In home context, it will be easy to inculcate or instil sportsmanship among children. When there are a few members in the family, children should be taught to be tolerant and adjustable to each other's cause. They should be encouraged to adopt a policy of 'give and take', and share each other's concern. They learn all this from their elders. Gradually they will shed their selfishness and egoism. This, in fact, is the first step to cultivating sportsmanship. When the elders are watching a sports game on television, it is better to have the children nearby. They should be asked to give their opinion about the way the players behave and play.

Children are taught how to react positively or negatively when they win or lose when they are little. This means that most likely the parents are teaching their children about sportsmanship. What every parent teaches the child is what matters. When the parents attend their child's sports-event, they should show good sportsmanship always. They should offer praise and encouraging words to all athletes, including their child's opponents. Never should they openly scold, tease, or demean any child athlete, coach, or referee while attending a sporting event.

Good sportsmanship is when teammates, opponents, coaches, and officials treat each other with respect. The youngsters are given opportunities to learn the basics of sportsmanship from the adults in their lives. They should provide them with examples from the lives of legends. Kids who see adults behaving in a sportsmanlike way gradually come to understand that the real winners in sports are those who know how to persevere and to behave with dignity—whether they win or lose a game.

The coach and the parents must set themselves exemplary in their conduct and behaviour during practices as well as during the actual competitions. This will have great influence on the children. The saying, "Actions speak louder than words" is very apt to be adopted. That is especially true when it comes to teach the children the basics of good sportsmanship. The caution, "Handle with care" is to be remembered always when we deal with children. All of the actions and reactions and expressions of frustrations and exultations manifested consciously or unconsciously by the parents, coaches or elders during or after the event are being watched assiduously by the children. There is always a tendency in them to emulate and imbibe these. Hence it is imperative that these eiders behave responsibly especially in presence of the children. During the time when the sporting event involving their ward is in progress, they should not give directions to the team or its individual members from the sidelines. There could be no harm if they shout encouraging words. After a competition, it is important not to dwell on who won or lost; instead, try to get feedback or his version of the performance from the child in either case. If his team loses, take corrective actions. If the opposing team wins, help him analyse impartially the good strategies the opponents followed and emulate those. No coach should expect too much out of his own trainee.

"A good coach will make his players see what they can be rather than what they are." Neither the parents nor the coach should push their wards to any game. The children should be given freedom to choose their favourite game. The coach and the parents should keep their perspective and understand that it is just a game. Even if the team loses every game of the season, it's unlikely to ruin the life of their ward or chances of future success. They should not isolate his trainee from the team and show any favouritism to him or her alone.

They should point out examples of good sportsmanship in professional athletes to their wards. Also point out bad examples, too, tell them why they upset them. They should set a good example with their courteous behaviour toward the parents of children of the other team. Congratulate them when their children win. Finally, they should realize that their ward is not a star, and enjoy the game, thinking of all the benefits that he is gaining—new skills, new friends, and attitudes that can help all through life. Applaud good plays no matter who makes them. Parents, if unsatisfied with the way the practices are conducted, should keep their comments positive, and discuss the problems privately with the coach.

Sportsmanship can be conceptualized as an enduring and relatively stable characteristic or disposition such that individuals differ in the way they are generally expected to behave in sport-situations. In general, sportsmanship refers to virtues such as fairness, self-control, courage and persistence and has been associated with interpersonal concepts of treating others and being treated fairly, maintaining self-control in dealing with others, and respect for both authority and opponents. Seven facets of sportsmanship have been identified:

- Full commitment to participation (e.g., showing up, working hard during all practices and games, acknowledging one's mistakes and trying to improve);
- Respect and concern for rules and officials;
- Respect and concern for social conventions (e.g., shaking hands, recognizing the good performance of an opponent);
- Respect and concern for the opponent (e.g., lending one's equipment to the opponent, agreeing to play

even if the opponent is late, not taking advantage of injured opponents);

- Avoiding poor attitudes toward participation (e.g., not adopting a win-at-all-costs approach, not showing temper after a mistake, and not competing solely for individual prizes);
- "Teamwork is the fuel that allows common people to produce uncommon results"; and
- "The purpose of any athletic endeavour is to challenge human limits both on and off the playing field."

Some eminent sports-personalities say thus:

> "Do you know what my favorite part of the game is? The opportunity to play" (Mike). "Sports do not build character. They reveal it" (John Wooden). "The Spirit of Sports: The spirit of sports gives each of us who participate an opportunity to be creative. Sports knows no sex, age, race or religion. Sports gives us all the ability to test ourselves mentally, physically and emotionally in a way no other aspect of life can. For many of us who struggle with 'fitting in' or our identity—sports gives us our first face of confidence. That first bit of confidence can be a gateway to many other great things!" (Dan O'Brien)

> "These answers to these questions will determine your success or failure. (1) Can people trust me to do what's right? (2) Am I committed to doing my best? (3) Do I care about other people and show it? If the answers to these questions are yes, there is no way you can fail" (Holtz). "Victory is in the quality of competition, not the final score" (Mike Marshall). "The most important decision I ever made in my career was to live my life in sports as honestly and ethically as possible. Never having compromised my values allows me to look back on my life with no regrets and feel satisfaction in what I was able to accomplish" (Greg LeMond). "Good coaches teach respect for the opposition, love of competition, the value of trying your best, and how

to win and lose graciously" (Brooks Clark). "Our greatest glory is not in never failing, but in rising each and every time we fail" (Confusicius). "Remember that sports are meant to be fun. Don't let someone make the sport unfun for you" (Kitt). "We cannot fail to win unless we fail to try" (Tom Clancy). "One man practicing good sportsmanship is far better than 50 others preaching it." (Knute K Rockne)

The authorship of the following great sayings is not known:

"The higher the goal, the harder the climb, but taken each day, one step at a time. The goal is accomplished, the dream is attained, and the prizes? The wisdom and the strength that are gained." "T.E.A.M. stands for (T)ogether (E)veryone (A)chieves (M)ore." "You win some, you lose some, but you always try again." "Some people dream of success while others wake up and achieve it." "Gold medals don't make champions...hard work does." "The greatest test of courage on the earth is to bear defeat without losing heart."

9

Sarcasm, Derision, Insultation and Cynicism

Sarcasm, derision, insultation and cynicism are part of a group of profane and sinister and hence undesirable way of interaction among human beings. They all stand for behavioural aberrations. These are peculiar and patented patterns of human behaviour; other members of the fauna do not indulge themselves in any of these. Humans employ these among themselves rampantly to ridicule themselves; they use freely selecting appropriate abuses from the 'Encyclopedia of Abuses' at each other: they do not even mind animalising each other, wrongly assuming that animals are a cursed lot. Humans try to look down on each other as a part of this culture. While deriding, insulting or being sarcastic, they call each other "borrowed" names such as "monkey" (for unstable mind), "ass" (brainless and slow) "insect" (mini, irritable and contemptible), "dog" (used when the abuser does not get another suitable name), "pig or swine" (dirty and contemptible), "giraffe" (long-necked), "elephant" (huge size), "rhinoceros" (shameless or thick-skinned), "rat" (small but menacing), "snake" (venomous and lurking), "fox" (cunning), "cock" (voluptuous) "cat" (for eye or cleverness), "vulture" (dirty and for eye-sight) and a few others. Selection of appropriate names for allocation is very assiduously and imaginatively done. The humans will not be blamed or punished by these creatures for the offence of trespassing or profane misappropriation of their names and other characteristics because they are not aware of the fact that humans have christened them with these names—a monkey, for example, does not know that it is christened, "monkey" or an elephant does not know that it is known as "elephant" among humans and so on. When a person shouts, "Hey, elephant, look here" the elephant looks at him not because it understands that humans christened it so but because it is responding to some sound-stimulus. Even if the person calls it a 'monkey' the elephant would have responded in the same manner.

In black and dark background, white objects become whiter and brighter. This world would have been an unworthy and monotonous place to live in, if only good people have been living. Good is good only if bad is beside it. A wise man has once said that one should not move away from the person who is indignant, derisive and contemptuous towards him. If possible, he should build a house for that person opposite to his own; because that is the way he can reform and cleanse himself without soap and water. That person's contempt and criticism will be tantamount to a mirror, wherein he can look and get his drawbacks highlighted and focused. He will thus be able to reform and purify himself. So it is a boon that such persons exist in this world. The black becomes foil for the white.

Sarcasm is a terrible and destructive kind of communication. It usually comes out of a cynical mind. Sarcasm, normally, does not have a truth-base. It emanates basically from one's heart, and rarely only designed by the head. If it is only of the heart, and not from the head, then he can be excused to some extent, for, the latter's role, if any, could be more detrimental. The person resorts to employing this heinous weapon called sarcasm in order to pulling down one in front of others in the society. He gets sadistic pleasure. He manifests his meanness at heart. His satires or jibes speak of the working system in him. This is a disorder. One fine morning, if the head placed on him realizes about his problems, consciously or unconsciously, deliberately or accidentally, then he may tumble upon self-analysis which is the only cure for his disease.

Derision is a peculiar behavioural output wherein there is a propensity on the part of some people to laugh at others, thereby trying to gain some ground for enhancing their stature in the eyes of others. Hence this is usually done in public. In fact they themselves are having the same traits of behaviour as those others whom they laugh at. They use it as a cover for their own hiding. It is smartness or cleverness. In fact their mocking at others is equivalent to mocking at themselves. But they do not seem to understand the same. But others understand the truth. They are resting foolishly in their 'paradise'. Their efforts to make others laughing-stock, recoil on to themselves at times. They are clever, but others are cleverer. They too get sadistic pleasure like cynics and 'sarcasters'.

Derision has two aspects—positive and negative. The positive relates to helping others in subtle way to know what their drawbacks are. Some children, for example, say proudly that they want to become crane-operators when asked about as to what they would want to be when they grow-up. If their parents want them to take-up some other profession which they consider 'loftier', it may be good to laugh at such ideas and deride them repeatedly in light manner when they are in their receptive veins. This sort of derision will bring forth positive results. Deriding people in the presence of others will tantamount to insultation. This is the negative type. This is the result of superiority complex combined with cynicism on the part of the insulter. Sometimes someone resorts to insulting another at an opportune moment later to avenge an insult or injury to his ego suffered on an earlier occasion at the hands of the former. This is a case of late reaction by physically or mentally weak persons. In all cases, the primary end of insulting is to derive sadistic pleasure or satisfaction.

Cynics usually employ sarcasm in whatever they utter in presence of others. The basis of cynicism is jealousy. The cynics do not hide their inner feelings unlike hypocrites. They are jealous of someone else's prosperity which the other person has earned due to his goodness and hard work. What can be done? The minimum that the cynics can do is to envy those who have achieved and by his cynical attitude to derive sadistic pleasure from it. They express their feelings of contempt by overt behaviour. They refuse to recognize other's goodness and do not mind extending this impression to the whole of humanity.

Such people do not get proper sleep and are disturbed. Cynics experience bad dreams. Their body-constitution does not provide place for hearts, the space is given on lease to wickedness, malaise and hatred. They are usually surly in their behaviour as well as attitudes. They are prone to looking at people with suspicion. This is also a disorder. Cynics are misanthropes.

It is interesting to watch, observe and study the behavioural patterns that these 'sarcasters', deriders, insulters and cynics present to us. All of them have similar traits to manifest. Although they look different, they essentially belong to the same class of people. All of these people are intrinsically of the same material. They developed these behavioural aberrations without their being conscious or knowledgeable. There are many contributory factors like hereditary and socio-psycho syndromes bringing about these aberrations. One must have sympathy for them, because they are haplessly mentally sick.

The people who are now deemed 'sarcasters', deriders, insulters and cynics might not have been like that, right from the beginning of their lives. They might have subsequently changed to become like these because of their adverse and unhealthy conditions in their family and also social environment. Or they have been mishandled by their 'best' teachers, namely, their haunting and harrying experiences in their lives. They start hating people around, and thereby developing allergy to interacting with them, especially with those who, in their perception, are luckier, happier or more successful and progressive. Loneliness in old age is another reason for such anomalies.

Even though introspection and self-analysis are the remedies, we cannot easily get around and convince such people to adopt these. They pay no heed to advice rendered by their friends or their seniors, as in the case of any other type of delinquents. Hence counselling by some wise men whom they genuinely respect will have some positive effects. It is a laborious process, because their willingness to co-operate cannot be easily purchased. We cannot afford to discard them; we have to salvage them, because they are problematic to themselves and detrimental to the harmonious existence of society.

Mutual Admiration—A Fantastic Interaction

10

Mutual admiration is a natural way of approach wherein two or more virtuous individuals or groups of such individuals involve themselves in acts of goodwill. This is a case of philosophy marrying philosophy. Goodness has an ardent affinity and attraction for goodness. Goodness begets goodness. This is a natural phenomenon. It is, however, dissimilar to cases where opposite poles attract each other. Here like-poles attract each other, that is to say, positives attract positives. If one virtuous person likes virtues of another, there is bound to be reciprocation. Here each other's philosophic approach and actions resonate through and through. Good goes good-ward. Hence, logically, cases wherein two or more wicked individuals involve themselves in acts mala fide cannot be brought under the precincts of 'mutual admiration', as is conceived. This is not thought of as a universal benefit scheme, which should be benefiting the wicked too. In the realm of mutual admiration, 'entry is strictly restricted to good people only'.

I remember having heard one 'crooked' person appreciating and extolling another crook, and *vice versa* too, in the presence of other people, when each of them know each other very well. They indulge in such acts only to serve some sinister ends of theirs, by misleading others and wooing their confidence/trust. It is simple to conceive that only wherever trust is cultivated, can there be mistrust, deceit or defrauding. This is sharp practice and hence stark misdemeanour. The 'shelf life' of this type of approach is very short, and hence the benefits accrued would be very transient, and the 'others' understanding their real game plan, would despise them. These people take others for granted as idiots like themselves. They are 'myopic'.

According to *Chamber's Dictionary*, the word "good" bears the following meanings: "having suitable or desirable qualities, virtuous, pious, kind, benevolent, well behaved, not troublesome, of repute, worthy, commendable, genuine, pleasing", etc. The word, 'good' is one of the finest words. The dictionary cannot hold the exact meaning in its entirety through few words. To get the total meaning, one has to add-up all and understand them together. Admiring any person or anything is a very difficult thing to do. Each and everybody cannot do it genuinely. Only refined, developed, self-analyzing and civilized person can admire another genuinely. It has to be through and through honest appraisal of the other person, devoid of hypocrisy and jealousy. There is a general propensity prevalent in most of us to view other's achievements or goodness in belittled and diminished manner. For this, special spectacles are available in the market. To see as to how people generally behave, let us scrutinize the following Table:

(A)	(B)	(C)	(D)	(E)
(Awards deserving) awarded)	(Awards actually awarded)	(Awards actually awarded)	(Awards (actually awarded)	(Awards actually awarded)
Excellent	OK	Good	Very Good	Excellent
Very Good	OK	Not Bad	Good	Very Good
Good	Bad	OK	Fair	Good
Fair	Very Bad	Not Good	Not Bad	Fair

The table above is self-explanatory. A key to the above table, however, is appended below:

(A) Denotes what people deserve.

(B) Denotes what people actually do not deserve, but adjudged and awarded.

(C) Denotes what people actually do not deserve, but adjudged and awarded.

(D) Denotes what people do not deserve, but adjudged and awarded.

(E) Denotes what people deserve as shown in (A) and adjudged the same unhypocritically.

People classified and grouped in (E) have the same frequency wavelength as those adjudged by them and hence they develop natural relationship between them. What (E) had awarded to them would have been the same had the adjudged had to do for (E). They will have developed 'admiration' for each other. No question of any element of surprise. This is, undoubtedly, a beautiful and spectacular scene. Adjudges pertaining to (B) to (D) manifest the varying degrees of cynicism and hypocrisy they hold within. Others can easily discern and adjudge the working of the minds of these adjudging judges. Cynicism of 'judges' included in (B) is more pronounced than those in Class (C) and that in (C) is more than that in Class (D) and that in (E) is naught. There is no real reason or cause offered by those who are adjudged; these 'judges' simply automatically manifest their intrinsic trait of cynicism and hypocrisy. Those adjudged are not to be blamed. They innocently offer themselves as objects of acrimony to these uncouth and squint-eyed 'judges'. Cynicism is a mental disorder. Now what do we do with these adjudging people in the groups (B), (C) and (D)?

Some promotions and transfers would have to be done. Promote (B) to (C) and gradually (C) to (D) and further gradually (D) to (E). Even though it looks very simple on paper, it will be difficult even for Hercules, to undertake such a task of training and promoting these people. It is practically impossible to turn all of them good. People sitting on the fence can easily be pushed to the favourable side. Those who have subsequently developed inclination or affinity towards goodness owing to changed situations and experiences can be trained to be good well before they become worse due to circumstances. By and large all are born good. Some may inherit bad character and some others acquire from the prevalent social systems. Most of them supplement their inheritance with the easily available and acquirable ones from the society they live in. Whatever may be the case; they can be influenced and changed by proper deliberate conscious training. An earnest and deliberate attempt by all is what is required. But, who would undertake such a hazardous task? Society. Most times, society behaves in a nonchalant, unconcerned and callous manner. It is neither reactive nor proactive which is tantamount to a silent agreement and hence this trait has been rendered acceptable by the society.

One man's admiring another is reversible process when both are like-minded. In this, both stand to advantage. It is a game of gain. In normal life somebody's gain implies loss to someone else, but in this cult case is otherwise. Mutual admiration brings about harmony through goodwill. When mutual admiration is perceived in the foil of morality it is seen clearly that it creates and fosters benevolence and philanthropy among people. This way of approach encourages one to think of goodness and search for goodness in others. One need not and does not try to see evil tendencies in others as it is an unnecessary and wasteful effort. Everybody thinks good, smells good, and the largesse of goodness spreads throughout the world and thus the world becomes good, a worthy place to live in.

Act of Compromising—An Interactive Syndrome

11

Our day-to-day life is full of discord or dissonance, especially with regard to interpersonal interactions that inevitably impinge on us in our everyday life. Each of us individually may be good: but the picture is quite different when two or more of us try to interact between or among ourselves. Everyone's latent intent, consciously or unconsciously, is to have peace, harmony and equanimity with his/her environment. If it were the case where only a single person were living on this planet, then the said intent, in theoretical sense at least, would have been tenable. This intent is not palpable in our social life until and unless one is at peace with oneself, to begin with, and extend that peace magnanimously to fellow beings in the society. This is easier said than done.

The 'pendulum' of mind has a tendency to oscillate between two extremes, of sorrow on one side, and again, sorrow on the other. The mean point represents equanimity, tranquility and happiness. We are determined, so to say, not to bring this pendulum to the mean point. A few, by nature, by birth, have propensity to bring it to the mean point irrespective of what happens around them. They, I reckon, are the fortunate ones. Most of us purchase discord at a premium, struggling hard to get there. This may be due to lack or total absence of built-in 'ingredients'. Those who aren't bestowed with this natural faculty, in majority of cases it is so, must strive hard to impede this tendency to acquire dissonance, is it possible?

We claim ownership of our minds. This claim, mostly, is an illusion. In fact we possess everything except our minds. We have presented, out of love, with wings to our minds, and they fly nonchalantly wandering in the wilderness. One must establish his ownership and bring it under control—'self-possession'. One who possesses his mind will be able to place it on his palm, as it were, and watch the system of its working. If any anomaly is detected, by an alert monitoring mind, necessary balancing act can be effected to adjust its scheme of behaviour as desired by a determined mind.

According to *Chamber's Dictionary*, 'compromising' means, 'arbitration, settlement of differences by mutual concessions, partial waiving of theories or principles for the sake of settlement, anything intermediate or mixed kind, neither one thing nor another'. Compromising is the art of 'giving away', without even an inkling of any desire or hope of any *quid pro quo*. At times it may become a negotiation or exchange. It is immaterial so long as the result is positive and hence desirable. Compromising is not merely being 'permissive' in a passive manner. One has to be deliberate and resolute in the beginning, but later on, it becomes a second nature in oneself. People like to cling to their points of view, at any cost, irrespective of their being right or wrong. It is the manifestation of their inherent urge to preserving their individuality. They are afraid that their very existence as individuals may cease. This we may name as 'self-securing'—'self-preserving' syndrome. If I agree to compromise on any issue, it is perceived by me, or even by 'outsiders', as a sort of humiliation or surrender, according to the degree of perversion of one's own imagination. I remember an occasion when a person had stated vehemently that a rabbit he had caught the other day had 'three' horns. He did not mean a joke. Any disagreement by others present there was flatly repudiated, and insisted that he was only correct. This is nothing but obstinacy.

An act *per se* or the motive behind an act is an expression of the working of the mind of the person behind it. If a mind is '*saatwik*' (pure and devine) then the act or thought brought about by such a mind would automatically be *saatwik*. An '*asaatwik*' (opposite of *saatwik)* mind can only prompt an *asaatwik* act or thought. Thus, we can understand the characteristic traits of the mind by observing, analyzing and retracing the cause or source of such act or thought. We are sure to reach the originating point. One should observe the behaviour of other people and draw healthy conclusions. Observing others and criticizing them have two sides or aspects: one is to derive sadistic pleasure, and the other is to identify the 'beauty' of those minds with a view to amalgamating and assimilating desirable elements of their behaviour in the observer's own cognitive system. The first one is negative and hence not to be adopted: the second is considered positive and hence worthy of adoption and emulation. This will lead to sedulous introspection and self-analysis.

Let us be good to ourselves and then to others. Unfortunately we are not good to ourselves: we tend to be partial when our case is brought to focus. In order to be an unbiased self-analyst one should think like Saint Surdas who said, "There is none who is more crooked, wicked, greedy and ungrateful than I." This will set the tone for self-analysis. This has to be a genuine admission without being sceptical or critical. Then one becomes purified making the 'mental slate' clean. Anything, if one wishes, can be written on that clean slate. Keeping it in that condition is most desirable. There will be many thoughts like the ones abandoned earlier rushing in with vehement thrust vying to regain space on the slate. If one ignores these unwanted thoughts wilfully at the threshold itself, one can become purified and remain so. The mind becomes light and ready to take off into the realm of simplicity and piety. There emerges a sense of 'feel good', and it permeates into the whole body-mind system. The result is *mens sana in corpore sano.*

The malady which has befallen upon us humans is our egoism. This 'special gift' is given only to us, not to the other members of the fauna. Thinking power and imagination are two factors creating and fostering this 'curse'. Even our society and its systems are to blame. Wars have been fought, and won and lost for satisfying this madness of egoism. This is the main hurdle in our march towards spiritualism. One wants to come to terms only with one's requirements to satisfy his egoism. At the same time one does not think that the 'others' too have the same problem. The moment one finds that his peace is disturbed due to unhealthy interpersonal transactions, without finding fault with the 'other side', one should resort to judicious introspection only to find out that the one alone is at fault. One should see only the other's perspective. This will lead to compromising. In many respects, on most occasions saying a real 'sorry' for any mistake is the result of introspection and self-analysis and hence compromising. Even in cases where one has perceived that no mistake is perpetrated on the other, if the latter has perceived that he has been wronged, the latter deserves a 'sorry'. This might bring realization to either of the parties and then there is a chance that a tear may be shed. Happiness!

Yes. Unhealthy egoism is not allowed to be rampant. This will help transcend one's mind, leading to spiritual development of each one of us in particular and society at large. Let the 'pendulum' be at rest!

In the light of the foregoing, I am apt to offer a definition to act of compromising as following: "diminution or banishment of egoistic syndrome in individuals by resorting to unbiased self-analysis with a view to cultivating accommodative and tolerant minds".

Exploitation—A Universal Phenomenon

12

Exploitation is a universal phenomenon. It occupies an important place in the realm of human interactional relationships. It involves covert as well as overt and specific as well as general dimensions in its manifestation.

The term 'exploitation' has two connotations. The first one concerns an act with a positive intent and the other with a negative one. When it is employed with positive intent it would relate to situations (real or virtual) and resources (tangible or intangible) that are offered to anyone who is to make most of them, by availing and utilizing them in an honest and genuine manner. One should think of them as opportunities and respect them as such. These situations and resources often come about in clustered plurality. Here there is an element of healthy competition internally among themselves, within an encompassing ambit, even sacrificing or undermining one in favour of another, in accordance with priority designed or earmarked, keeping in focus only the main objectives to be attained. These opportunities include his well-gotten name, fame and material wealth, sense of love, intelligence, imagination, satisfaction, capacity to work and so on. Here in this case only one person is isolated and considered for the sake of sacred study. He is at liberty to make most of the opportunities that are offered to him and derive optimal advantage for his self, but by doing so he is not to interfere, damage, usurp, snatch or deprive the rights of others. This is one aspect of 'exploitation', the positive one. It is ethically and morally sound concept and, as such, it is very difficult to imbibe and practise because it is against the natural propensities of human beings. Such humans are in a minority. Exploitation may be physical, physiological, psychological, moral, sensual, political, religious, emotional, financial, cultural, intellectual, spiritual and even notional.

There are exploits performed by heroic men. Through their heroic feats they become achievers. They make gains of satisfaction and pride through them and they happily share these gains with all others in the society. Here they do not exploit others; they 'exploit' only their own potential of valour to optimal level. In an organizational context, an efficient hierarchy tries to enhance the man-power output in order to take organizations to new heights. Here it tries to exploit and make full use of the capabilities of its people, making sure that they are fully employed, not under-employed and at same time not over-employed. They are adequately compensated in all respects; then there is no exploitation of any kind. This is a noble scenario.

The use of this term in a negative mode, its second face, relates to unhealthy, immoral or undesirable handling of prevailing situations or resources by one person solely to his own advantage, depriving others of their genuine, moral and legal rights of enjoyment, when it is known and recognized by all that these are made available commonly for the enjoyment of many others too. In most cases one's vile eyes, coloured with greed and selfishness, focus on other's weaknesses in order to availing advantages for the self by exploiting them. These form invaluable inputs for them for furtherance of their evil pursuits. These so-called weaknesses are conceived of originating, as variations or aberrations vis-à-vis the existing norms of societal behaviour. Man, the male, is basically lazy. If one looks for, he is sure to get hold of many a weakness in all human beings. Weaknesses are due to financial inadequacies, health-reasons, physical statures, intellectual handicaps, over-sensuality or the opposite, greed or undeserving desires and in some cases, even skin-colour and other beauty quotients. The society as well as its members is conditioned in this regard. This would be tantamount to blatant expressions of shameless selfishness. Here in this segment someone presumes that this world with all its paraphernalia is created only for his sole benefit. This is thus another aspect of 'exploitation', the negative one which is ethically and morally unsound. Majority of humans exploit them in the negative way and because of this, this term 'exploitation' is generally conceived in the negative sense only.

In some cases it is seen that some of the people in authority extract extra-work from their employees after giving attractive promises of promotion, awards, incentives or other rewards, and subsequently when the job is finished they tend to go back on their promises. This shows that there is no healthy organizational culture. This is negative exploitation prompted by fraudulent acts of those people.

An extreme case of exploitation is perpetrated by the 'institution of bonded-labour'. This is a bad set of words and not to be used in civilized societies. Necessary legislations have been effected to abolish this system. It does not exist *de jure* but its *de facto* existence in a lackadaisical or latent manner cannot be repudiated. Earlier days, even in our so-called modern societies throughout the world, till recently, these exploited were known as 'branded slaves'. They were being traded like cattle. Nowadays, we even need prior permission from cattle themselves before we undertake any such trading!

Members of the fauna other than humans and the flora too exploit the resources of the world to their advantage, but only in a limited way for the sake of their sustenance and existence. But that is in the positive manner only. The exploitation by other animals partially has a semblance of negativity while they do it as a part of their 'struggle for existence': it may be perceived as an expression of their 'selfishness', but a pardonable behaviour on their part. A small tree, to cite a case in point, existing under a big tree cannot grow in its natural way because the latter monopolistically consumes food available in the earth below and so also the carbon dioxide available in and around proximate atmosphere. One can perceive this action of the big tree culminating in deprivation of the invaluable ingredients for growth to the small tree. There is no deliberate conscious efforts on the part of the big tree to deprive those growing under it any of the needed resources. This intent of the big tree is to be understood. There are innumerable examples discernible in this world. It is all Nature's ways and, therefore, one should not name this action as a harsh and unscrupulous exploitation. This is thus an example of positive, sound and excusable type of 'exploitation'.

The term thus relates only to the humans. It is they who want to rule the world by taking control of anything and everything available in the world. One person exploits another in order to meet his private ends. He wants to avail maximum advantage for himself. He may not be even aware as to why he wants it. If he analyses his subconscious mind, he might get an answer to this question. He is afraid of going to the subconscious mind because he is probably sure of the answer which would be an unwelcome one. He knows or is aware that exploitation is undesirable trait and hence he is keen to ascribe this trait cleverly and safely to others.

Exploitation is very commonly employed practice by human beings. Governments exploit the people they rule, husbands exploit their wives, teachers their students, parents their children, leaders their led, trade unions their members, supervisors their subordinates, lawyers their clients, doctors their patients, the rich the poor, masters their slaves and so on. Wherever fiduciary relationships exist, it is easier to apply undue influence on the other and exploit the hapless predicament of such people. In all these above-cited examples, the exploited too exploit the exploiters. It is interesting! But it is noteworthy that these reverse actions may not be as strong as what they would have undergone at the hands of the exploiters. The exploiters are stronger and more powerful and hence the effect of their perpetrations would also be stronger and more severe. In most cases the exploitation from the exploited will merely be an expression of resentment. They can, at best, turn to Nemesis to get retributive justice. It can not strictly be called exploitation. It is like the fight between a tiger and a lamb, the latter knowing fully well that it is fighting a losing game.

People having fiduciary relationships with others resort, with great ease, to emotional blackmailing of some among them, at opportune moments, and thereby they would be able to get them where they want them to be. They look for the potential victims' Achillean heels to settle scores. They take advantage of the latter's precarious predicament. They apply all sorts of strategies and tactics while serving emotional blackmailing. They try to earn sympathy from the latter by pretensions. Crocodile tears are often shed. Success depends on the extent of their capability of hoodwinking the latter, and the latter should 'fall' into the trap. If they do not fall, then the game-plan will turn out to be a fiasco. For the success of these fiendish games, they have to be efficient psychologists, besides being dramatists.

Let me cite a true story in this connection. I was posted in a small city in one of the states. I was living in the third floor of an apartment, and the ground floor was occupied by a family consisting of a man and his wife. The gentleman of the groundfloor house was fond of having 'two pegs' everyday, and his wife was strongly against that. There was no chance of their indulging in altercations or fights between them, because, as he was a very docile, domesticated and hen-pecked husband, he used to submit himself to taunts and insults thrown out by the wide mouth of his wife, most probably, because he had strongly believed in the philosophic saying that 'there should be a minimum of two hands required to make out a clapping sound'. But as she was clever and intuitive, she could easily perceive her husband's predicament as a case of strong weakness in him. She had decided, consciously or otherwise, to take advantage of the situation. As usual when he developed his '8-pm itch', he requested his wife to give permission for his 'two pegs'. She then confronted him with a question, "Can you wash all the dishes? If you can help me in this, I would give you permission". "Yes, I will do it", and ran to the kitchen and started the job. Seeing this spontaneous response on the part of her husband, she got encouraged to move further. She planted a kiss on his bare upper-right arm and said, "Darling! There are only a few dishes today. You are a very healthy and strong person. I love you. When you finish dish-washing, please clean the floor of the living room also. OK?." He did do both the jobs 'happily' and earned his much-required reward. Man, the male, is basically lazy. The woman, the female, perceives his laziness as his weakness. And weaknesses make anyone vulnerable to exploitation. One can always find weaknesses in others. If one does not find any 'ex-shelf', he can manufacture a few and ascribe them to anyone targeted.

In this case, both of the individuals probably were unaware or pretending to be so of the fact that it was a case of exploitation. And they would carry on, on the same mode: but sooner or later the husband would wake up to realize that he was being exploited. The husband would await an opportunity for retaliation. He would try to exploit his wife and thus take 'revenge', so to say, and he would surely get appropriate opportunity sometime later. What he needed was patience. Some day her exploitable weaknesses would emerge and they would offer themselves for exploitation. It is this 'weakness' that is what an exploiter always looks for in order to fructifying his game-plan, i.e. exploitation.

There is an emotional dimension to exploitation. Emotions are highly volatile, vulnerable and sensitive softwares. They can be easily influenced by other external stimuli of emotions when impinged on them. Emotional exploitation is of the worst kind. Wherever there is emotional ethos between and among individuals, there always exist chances of this sort of exploitation. The severity or otherwise of the effects is directly proportional to the degree or intensity of emotional bondage existing. These often intrinsically belong to the negative type. But there are positive types too.

Terrorism—A Perspective

13

Terrorism is a childish act. It stands for immature behaviour. Terrorism is the 'effect' and resentment, dissatisfaction or complaint is the 'cause'. All human beings resort to terrorism in order to remedy the cause of resentment, and restore happiness and peace. Even though reactions of all the people who resort to terrorism are of the same kind, there are lots of variations in their expressions, in terms of degree, intensity, content of horror-element, and *modus operandi.* There are similarities as well as differences discernible in responses to same stimuli from children and adults.

A child becomes resentful, if something he wants is denied to him. It may be a particular toy, a special food item or clothing, books, or school-bag, or even a particular school itself, or any other requirements, becoming the cause behind 'cause', i.e. resentment. These requirements are borne out of his 'exchanging of notes' with his friends, or owing to his own perception or learning. Here, no logical persuasive suggestions or dissuasive arguments will have any effect on the child, because the originating point of emotions such as dissatisfaction or complaints is one of heart. We know that sentiments from the heart and logical reasoning from the head can never confluent. The result is persistent resentment.

The child reacts in such a way as to enable him to highlight and bring it to focus and address those who, he thinks, can solve the problem. If the older one buys a beautiful book or bag or anything and give to the child, he would throw it away, as it is not the one he has conceived of. This is terrorism by the child, manifested in his own way, stretching to his maximum potentialities and capabilities in order to render its effectiveness to its optimum level. In his next outing, it is likely that he might inject more intensity, and terror-content, and might change mode as well. If the parents do not view this anomalous behaviour in the correct perspective, and that too on the first occasion itself, and do not handle it tactfully and appropriately, there will be cause of anxiety earmarked for future.

Normally parents try to redeem the situation by buying another book or bag or anything according to the child's wishes, and the child accepts it. But, by this, he has understood the tactics he has to adopt in future to get his parents succumbed to his wishes. This is a dangerous trend. Unwise parents resort to bribing the child in order to tide away or escape from the present predicament as a 'first aid' relief. Parents should have avoided such situations by thinking ahead what the child would have liked. It may not be possible always to accede to his demands. He has to be convinced of your inability to agree to his demand at that time. But a false promise is never to be resorted to, for he has nothing else to remember. He has the memory of an elephant, especially in such matters. He would be watching you, might be, he may not be reminding you. He will be retributive in his mind. As he grows up he may show up a tendency to terrorize them sometimes. He may resort to, for example, rash driving later at the earliest opportunity. Take him to confidence first through a dialogue and then only should they proceed. This is to nip in the bud-stage of terrorism. Let us not bring up terrorists.

'Terror' means extreme fear or an object of dread. This is a sort of intimidation, may be organized or systematic. Looking at word 'terror' creates a horrifying effect. Terror unleashed in rampant manner is to achieve some objectives. The actions may manifest in many variant ways depending upon the issues on hand, or capabilities or otherwise of others to whom reactions are addressed, and the overall situation prevailing. Some people tolerate and ignore or suppress such sentiments and carry on with life, philosophizing that these are parts of life, and they bring their 'disgruntlement' within their 'tolerance limit'. For some others, they may be beyond tolerance limits. They perceive their 'limits' by themselves. In some other cases, they are provoked or prompted by others or situations. In this case, the result is terrorism. Terrorism originates out of the feelings of 'deprivation' of some 'legitimate rights' of theirs, as perceived by them. Here, 'legitimacy' or 'illegitimacy', as they conceive, is a debatable issue in the eyes of others.

Terrorism *per se* is undesirable. Terrorists are very ordinary human beings with overworking hearts and rusted intelligence. They are highly emotional and lowly intelligent hence intelligence has practically no role to play in their activities. Hearts always cheat, and, therefore, depending on heart alone is idiocy. This idea cannot be sold to the terrorists. Through their acts of terrorism, they inflict heavy casualties on innocent people and heavy loss of property and overall peace in the society. These are the only methods they adopt in order to focus the attention of those who can redress their woes. When their 'struggle' gets long-drawn they even forget their ideology or mission. They keep running in the groove automatically and helplessly. They forget the fact that they are running, because they are conditioned and have become senseless. They become some sort of 'guided missiles'. Some of them get 'fed up' with carrying on with this sort of irresponsible, non-sensible, monotonous pursuits. They are like long-distance runners who, even after reaching the finishing point, keep running for some more distance. Those who want to leave the stream will be killed by the organizational set-up, thereby with no escape for them. They become 'victims' of fear-psychosis. Those who manage to leave such outfits feel like 'fish out of water' or like a child dispossessed of his only favourite toy. They become confused and frustrated, with no aim in life.

The organization wants to perpetuate this 'industry' called terrorism. This outfit has the semblance of a business organization, with proper hierarchy, mission and strategies. It recruits fallible young people to throng their midst. These young recruits are brain-washed, conditioned and trained, and are emotionally captivated through indoctrination programmes. In this it uses emotive and inflammatory speeches by their 'lords' through which their mission and objectives are spelt out.

The operating commanders are to execute them and achieve results. The organization is a tight-fit entity.

Terrorism originates from hearts. So, if anyone wants to control or fight it, he has to tackle and win over these hearts. It is a very difficult task. In order to move towards a solution, 'both sides' should adopt a 'give-and-take' policy, a positive step in the direction of negotiation. It is not easy to 'sell' this idea to the terrorist. Here are two sides with diametrically opposite parameters of perception, one side obeying their 'hearts', the terrorists; and the other their 'heads', the majority entrusted with the responsibility of general welfare. Both of them are unwilling to dilute or discount their dependence on their respective 'items', heart and head. It is, again, a difficult situation. Sometimes it appears that none is interested. They should mutually offer concessions that are genuine and pragmatic. The approach by both sides should be serious and based on mutual trust and confidence. Even if one manages to take a horse to water, he can't force it to drink. As confidence-building measure both the sides must come forward and relax their stance or demands. An 'open heart surgery' or even 'heart transplantation' is recommended for terrorists, for these are the two ways of 'changing their hearts'.

These terrorists are like 'prodigal sons' who should be brought back 'home' at the earliest. The onus mainly rests with the major side and hence a pro-active stance should be adopted by them. The moment one party gives an impression that it is a bit relaxed on terms of negotiation, the other takes undue advantage. This gives rise to exasperation to that party who is in a mood to offer concessions. Terrorists approach this offer with suspicion, like anyone under the grip of fear psychosis. Children too behave in this fashion. That is why one is apt to suggest that terrorism is a childish behaviour. It is like inviting a ferocious hungry lion trying to pounce on a prey, and the latter pleading, "Look, sir, please hold, have a glass of cold water and relax. We will discuss our points and negotiate." Similar is the situation when the major side deals with terrorists in an effort to bring them to negotiation.

The terrorists are mostly adamant even on whimsical demands. In order to avail better bargaining power they keep their demands very high and climb down a bit to give an impression to the other side that they have condescended. In fact they are unwilling to concede. They are afraid that if they concede, their 'cause' or mission may be jeopardised or undermined. They can't afford it; they don't want to retrogress because it challenges their very existence. They suffer from anxiety and fear. They may reach a point of no return. When there is a chance of solving their problems they themselves spoil it by intensifying terrorist activities in order to arming themselves with strength at the time of any possible negotiation process. It is like 'heavy-discount-sales' by retailer shopkeepers. They increase the price by one hundred per cent and offer an attractive heavy discount. How can any sensible customer succumb to such unethical tactics? The other party will have to wait and watch till the terrorists get 'deflated' and frustrated and it becomes practically difficult for them to sustain such prolonged operations. They lose their will to continue their activities and agree for negotiations at some stage or other. It is a wishful thinking on the part of the major side. But, by then, they would have inflicted severe damage and destruction to life and property of innocent people.

"Prevention is better than cure" is an old adage which is borrowed for this case. By better transparent, austere, judicious policies and timely decisions by those who are at the helm of affairs, disgruntlement of people can be minimized if not avoided. Any small groups championing the cause or interests of a few will not come into prominence. But due to some misunderstanding or inhumane policies it is possible that a minor group might get hurt or get on to the wrong side. This might become an 'itch' and later on an 'ulcer' and if nothing is done to heal it in time, it might become 'cancer'. There is hardly any cure for cancer. This cancer is terrorism.

Superstitions—A Profane Institution

14

According to *Chamber's Dictionary*, the word, 'Superstition' means, "a false worship or religion: an ignorant and irrational belief in supernatural agency, omens, divination, sorcery: deep-rooted but unfounded general belief." Superstition, Latin word, 'superstitio', stands for unreasonable or excessive belief in fear or magic, especially foreign or fantastical ideas. It refers to a belief or notion, not based on reason or knowledge. It is commonly applied to beliefs and practices surrounding luck, prophecy and spiritual beings. It is a traditional belief that a certain action or event can cause or foretell an apparently unrelated event. Superstition is defined as "any belief or attitude that is inconsistent with the known laws of science or with what is generally considered in the particular society as true and rational; especially, such a belief in charms, omens, the supernatural, etc." It is also "any action or practice based on such a belief or attitude" (*Webster's New World Dictionary of the American Language*).

Based on these two definitions, superstition can be categorized as both concrete and abstract. Concrete superstition would relate to the belief itself, a belief that is not founded on the reasonable concepts of the world and human life. Abstract superstition is related more to the disposition to attribute normal everyday occurrences to the spiritual or occult. Within the idea of abstract superstition, we could define superstition as a readiness to accept unverified statements regarding the supernatural interference in this world.

In the case of scientific knowledge, the contours and parameters of theories and doctrines are clearly defined, and hence there is no question of any ambiguity, erosions, encroachments or confusion arising. Various theories and postulates in science, at first, appear before us as phenomena or revelations which subsequently turn into empirical knowledge; later on they are rendered established facts, beyond doubt, supported by conforming results through elaborate experiments conducted in laboratories. Most of them become permanent and universally true. They stand the test of time. Those that can not be proved experimentally will be discarded. Religion, on the other hand, is belief in, or recognition of, a higher unseen controlling power. Since this power is believed to be omnipotent, an attributed potency, and omnipresent, but imperceptible to the five human senses, there is a lot of scope for conjectures, manipulations and misconceptions creeping in the realm of religion. Several superstitious beliefs and practices thereby get begotten. Their growth is phenomenal and rampant. Religious establishments, in order to serve to perpetuate the ulterior motives of those at the helm of affairs, solicit, harbour and perpetuate many beliefs and notions that do not have any logical footing. These superstitious beliefs once integrated with the religions are required for the very survival and existence of religious denominations themselves. It is easier to market undesirable and harmful products to unsuspecting and innocent people either by aggressive strategies, creating fear-psychosis or by coercion. People get succumbed to such tactics and buy them. Gradually they helplessly develop addiction-syndrome in respect of this drug of superstitions. We practise superstitions because of fear, whereas we obey God because of genuine love and respect for Him.

In keeping with the Latin etymology of the word, believers of one religion have often seen other religions as denominations of superstitious outfits. Likewise, atheists and agnostics may regard religious belief as superstition. Religious practices are most likely to be labelled "superstitious" by outsiders when they include belief in extraordinary events (miracles), supernatural interventions, apparitions or the efficacy of prayer, charms, incantations, the meaningfulness of omens and foretelling. The followers of the preachings of the Buddha,

Jesus, Mohammed or/and many other god-men established religious orders naming after these great souls. Because of that, a person may not recognize superstitious actions coming from themselves, but are quick to point fingers at others and consider them superstitious. Every country in the world has its superstitious beliefs. Every group of people has its set of beliefs. In fact, it is hard to find an individual even among the educated lot who doesn't have some sort of superstitious belief. We may even practise it subconsciously, but nevertheless, it is practised. It is easy for us to view other cultures as superstitious, or to view other individuals as superstitious, but when it comes to us, we tend to put it in other terms or simply not acknowledge what we do as superstitious practices. Atheists and communists condemn superstition; they do not visit places of worship, except, it is alleged, under cover of darkness. Atheists utter, 'Oh, God!' unknowingly or unconsciously, when they slip and fall on the ground accidentally. When they regain balance they look around to check if anyone heard them saying so. If it is all true, it is all hypocrisy; may God bless them!

The Greek and the Roman before the advent of the modern religious orders modelled their relations with the gods on political and social terms. There was no room for fear at the thought of the gods. Fear of the gods was what the Romans meant by 'superstition'. The Roman Catholic Church considers superstition to be sinful in the sense that it denotes a lack of trust in the divine providence of God; for them superstition in some sense represents a perverse excess of religion, and dispels commonly held pre-conceptions or misunderstandings in relations to superstitious practices. Superstition is a deviation of religious feeling. It can even affect the worship we offer to the true God. To attribute the efficacy of prayers or of sacramental signs to their mere external performance, apart from the interior dispositions that they demand is to fall into superstition. Some superstitions originated as religious practices that continued to be observed by people who no longer adhere to the religion that gave birth to the practice. Often the practices lost their original meaning in this process. Every religious system tends to accumulate superstitions as peripheral beliefs—a Christian or a Hindu, for example, may believe that in time of trouble he will be guided by the Bible or the Ramayana if he opens it at random and reads the text that first strikes his eye. Often one person's religion is another one's superstition. Christians, Muslims or any other religions regard many Hindu practices as superstitious, and *vice versa*. Finally, all religions' beliefs and practices may seem superstitious to the person without religion. An interesting thing to note about superstition nowadays is that it is not considered "cool" to be superstitious. Because of that, a person may not recognize superstitious actions coming from themselves, but are quick to point fingers at others and consider them superstitious.

Superstitious practices as we know them today, especially those practised in the western world are considerably different from those practised originally. It is important to realize that most, if not all, superstitious practices can be traced back to several thousands of years. In ancient times, superstition was a lot more widespread than it is today. The reason for this has been mainly due to our subsequent ingeniously developed scientific explanations for many of the simple things of life. The fact that a flower could grow from a little seed was considered to have something supernatural about it, because they did not understand how the seed worked. With the advancement of technology and subsequent scientific progress, superstitious beliefs have sharply declined. In the ancient world, superstition was common even among the Greeks, who were known for their intellect. Most superstitions can be traced back in time to when ancient people had no understanding of the natural world, as we know it today. Ignorance of laws of Nature generated scepticism and fear in people which culminated in superstitious beliefs. And most superstitions that began thousands of years ago still persist in our society even today!

Throughout human history, as one can see, existence of superstitions in human societies has been relevant. They have been playing an important role. There can be no exceptions; all persons, the rich or the poor, educated or uneducated, tribal or aboriginal act superstitiously at times. Superstitious beliefs and practices have established their strong influence on each and every human activity and events in life; eating, sleeping, playing, working, getting married, having a baby, falling ill, birth, entering adulthood, marriage, pregnancy and even dying. Superstitions are designed to protect them and ensure safe passage from one stage of life to the next. They relate them to clothing that humans wear, the names they adopt, the numbers they deal with, animals, lakes, mountains, the planets, stars and the weather. In the past century, superstitious beliefs have suffered another large decline due primarily to the rise of education that is more intertwined with science. Our educational system deals more with the scientific, and though it makes a good case for the spiritual significance of life, it is by no means compatible with superstition. The reason is that by definition, superstition is 'unreasonable'.

Many people scoff at superstitions because they consider such beliefs to be unscientific. Even some of them adopt a few unconsciously and come under their spell. Even in so-called modern times, in a day when objective evidence is highly valued, there are few people who would not, if pressed, admit to cherishing secretly one or two irrational beliefs or superstitions. Some of them ignore, discard and deride the existing superstitions, but unknowingly adopt a few others to replace them. It is, as though, unfashionable not to have some superstitious beliefs; they have to fill the 'vacuum'. There is some sort of addiction about them. Some superstitions belong to the cultural tradition. Some of them have nexus with religion and its superstitions. Many persons, in nearly all times, have held, seriously or half-seriously, irrational beliefs concerning methods of warding off ill or bringing good, and healing or preventing sickness or accident. A few specific folk traditions, such as belief in the evil eye have been found in most periods of history and in most parts of the world. Others may be limited to one country, region, or village, to one family, or to one social or vocational group.

People develop personal superstitions. A schoolboy, for example, believes that he gets good high marks only if he uses a particular pen at his examination. He considers that pen to be lucky. A horseplayer, to cite another example, may be convinced that gray horses run well for him. Superstitions thus relate to:

(1) Religious faiths, beliefs and practices,
(2) Folklores,
(3) One country, region, or village, to one family, or to one social or vocational group, and
(4) Individuals.

There are thousands of superstitious beliefs existing in the world. A few of them are considered universal. They exist irrespective of religious, regional, social, vocational and cultural groupings. They relate to urban and rural settings, and so also to certain families and individuals. Though it is impossible to enlist all, a few as illustrative examples are appended below:

(1) Some believe that if a black cat crosses their path, it will bring about bad luck.
(2) Dropping of a knife or fork on the floor means a company is coming.
(3) Rabbit's foot is associated with fertility.
(4) Many may joke about avoiding bad luck by touching wood. "Touch wood", they say.
(5) Many avoid walking under a ladder.
(6) Some believe that a person born on a Sunday will always have good luck.
(7) A bride and bridegroom will have bad luck if they see each other on their wedding day before the ceremony.
(8) A pregnant woman must eat the night food, or she will have her child an unwanted birthmark.
(9) After a person dies, the doors and windows of the room should be open so that the spirit can leave the dead.
(10) A newborn baby must be carried upstairs before being carried downstairs. In this way, the child will be assured of rising in the world and having success.
(11) Putting money in a purse or wallet being given as a gift to make sure that the purse or wallet will always contain money.

(12) Some people will not start a trip on a Friday, especially if it falls on the thirteenth day of the month. Friday and the number 13 are both associated with bad luck.

(13) For Japanese, number 4 is unlucky. As a result many buildings in Japan have No fourth floors.

(14) Wedding guests throw rice at the newly-weds to ensure that marriage will result in many children.

(15) Finding a horse-shoe means good luck.

(16) Breaking a mirror brings bad luck.

(17) Spilling salt brings bad luck. The bad effect can be avoided by throwing a pinch of salt over the left shoulder.

(18) A howling of dog means imminent death.

(19) A ring around the moon means rain will soon fall.

(20) A person with red hair has a quick temper.

(21) Hang a horse-shoe over a door and prevent witches from entering the house.

(22) One does not sleep keeping his head facing in the direction of the North Pole.

(23) A bird in the house is a sign of a death.

(24) A loaf of bread should never be turned upside down after a slice has been cut from it.

(25) Never take a broom along when you move. Throw it out and buy a new one.

(26) If the first butterfly you see in the year is white, you will have good luck all year.

(27) An acorn at the window will keep lightning out.

(28) It is bad luck to leave a house through a different door than the one used to come into it.

(29) If you catch a falling leaf on the first day of autumn you will not catch a cold all winter.

(30) Dropping an umbrella on the floor means that there will be a murder in the house.

(31) If the groom drops the wedding band during the ceremony, the marriage is doomed.
(32) To dream of a lizard is a sign that you have a secret enemy.
(33) If a friend gives you a knife, you should give him a coin, or peril your friendship.
(34) Dream of running: a sign of a big change in your life.
(35) If an non-working clock suddenly chimes, there will be a death in the family.
(36) It is bad luck to light three cigarettes with the same match.
(37) A pregnant woman should avoid going outside during an eclipse in order to prevent her baby born with a facial birthmark.
(38) "Keeping fingers crossed" is said while making a wish.
(39) "God bless" is said while someone sneezes.
(40) Do not open an umbrella indoors.

The catalogue above can not be exhaustive. There are many other countless superstitions all around us, many of which we don't even notice or recognize as superstitious. Superstitions are attached to countless things in our everyday life, and most of them are simply traditions passed on from ancient beliefs. They started because of ignorance or fear of a certain fact; not that we know better, we still are superstitious. They may have started as folk religious beliefs, and we practise them out of ignorance. The reason is, for the most part, tradition. Most people who practise tradition have no clue why they are doing or what they are doing. They do it because their parents and grandparents did it. And that is how it works most of the time with superstition. Most of us do not accept our culture as superstitious; we believe that there are no superstitions among us. We practise superstition everyday, even when we say, "God bless" when somebody sneezes.

As we saw from the illustrations of superstitions, we can use virtually anything to create superstition, and superstition is associated with virtually everything one can imagine. There are endless things in our culture associated with superstition. The fact is that all of us engage ourselves in superstition whether we try to or not. It is embedded in our culture, and is part of our tradition. We don't think about why we do a lot of the things that we do. Not all of it is bad in itself either. But superstition can make way for fear and uncertainty in any person's life, because that is essentially what it preaches. That is why it is important for us not to lay too much at stake when it comes to superstition, because it breeds fear and uncertainty. We need to plant our feet on the solid rock of God. He is our rock and our fortress, and we need not fear. And that is what life is all about. We should resort to loving submission to God. Superstition is the devil's way of taking our focus away from the solid Rock. Why do people of some religious denominations bow to images when the religious books say not to? They say it is not wrong and so they do it. None would say it is superstitious, but it is definitely tradition. A long time ago, a practice was developed to make the images to help people focus on God, but with time, people started praying to the images themselves, forgetting God. Any attempt to remove the images from these places of worship now would be very difficult, if not impossible. It may not be superstition yet, but that is how superstitions start traditions. There are many superstitions practised that we do subconsciously; we have no clue in most cases as to why at all we practise them. The question is if we would continue to practise them if we knew how they came about. All of these superstitions now have been passed down as traditions, and we unknowingly practise them. Most of us do not know the meaning behind them either.

During the Renaissance and Reformation period, the influence of superstition suffered a severe blow, and was almost wiped out completely. However, superstition persisted stubbornly in the hearts of people. When man has no intelligible reasoning for something, he always wants to know more about the supernatural and spiritual world, and will very readily and willingly submit to any authority that has a traditional and even maybe a divine sanction.

It is interesting to note that people are interested to have only good luck in everything, not bad luck. Most people are undesignedly pessimistic, and they hate being so. They desperately want to be optimistic. They want good luck in every aspect of life at all costs. Most people have fears that make them insecure. Superstitions help them overcome such fears by providing insurance on security. Superstitions thus have a part in life as long as people remain pessimistic, anxious and uncertain about the future. They are scared, and the religious orders as well as social systems take advantage of this predicament, and propound and market superstitions and allied things as good products. They accept them helplessly, as they are conditioned that way. That is why we see that these superstitions have a good market. There may not be any logic behind any of these superstitions, but logic behind them will be ascribed and supplied to them by those people themselves. With lots of ado they construct background stories about their origin, in their 'sincere' efforts to 'baptize' and solemnize them, and serve these stories to gullible people. Some success-stories too would be in circulation as appetisers or temptation tonics. The business carries on.

It is a fashion among 'modern' people to decry superstitious beliefs. Anyone believing in or practising superstition is condemned vehemently. They hold an air of superiority over those people. When someone attributes that they too are superstitious about something, when specifically pointed out, they flatly deny such allegations. They even advise the former to desist from making such calumny against them. This is hypocrisy.

Sycophancy—A Universal Phenomenon

15

Sycophancy is flattery-syndrome adopted by fettered loyalists of some important personalities or leaders. Sycophants do not mind stooping even to the levels of servitude while they are engaged in this business of conferring overdose of praise to these 'respectable' leaders. It is a voluntary act, whereby the 'subject' and the 'object' are equally satisfied and happy. The objective of this business is, 'I scratch your back, and you scratch mine'. It is a mutual benefit scheme. Sycophants and the leaders are mutually dependent, the former to serve their private selfish ends through the latter, and the latter to be able to ensure continued enjoyment of the positions they have gained with the help of the former. Both have an existence similar to that of the Siamese twins. Both have a common concern for existence.

Sycophancy is a universal phenomenon. It emanates as a bye-product of interactions among self-centred human individuals. It is a commodity of high-value and of flippant marketability. Archeological excavations in the vast 'field' of History could unearth traces of sycophancy even in pre-historic eras. In the recent years the rate of growth of it has been phenomenal. Its rate of growth maintains direct proportion to that of 'thick-skin culture' as well as shamelessness of the 'modern' people of the present times.

If, due to some exigency caused naturally or artificially, a leader's slot has become vacant in an organization, the people select or elect a new leader, usually the second in the hierarchic ladder. If there is none readily available 'ex-shelf', a stooge will be found out to fill in the vacuum. The suitability of that person is a debatable point among those who do not form part of sycophancy group, or fence-sitters. The sycophants select the leader undermining or overruling the accepted norms of qualities required for a leader, and their selection is based on their 'convenience'. They 'challenge' the list of generally recognized qualities that a leader should possess, and incorporate certain changes, including total deletion and substitution by some other 'suitable' criteria. They first recruit a person and then ascribe certain 'desired' qualities to such a person. It is not the reverse process that is adopted, viz. finding out a person who has the qualities of a person and recognize him/her as the leader. They don't want to wait for any natural emergence of a leader. If one emerges in that way, they are afraid, the qualities they look for may be absent in such a person. This could be frustrating for them for obvious reasons. It is all nothing but manipulations. This is their self-protectionism.

Sycophants form many concentric circles around the leader. There is an inner circle around the leader. It is like a circular concrete wall, with semblance of an impregnable fortitude wherein entry is restricted only to those who have special 'passes'. Those who are occupiers of the inner circle have been granted monopolistic and exclusive rights to remain there. They are ardent followers of the leader. It is their duty to 'guide', nay, even 'misguide' the leader who listens only to them. The leader enjoys their melodious songs of flattery sung on him/her. These members wield enormous authority, in most cases 'unconstitutional' or 'extra-constitutional', unofficially extended to them by the leader, or sometimes in the absence of expressed or implied 'nod' from the leader, even self-assumed by these people. There are many more circles called 'outer circles' around the leader. Those in these circles have no noticeable authority. They derive a bit of taste of authority by being in 'close touch' with those in the inner circles. They are optimistic aspirants of promotions, inwards, into inner ones. This is 'chain reaction' syndrome. Some of them succeed or pretend to have succeeded. They often meet those in the outer circles to convey, "We have appraised the leader of your problems and the leader has promised to 'look into' them. Don't you worry." Firstly, they might not have told the leader anything at all or secondly, it is likely that they could have twisted or misrepresented the facts to the leader, taking the full advantage of the latter's inability due to insulation to meet the leader directly. Some of the people in the outer ring do not succeed in reaching the coveted inner circle and get frustrated and gradually vanish into oblivion. They muse and console themselves by muttering, "Hard luck! Let us try our luck elsewhere." These things do happen in the field of politics. Shifting loyalties is very common in politics. They condemn party leadership of the party they have just left, employing some choicest vehement, impugning and unholy words and in the same breath extol the one they have just joined. These are all natural, organic and dynamic processes.

India is a country of godmen. Each of them has entourage and large followings. Each has many 'circles' around him. All of them believe in, and maintain strict and tight hierarchical set-ups. Here the followers are disciples who are highly disciplined. Godman's orders normally by words or bodily gestures will be taken as God's own and followed implicitly. These followers do not need any materialistic advancement. They have aspirations for spiritual advancement only. Hence, there is no competition in the material sense. There are evidences of sycophancy among these disciples, but this tendency is totally discouraged to come to surface at the threshold stage itself.

Sycophancy is a universal phenomenon. Even in times immemorial, sycophancy was prevalent in the courts of kings and emperors. Nothing unpleasant was ever said in those courts. Those rulers were used to listening to praises and flattery. They always tried to look at those things, at best, as the expectations of their subjects from them, and tried to deserve such praises in reality. Even today sycophancy is a fashion. It is very much there in all the spheres of human activities, in public or private organizations, academic institutions, sports bodies, defence organizations, political parties, banking services.

Sycophants belong to a special tribe. They have their agenda, viz. 'serving their private ends'. Their strength in their ranks is mutable, waxing and waning. They market their 'leader' cleverly by projecting him as the best choice. Then they elevate such a person to a very high pedestal. It will be embarrassing for that person to condescend from that height. He may fall from there and meet with an accident. Such a 'leader' need have only an average or below average intelligence level. Another qualification would be an affluent family background. He/she should be of fair complexion and handsome/ beautiful. Even if such a person makes some strategic mistakes, the clever sycophants would cover him up. They do not mind owning up the mistakes on the leader's behalf, thus projecting a sacrificing demeanour.

The originating point of sycophancy is the heart. It is an expression of one's selfishness and self-centredness. Such people are interested only in the 'ends' and not the 'means'. They forget all moral norms while trying to achieve their 'ends'. They form part of the leader's entourage because it is from there they can proceed to serve their selfish motives. If someone keeps telling another that he is 'great' repeatedly, it has a 'drug-effect' on him. This 'treatment' gives a smoothening effect to the ears. The flattered becomes vulnerable, gullible, and even blind. None can escape from this trap. Even great kings had fallen prey to these kinds of strategies. Along with it, the flatterer administers his 'servility-dosage' to the flattered, equivalent to 'icing of the pudding'. There ends successfully his game-plan. And thus the flatterer wins. Now the roles of the leader and the led interchange; and the reverse will be the order, *de facto*. An old adage says, "One does not mind paying obeisance, even in front of an ass, if the latter can provide with what one wants." This is the ultimate in shamelessness!

Sycophancy is a drama enacted in actual life, wherein villain ultimately becomes a *de facto* hero. Here in it, there exists an element of deceit, circumvention and manipulation. In actual drama-settings, anything of this sort is not depicted. Even if such things are done, we know that it is, after all, only a drama, meant to entertain people and hence we can ignore this sort of a theme. But in actual life, such scheme of things cannot be 'digested'. In the cine-world, we can see a senior and well respected artist accepts 'roles' like that of a beggar in clothes torn to tatters, and he performs very well. One does such roles primarily because he is answering 'inner calls' from the 'resident actor' within him, telling him that the subject role is a challenging one, and that he should play it. His rewards are applauses of appreciation, of course, some 'mark of the mint' too. Here there is no deceit or circumventions. This is only an artificial performance, for the purpose of entertainment of the public. There is honesty of purpose. But the case is different in case of sycophants whose 'drama' is for achieving their own private ends through unethical and hence undesirable means, often at the cost of innocent members of the organization or the general public.

Appreciating Nature 16

All in the fauna or flora kingdom exist at the mercy of the Nature. In fact, all of them form an integral part of it. While sailing in a boat, we cannot afford to ignore the boat in which we sail nor the presence of water on which our boat floats. We pray to God instinctively for our safety 'at least' while we are in it or till we reach the other shore. We feel grateful to both the boat and the water provided by the great Nature and to God for providing the Nature itself. This gratefulness, expressed or unexpressed, is considered as a matter of interrelationship. Nature is God and God is Nature. Communion with Nature or God is as well a bionomic transaction. We are apt to forget about all of them—thc boat, the Nature and God—after reaching our destination, if we can afford, at least for the time being or till such time another 'requirement' of help crops-up! There is a saying—till we cross the bridge *en route*, especially if it is a dilapidated one, keeping our 'fingers crossed' we pray to God for our safe passage, and after the successful crossing, instead of being grateful we are apt to advise Him 'to go to hell'. It is all expression of insincerity and self-centredness; perpetration of hypocrisy and blasphemy!

There is direct evidence on the existence of God, the greatest supernatural power of the universe, at least on three counts: the Gravitational force which is responsible for the very existence of the universe in the present form as we see it, the Sun who heads a family called Solar System of which our Earth is a member and the great manifestation, we call it Nature. Watching as well as knowing of this Nature offers one of the greatest and the most exciting experiences that one would have. What is required is keen intelligent observation of some of the simple manifestations that it naturally emits and offers. We have only to watch them as they occur. One question comes always to our mind, "What is happening?"

I had sprinkled some chilli seeds in an earthen flower pot kept in the balcony of my flat. Some of the seeds germinated and tiny little plants came up, and as they grew up they started flowering. The balcony is a closed one with sliding glass shutters. I had kept one of the shutters open, to allow a bit of sunlight and fresh air to come in. They had no direct contact with the mother-earth, but for the gravitational force. I was worried as to how pollination would take place, as the pot was not in the open, which fact would have prevented the flowers from 'inviting' the pollinating agents. To my surprise, pollination took place. But, despite my keen watching, I could not see any pollinating agent arriving and doing the 'work'. I could get what I wanted—fresh green chillies from my 'mini garden'. Who called the pollinating agent to come there and do its 'job'? It is the great Nature that has brought about this phenomenon—a manifestation of Nature's sense of natural sciences in the applied form! One would often get excited by thinking about the various games that Nature plays.

I happened to observe a cow in a herd. One of them felt an itching sensation behind its left ear. If a human being had the same problem, he would have sorted it out himself or he would have taken help from his willing or unwilling fellow beings. They have some 'audible and understandable' language to come to their rescue. But what of a cow who, as far as we know, has nothing of that sort of facility at its disposal. But another cow came forward and solved the problem within seconds by a 'tongue action' at the exact point behind the left ear. How did the first cow convey its specific problem to the other and how exactly the other one understood the problem? It is not mere 'instinctive' communication that had taken place. One must better ask them. Probably they 'speak with their eyes'. We often emphatically declare that these animals do not have any intellect and they understand nothing. This is equivalent to a cat's hypocrisy in closing its eyes, while it drinks the stolen milk, pretending that none is observing and going to catch it red-handed. Our bold, but shameless declarations or assertions that animals other than humans do have only instincts unfortunately are one-sided, since no confirmation or otherwise is obtained from the animals. We, for our convenience, take their so-called 'silence' for their non-existent concurrence. Here we are unjust and cruel. This predicament of theirs can be understood only if we have some sense to empathize with them.

Similarly a female antelope had some vexing problem just below one of its eyes. The male-companion promptly solved the problem by employing gently, softly and with care and caution its tough sharp-edged huge heavy paraphernalia called horns. If at all we happen to witness this 'operation', we would have been scared, thinking that these tough heavy sharp-edged horns could cause damage to the eyes of that female. We would have only wonder to fill our eyes and hearts when we realize that nothing untoward had happened in this 'eye-operation'. Again, it is a fantastic phenomenon.

When wildest of wild animals like lions and tigers stealthily move about looking for their prey, the monkeys 'supervising' and 'circumspecting' all happenings from tree-tops make loud noise and move and jump from branch to branch or tree to tree, giving alarm to the hapless potential preys about impending danger, so as to enable them to run to safety. Even, birds join monkeys in the latter's pursuit for this 'noble cause'.

Nature tells tigers to hunt, kill, and eat deer; deer to eat grass; elephants to eat vegetation; ants to enjoy sweets; bees to collect honey from flowers and live on it; cows to live on grass and young calf on its mother's milk; birds on fruits; giraffe to stretch its long neck to reach its food, kept above, on tall bushes and trees; plants to draw their food from inside the earth; flowers to look at sun and blossom; micro-organisms to our development as well as destruction, grass to grow on the surface of the earth; rivers meet water requirements of everybody and everything; and above all, most importantly, air is supplied to all under Nature's own personal supervision and control in order to avoid any breakdown in supplies of this vital ingredient. What a flawless organizational set-up our Nature has made!

We often observe anticipatory reactions of animals in case of advent of thunder storms and heavy rains. In fact the nature, degree and intensity of these anticipatory reactions could provide a measure of the nature of the impending natural phenomenon. They anticipate quite well in advance, whereas human beings understand such things much later than these animals do. In this anticipation, these animals move about fast in restless manner and start making various types of peculiar noise. They get 'weather forecast' in advance. They are, as if, having an efficient meteorological department to support them, even much superior to ours own! Birds fly about aimlessly here and there, fluttering their wings to convey to their friends and relatives to move into suitable safe shelters.

Urge for survival is quite prominently discernible in members of both fauna and flora. But in the case of humans, this survival instinct is of low intensity. They tend to perish more easily under heavy odds than others. They are physically weaker, but intellectually stronger than others, but an ideal combination is what is wanted. In the case of young ones, infants, children, cubs, calves whatever we may call them, they need protection from their older ones. In case of young ones of animals, their survival instinct is much stronger than that of human children/ infants. The latter needs care for very much longer time, maybe because their life-span is much longer. The young human child remains under the care of their older ones for years, whereas those of other animals, the period may be of a few hours or days. The elders do not believe in perpetuation of dependency of the young ones on them. "You see, they get spoiled, and remain dependent for ever. We cannot afford such a situation to continue because of our peculiar environment prevailing in our jungle" they say. Too much protection weakens them, both physically and mentally. Hence animals virtually 'kick out' their young ones at the earliest opportunity. The birds start flying training for their young ones very early. It is only humans who lag behind.

Out of all creations, human beings standout as a special and unique product. They have more ostentatious intelligence than any other member of the fauna has. Moreover, they have been bestowed with great imaginative power. Both of these make human beings very special. We ourselves claim that we are a great creation and we are very near to God. None else from the animal world is overtly contesting this unilateral claim. Human beings are thus really lucky, because they have won the coveted position without contest or competition.

Men claim that they are the most intelligent of creations. How did they arrive at this conclusion? They have invented 'measuring dip stick' for themselves by themselves, and adopted a 'compare-and-measure' method to assess IQ levels among themselves. How can this system be made applicable as such to other animals, keeping human data as the base? Is there any system available to assess or evaluate different manifestations in which they are key-players? Can we pass off an architectural beauty like honey-comb made by tiny slave-bees or hanging sparrow-nests, symbol of perseverance, artistry and elegance, as sheer evidence of instincts, and not sign of naive intelligence? There could be thousands of such examples.

'Other' animals too have emotions like humans have. There is no element of hypocrisy in these expressions. We can often notice the eyes of goats that are given a notional extension of life-span by few minutes, by the butcher, while another one is being butchered in front of their eyes. They don't seem to cry. They also do not laugh, but their eyes occasionally gleam, a semblance of a smile, when they are happy. Lambs frisk and play, when they do not face dangers. It is, probably, not due to any mental deliberations, but it occurs instinctively, but instantly. We are not sure if there is any element of mental work involved in it.

Humans make use or misuse of both of their assets, namely, intelligence and power of imagination, to create disharmony in the world, due to their thoughtless acts. They don't follow many of the dictates of the Nature. They flout the rules of the game and make chaotic situation for themselves. The human beings disturb the Nature's balance in many ways and pay for all that very dearly. Trees are cut unscrupulously from beautiful forests, making the latter a barren place which will ultimately be converted into a 'beautiful' cricket field or residential or commercial complexes all of which stand for 'modernity' and 'progress'. Because of these thoughtless acts of theirs, there will be less rainfall and the resultant drought situation. Our globe is getting hotter day-by-day and time is not far away when it will be re-christened as Planet Mercury II or Venus II, even while it moves around the Sun in the same old trajectory. Even the Sun might feel embarrassed. Humans, it seems, have realized their mistake. Through insincere half-hearted approach they try to do futile 'damage control exercises' like the Copenhagen Conclave 2009. A representative world there expressed their anguish and concern over the existing predicament. Most of the elite members delivered eloquent speeches stressing the need for pragmatic approach to the problem. Most of them individually have been sincere and serious about what they wanted to convey, but one could not witness any collectivism in their approaches. The conclave has ultimately been a fiasco. They even shed crocodile tears at the miserable plight of the whales and penguins of the Antarctic region and even Yeti of the Himalayan region, besides their own future generations. This sort of 'fire-fighting' exercise would go always futile. This, in fact, is self-deceit and hypocrisy. We pollute water with toxic, hazardous chemical effluents that are highly injurious to health of the entire living things. We, thus, have been 'successful' in converting a beautiful 'heaven' into a cursed 'hell'!

The humans, it seems, have realized that the Earth is no more a conducive place to live-on. They are looking for living planets in the outer space. It is like some curious person looking out through the broken glass windows of his dilapidated house. When one does not want to renovate his dilapidated house he is occupying or when according to him it is beyond any repairs, he definitely needs looking for another better dwelling place. Now that he is an expert in 'house-breaking-and-globe-warming technology', he would be able to do a perfect job there too when such opportunities come-up! They have made significant strides in this direction. It seems that they have located one, a 'sister or grandmother' earth, several light years away from their earth, as a part of another solar system. Preparations are under way to go and live there. The only problem could be that one would have to spend half of his lifespan in travelling to reach there. It is, however, an ideal place for deporting criminals and terrorists as a punishment.

Conceiving God

17

From the time man became conscious of his having power of imagination, he, with the help of his intelligence, started conceiving about some power beyond him, superior to his own. He thus arrived at the concept of God. Then onwards his strife was directed at knowing more about that power. He conceptualized in his own limited manner and provided shape and forms to it, and started adoring and worshipping. Some of the humans concentrated on such a phenomenon and claimed that they could perceive and realize its existence. Some others followed them and thus various denominations of religions came up. These religions provided them with a platform or launching-pad to continue pursuit on the concept. He developed systems of communion with God, establishment of a sort of interactive syndrome and inter-relationships.

God is omnipotent, omniscient and omnipresent. It is believed that God resides in everybody in the form of what we call 'the spirit' or 'soul' in the mind. The 'mind' itself is a concept. It is not tangible, visible or audible. We can not call it an intuition or instinct-centre also. Some wise men assume that the mind and intellect are the same. Intellect also is intangible as well as invisible. It is an abstract entity. It is not synonymous with brain. Brain is the hardware while intellect is the software of the human computer-system. If it were tangible or visible, a brain surgeon could undertake a surgical operation of the brain and make it more or less effective or alter the IQ level. This is not done. So if the mind is intangible, the soul is much more intangible. The more we think about them, the more we become confused. The starting and finishing points of our thinking process would coincide. We are apt to believe only what we are able to touch, see, hear, smell or taste. But soul, mind and intellect do not present themselves before any of these senses for any sort of research, probe or experimentation. They are abstract and elusive.

What is absolutely clear is that the Force of Gravitation, the Sun and the Nature are the three manifestations which constitute enough direct proof of the existence of God. The Force of Gravitation is responsible for the very existence of the universe in the present form, as we see it; the Sun heads a family called solar system of which our Earth is a member; and the great Nature which nurtures us. We are tremendously grateful and respectful to all these three. For us they form God, and they are very near to us. There is no need for us to go further far away looking for God. If we go further we will enter the metaphysical realm, where all concepts about God and about our existence might become very unclear.

No creature, none with life, likes to suffer from pain or sorrow. We are all allergic to pain or sorrow. All of us want comforts, peace and happiness. In fact, there is no difference between sorrow and happiness. It is the way one looks at them. For some of us who are used to 'live in' comforts always, even a small discomfort or irritation can cause disproportionate anxiety and pain, and it will be unbearable, whereas, and for some others, it may not be even cognitive. Each one of us is a 'victim' of conditioning, self-made or society-made. Each one of us seems to be in the whirlpool of psychic-syndrome. If one 'marries' sorrow voluntarily or involuntarily, then there is no question of one's feeling sad at any time. Make sorrow one's life-partner. Similarly there is nothing like happiness. We unconsciously try to differentiate them and imbibe one of them for our convenience. This is the phenomenon of perception. Some people who have unflinching and ardent faith in God may philosophize and redeem themselves from sorrow, or in fact they may not be able to tell sorrow from happiness. This is a fantastic state, envious too. They name both sorrow and happiness by one name, 'fate'. This is an effective mechanism that can be employed for 'pain absorption'. We know that God is omnipotent, omniscient and omnipresent. When there is someone with all these unfailing powerful characteristics, we call him God, where is any room for anybody's worry? Whatever befalls on anyone, whether good or bad should be taken as a gift from Him, and accept it happily. They may say, 'For, we are all poised on a huge wave of fate which hangs uncertain to which side to fall'. He is destined to believe in his 'fate'.

Human societies are formed by natural organic processes. Human beings too wanted them, when they were formed millions of years ago. They had to live together for mutual benefits at that time. It is true of the present times too. The role of the societies has not changed even a bit, despite passage of time. Societies are for sharing happiness and sorrow of individual members, apart from other benefits. None is so much bothered about sharing happiness as sorrow, because one finds it difficult to consume or absorb it. He likes to share sorrow with other members of the society, because by sharing he will be able to dispel a large portion of it. He will feel relieved. Here comes the role of the society. It absorbs sorrow. Thus sorrow gets dissipated and its concentration gets rarefied by sharing, thereby one's burden is reduced qualitatively and quantitatively to a bearable quantum. This lessens its impact on that one person. The others' empathy is the essence of sorrow-sharing.

It seems that society for its own very existence created the concept of God. Man has intelligence and imagination in abundance which he employs carefully to conceive about God. It seems God is interested in continued existence of human societies. He has sent to earth his 'incarnations' like Krishna, 'son' like Jesus Christ, 'messenger' like Mohammed the prophet, and others to be amidst the members of the society in order to cleanse the society by annihilating demons and those others who threaten the harmonious perpetuation of societies. They then wanted to re-establish societies with only good people and good systems. This process continues continually, like periodic maintenance of machines and systems.

"I like this uncle. Yes, I love him. He gives me good chocolates everyday. But I do not like the other uncle. He does not give me even a toffee", says Miss Little, my smart neighbour. Man praises anyone who did, does and has potentialities to do favours to him. He is a keen aspirant awaiting always to receive favours from others. But he is not eager to extend favours to others, even by way of reciprocation. This is a paradox. It depicts only his self-centric approach to life. He considers that all others exist only to do favours to him. It goes without saying that if one does not do favours to another person, the former, the non-giver, will be despised not merely by the frustrated aspirants, but by innocent 'onlookers', who, of course, also belong to the same category of non-givers. It may not be uncommon to see people admonishing or despising God too if He does not 'give' favours, gifts or boons to these 'worthy, devoted and deserving' aspirants. Even God is not spared! Man usually does not despise Him overtly, because of public criticisms and some unknown fear, but may do it covertly in the hiding where there is no public criticism or auditing, or even God may not be a witness to it. This is crass hypocrisy!

Why does man worship God? It is to get some favours from Him. He has plenty with Him to give, if He likes and wants to give. Why does man praise Him, sometimes alone and sometimes in congregations? He takes things for granted and thinks that He likes appreciation, admiration and extolment, sometimes even 'thanks giving', and shower on Him all the good epithets available, in His praise. Man thinks, foolishly, that He is also like human beings who always enjoy flattery and adulations which blind them. When a man enjoys them he becomes willing to do anything that is asked for by the adulator or flatterer. One wonders if God succumbs to such tactics and strategies. He is not fallible and erratic like human beings.

18 The Positives and the Negatives

In this world of ours we notice a unique and one of the most interesting and intriguing phenomena in the form of a 'pair', called, 'The Positives and The Negatives'. These two have the status of a 'pair' because they are conceptually created complementary to each other. The existence of the one gives meaning to that of the other. It is like a pair of shoes or a pair of scissors. The positives and the negatives cohabit together to form a new entity. One cannot keep them separately for long. In a magnet we can not have only a north pole or south pole. Their independent existence is difficult, and if it happens it would be exceptional and artificial, and hence unnatural. It is also similar to the 'pair' concept of darkness and brightness. Here too the existence of one proves that of the other. But in this case, unlike in the case of the positives and the negatives, their existence is not interdependent and complementary. One replaces the other partially or completely.

An atom contains generally protons and electrons, representing the positive and the negative charges. They exist together by spatial arrangement of energy-levels and when they are thus 'together' they have certain equations, rules and regulations to be strictly complied with. Theirs is a sort of matrimonial arrangement. Cases of 'divorces' are nonexistent. There is semblance of a patriarchal system prevalent in every atom. The nucleus husbands the electrons. The atom as a unit maintains 'equilibrium' within itself. The positive proton stays at the centre and the electrons circle around it on pre-designed paths or orbits. If any external force in the form of excitation, known as fission process of extrication, tries to disturb this arrangement artificially and makes one of them live independently, it will not be 'comfortable' as well as stable in that state, since it is an unnatural set-up. They are all for natural existence. It will experience great 'discomfort' borne out of a 'feeling' of incompleteness. It would be similar to, but much more than, the sense of insecurity that a wild animal experiences when it is caught and forcibly kept away from its natural habitat, the forest. It would be like the case of a 'fish out of water'; the fish dies due to changed conditions of environments or over a period of millennia learns to adapt itself to the new environment. It may become by the process of evolution an amphibian or, later, an animal suitable to survive on land due to its earnest efforts in the struggle for existence.

The atom represents a microcosm of the Solar System. If we consider the Sun as the nucleus, all the planets like the Earth or the Jupiter may be thought of as electrons orbiting around the nucleus, the Sun. All these planets orbit in accordance with certain spatial arrangements. Similarly the moons of different planets too orbit around their respective parent planets. All these show that there is great amount of intra and inter-dependence existing within and among all these objects. We know that atoms cannot exist as independent units or entities. They form-up their 'groups' and these mini-groups are called molecules. These molecules can enjoy, by choice, independent existence to a limited period of time and extent. They too like to combine, for stability, with others of similar kind, at the earliest opportunity and form-up societies called chemical 'compounds'. They are all for equanimity and equilibrium. This is all caused by God, in the form of Gravitational Force.

Similarly, the humans as well as the other members of the fauna, based on commonality of their traits and tastes, form mini-groups initially and gradually many such mini-groups form-up major ones called associations or societies and they then live in them, within their 'four walls' harmoniously and happily. These are organic entities or establishments. They grow or decay, depending on dynamic conditions in and around them. They too have their laws and bye-laws governing the various aspects of their existence, sustenance and survival.

The configuration as well as the internal structure of these associations or societies remains intact so long as these rules are not circumvented or violated.

In the monsoon season we notice the phenomenon called lightning. This is due to the tendency or ardent affinity of high voltage positive charge, in terms of millions of volts, accumulated in the atmosphere to transcend to the negative-zero of the earth at the earliest opportunity, adjusting the potential difference between them, avoiding their 'discomfort' and bringing about some sort of equilibrium, balance and accord.

On this Earth of ours there lives the fauna. Each of its members is identified by its gender. Some are males, while some others are females. Somehow, by and large, Nature keeps their ratio of these two at fifty-fifty. The males represent the positive and the females the negative. The males beget the offspring, while the females bear them. All members of the fauna are bi-sexual to some extent. In some cases the balance between male and female constituents in their body-systems may be precariously maintained. This balance gets tilted to the 'other' side, in some cases, depending upon certain compelling circumstances or situations that the individuals confront, and as a result, such individuals might turn homosexuals. Others declare such sexual behaviour as unnatural because it does not conform to the already 'accepted' or existing set of behaviour. One can call such cases as 'accidents'. We categorize such cases as exceptions, as large majority of individuals are heterosexual, in conformity with the normal norms. Homosexuality is prevalent among all members of the fauna.

For the purpose of analytical study, we may make a vertical division and classify the human beings in two categories: The Males and The Females, the positives and negatives. The males, like the females, may be Asians, Americans, Africans, Europeans, Hindus, Christians, Muslims, Buddhists or of any denominations of nationality, creed, language colour or religion. There is no place for considerations based on any of these: basically they are either males or females. If one looks at the behavioural patterns of all these human males of the world, one will find that they are essentially of the same mould. Similarly if one endeavours to look at those of the human females, it would also be seen that behaviour of all the females of the world is generally of the same mould. But these patterns manifested by the females are entirely different from those of the human males. There are marked differences.

The females are termed 'the weaker sex', even though some of them are physically stronger than males. It is observed that some sterile females show some of male behavioural characteristics like lack of or shedding away of their patented variety of shyness. They are inclined to show typical male traits like aggressiveness and nonchalance when they come to know conclusively that they are barren. It is only an attitudinal or psychological change. There would be no physical or physiological changes.

The males are generally physically stronger and sexually overt, uninhibited and expressive and as such they exhibit dominancy in their sexual behaviour. There is always a tendency on the part of the males to advance very fast towards their female counterparts. The males reach the place where the females are, hence there is no need for the females to take any initiative. All things will automatically fall in line. They need to have a bit of patience only.

That is the reason why we see females hardly taking any initiative or exertion in romance or love-making or any other allied activities, because males are pro-active in all these. Moreover, since this system has been in vogue from the very beginning of existence, and both the parties taking such behaviour for granted, males do not like or enjoy if the females too behave the way the males do. Similarly, the females do not like or enjoy if the males behave the way the females do. One can not say, 'why can't women be like men or why can't men be like women'. The females silently enjoy every bit of all these in their typical feminine way. The females do not enjoy sensuous play except with emotional attachments, whereas the males do enjoy generally, without much of emotional involvement. That is why the latter is stamped as 'loafer beetles'. What a good arrangement the Nature has made!

The characteristics of the behaviour of the males and the females represent two parallel lines which will never converge and confluent to oblige anyone. It is this difference in their behavioural patterns that enables them to live together, notwithstanding their mutual sensuous equations. The sensuous equations will wane or change gradually with time, but it is only these anomalous patterns of behaviour that will take them together along. Husbands and wives have many common interests and causes between them and these keep them together, despite their different psychological inhibitions and notions. They sink their differences, consciously or unconsciously, to a great extent and try to move forward. We know that two male friends can not adjust themselves and live together for long, howsoever close their friendship may be. Similar is the case with females too. Cases of homosexuals are excluded here for obvious reasons. Brother-sister relationships are more stable and tenable than brother-brother or sister-sister relationships. We know that like poles repel each other and unlike ones attract each other.

Human beings unlike the other members of the fauna are obsessed with this gender-syndrome. Even in early childhood they start differentiating the gender. A female child will develop this consciousness when she attains the age of three or four, whereas a male child at six or seven. Besides their own observations in and around, they are conditioned and made conscious of it by their parents and elders. It is interesting to watch a young child trying to confirm for itself the gender of its younger one when none else is around. This curiosity has its origin in its conditioned gender consciousness.

Response to the same set of stimuli by both the males and the females differs considerably at a point of time, because the attitudes and propensities of these two types are wide and varied. The perception of the males towards procreation, for example, is entirely different vis-à-vis that of the females. For the latter it is *raison d'etre*, and they are very serious about it even before marriage and its consummation. On the other hand for the former, at least in the beginning, it is nothing but efforts to satisfying his sensuous needs. Only when the females conceive, the males give serious thought of having children. For many of the males the period of 'nine-months-plus' is too long a period. They start showing their patented impatience.

Relationships of the father and those of the mother with their children too are different. Fathers, the males, love their children in a very rational and pragmatic manner, whereas the mothers, the females, in an emotional manner. Children understand and enjoy the difference between both, but either of the parents does not understand it clearly. The 'male' residing in the father showers overtly more love to his daughters than to his sons, but the 'female' in the mother adopts the reverse order. They select their ways instinctively and as such nothing is considered wrong in both of these cases. It is believed that fathers who have many daughters have longer life-span and they remain more healthy, cheerful and handsome than those of them having many sons. Similarly, mothers having many sons look more healthy and beautiful and they too have an extended life-span. The opposite situation in either case can be imagined by anyone. Father's love is one, more of the head, whereas mother's love is one, more of the heart. Fathers, unlike mothers, seem to be less affectionate overtly because their expressing of sentiments is normally subtle and unostentatious, and hence they may be perceived mistakenly. Moreover, men are not provided with efficient lachrymal glands.

On this Earth of ours, there lives the flora which consists of many thousand types of plants. Most of them are bi-sexual but some of the trees and herbs are distinctly males and some others females. In case of Nutmeg, Papaya, Indian Gooseberry, and others, some of them are totally males and some others are totally females. Such male plants or trees generally produce male flowers only or some vestigial female flowers. Female plants also flower; but most of them will be females. Female ones fructify. Here we have some sort of proof of this. If a flower has fructified or produced seed, one can easily conclude *post facto* that the same has been a female one. But, if not, none can deny the fact that it has been a flower, but doubt arises only about its gender. There could be many reasons why it turned out to be barren; not necessarily because it is male. One reason could be that pollinating agents, due to their busy schedule of work elsewhere, could not visit it at the appropriate time. There are cases wherein some chaste human females, declared 'barren', because they failed to get conceived despite the passage of many years after marriage, conceived and delivered child/children subsequently. There could be many reasons, psychological as well as physiological, save spiritual and superstitious ones, for this anomaly. Barren females always remain as 'females', and not as males. This is universally true in cases of both the fauna and the flora.

In the flora-world there are hundreds of flowers that are beautiful, and their function, as though, is only to add beauty to the Nature or simply to feeding the 'ungrateful' bees, beetles and sparrows with their sweet honey. After doing this duty of theirs all perish without fructifying. One would wonder as to why they do not do their normal function, and why Nature is so cruel towards them. These plants and trees could have developed, by default, over a period of time some other alternate ways of performing their reproductive functions through their specialized stems or roots, rendering the flowers dysfunctional. One can ask the Nature, if one wishes to, as to why at all these flowers are asked to blossom! In a nutshell it can be said that all females need not fructify or produce seeds or eggs or deliver offsprings for procreation. There could be many reasons.

The Earth is talked about respectfully and is bestowed upon great status as 'Mother' or 'Goddess' which represents femininity. Her movement around the Sun resembles that of an electron around its nucleus. Just like the nucleus and the electrons, the Sun and the Earth too co-exist, maintaining some sort of equilibrium, between the positives and the negatives. The mountains on the earth are considered 'masculine', whereas the rivers flowing on her are 'feminine'. The vehicles of transportation like ships, aeroplanes, buses, cars, boats, bicycles are considered 'feminine'. Most of men's-wear like their caps, trousers, coats, shirts, even under-garments are considered feminine. The man's moustache and beard, considered most masculine, are of feminine gender. Similarly the woman's wear like blouse and petticoat, and, surprisingly, even her hair are considered of masculine gender. The German language, for example, considers 'door' as feminine, whereas the 'window' neutral. The word, 'book' in Hindi is of feminine gender, whereas in German it is of neutral gender.

Any 'giver' is considered of positive gender, and taker or accepter negative. An electric plug and its socket, filler-gas and vacuum, water and river and so on are thought of as pair of positives and negatives. One can find thousands of such examples. These classifications have naturally been evolved due to random usages in human languages owing to cultural ethos of different peoples and their societies. All of them differentiate all objects into two major sectors, viz the males and the females, the positives and the negatives.

Understanding the Meeker Sex

19

We are apt to bemoan an enigmatic question, "Why do the women represent the meeker sex?" The reason for woman's meekness could be of social economic or of cultural nature or combination of these. Let me, however, analyse some of the psychological elements involved, awareness of which could help women understand themselves and perhaps thereby transcend their seemingly precarious plight. This exposition here is the end-product of the author's empiricism and imagination.

Human societies by and large, it is alleged, are 'man-made' and probably 'male-dominated'. Human societies are not 'authored' by anyone, but evolved themselves through many processes over years. Societies like the humans themselves are organic. This organic evolution has been natural and gradual, in a cause-effect continuum. Well, in the ancient societies, for their very survival, they needed physically and intellectually strong individuals. They were the men who provided adequate protection, and that is why and how the societies survived over millions of years, despite many challenges and threats from Nature and its environment. Men, therefore, have developed a second nature of providing protection intuitively and instinctively to those requiring it. I have observed a five-year old boy accompanying his seventeen-year old sister when the latter wanted to cover a distance at dusk. Interestingly, the boy, the 'man-bit' was walking proudly by his sister, with or without holding her hand, as though he were capable of surmounting any difficulties *en route*. She too was enjoying this protector's company. She preferred this company to her twelve-year old sister's. The present day demands and requirements of the societies are probably not identical with those of the olden times. Even the present day thinking of women's liberation is a part of the perennial natural organic development processes which we have been experiencing or witnessing.

I often think as to what this world with all its societies would have been, had it been 'woman-made' and 'female-dominated'. To begin with, these complex words would have been in vogue among men who ought to have been in resentful and melancholic mode. Most probably, these words would have lost their relevance long time ago and nearing their extinction due to wear and tear. All the masculine genders used in languages would have been replaced by feminine genders and *vice versa*. Most of the objects would have been more beautified; functions, relevance and utility of many of them would have been different. Utility and beauty quotients would probably have interchanged their positions. Aeroplanes, motor-cars and other modes of conveyance would have been either not existing as they are now or if they have been existing, all of them would have been of different designs. The colour-codes of these would have matched with the various ones similar to those of lipsticks, like orange, pink. Fire-arms like pistols and hand-tools would have been of different designs, if existed, for example, a hammer would have the shape of a high-heeled sandal. To state in a nutshell all the objects and situations now existing would have not been existing or if existing would have been of different design and nomenclature. If one attempts to think in this direction, I am sure, one's imaginative prowess, however great, would have been wanting. The word, 'husband', for instance, would not have been there with the same meaning as it is having today.

Let us face a bit of a fact. It is easy to put blame on men for whatever 'wrongs' perpetrated over many a millennia on women and their cause. Well, some people get satisfaction when they are able to apportion blame to someone else. Blaming is for blaming's sake. The matter ends once the complaint is lodged. It seems means and ends are the same. I can cite an incident. A friend of mine had met with an accident on the other day on the road while driving his vehicle. It was clear that he was driving cautiously complying with all safety rules unlike the other person who collided with him. He could vociferously claim that the accident occurred clearly due to the other person's fault. Even passers-by who congregated on the spot subscribed to his contention. Though he got a bone or two of his broken, he was to some extent satisfied, because he got someone to blame. If the other person had done a vanishing act immediately after the incident, he could adopt another option, that is, to curse him and avail satisfaction. This trait is more fastidious in women than in men. This is the case of women who blame men for all their woes and maladies they face now.

In our day-to-day life in home-context, we come across many women educated and 'modern' who refuse to take any lead or initiative when a major decision is required to be taken, when men refer or pose problems to their women. They often come out with some peripheral issues and prefer to be orbiting or hovering over. They remain non-committal. If men take bold decision and go ahead, the watchful eyes and minds of women would be scanning through the effects of such decisions with a view to pin-pointing the mistakes, lacunae and deficiencies in those decisions. Women are found to be good 'post-mortem' analysts. Well, women would always attribute this behaviour of theirs, when confronted, to the question of not having been given chance to go ahead with their initiatives for generations. They could not acquire decision-making habit and skills due to non-utilization of the faculties, resulting in hibernation and rusting. So, in order to remedy these anomalies, I am afraid, time would be required to be allowed, at least one-fourth of what can be called 'deprivation period'.

The meeker sex has remained under-privileged or even left-out, if it is so, for centuries. The reason, if one of women undertakes introspection unbiasedly, can be seen attributable to her own inherent instincts, fastidious traits and inhibiting trends, founded on her part of human psychology. Her behaviour is determined by her socio-psycho system—her instincts, intuitions and perceptions.

Women have strong child-bearing and child-rearing instincts which Nature has bestowed upon them. This is a fantastic phenomenon. Any effort by any of them to swim against the tide only creates severe adverse effects and none would be happy and comfortable. She is very keen to realizing this child-bearing and rearing need. She wants help in realizing her *raison d'etre*. She is like a sparrow hawk waiting patiently for drinking water if and when it rains. She is like a flower awaiting the arrival of the pollinating agent. She contracts patience. This sort of patience affects her psychology resulting in a subdued or meek predicament. Here the physiological system is affecting the psychological set-up. This nexus between these two cannot be undermined, at the same time it is worthwhile becoming conscious of it.

One of the most important virtues that women exhibit is their shyness. Being shy is shrinking from notice or approach, feeling secluded, warily reluctant to come forward. This results in timidity, a perceived trait. Shyness enhances her beauty which is required to attract the opposite sex. This is a game played by Nature and none can defy it in the normal course of life. Positive and Negative poles attract each other. This is probably the only way that can help them achieve their *raison d'etre*. This shyness or timidity makes women meek and they develop ardent propensities to be in their 'shells'. In fact they bring with them this virtue of shyness on their birth as females and is imbibed and fostered by the societal set-up in which they grow. Many married women prefer to be known as 'Mrs or Ms' of their husbands, even when they hold beautiful names. Their names are generally held, especially in Indian context, as 'secrets', or as 'security cover'. It is an expression of shyness or delicacy. They prefer to be known as their children's mothers, or their fathers' daughters or their husbands' wives, not as themselves. They do not 'open up'. They prefer to remain in the background, playing very decisive roles. Women enjoy a one-down position. They don't like to be 'opening batsmen', to borrow terms from the game of Cricket. This trait in them is amply manifest in almost all situations which includes that wherein they co-operate with their men during their common efforts towards realization of their very *raison d'etre*.

Women are very intelligent and capable of designing strategies to bring their males under their control. Why they want to bring their husbands under control? Because they know very well as to how the males behave if let loose. They are basically nonchalant. Women accomplish this very efficiently and effectively. I have come across many married women; though well-educated and well-informed talk childishly things to their husbands. This is, probably, to gain favourable attitude or sympathy from them which can be effectively translated later on at appropriate times into a 'control syndrome' over their husbands. 'Weak' can conquer the 'strong' by 'lying low' in the beginning in order to provide a false notion of their 'surrender' to their husbands. Such stimuli applied on them provide the latter with egoistic satisfaction. They get intoxicated over this and with out their knowledge they get conditioned. Women like the situation and they would encash it later at opportune moments. This is accepted as an honest and ethical strife.

Women want to look pretty and attractive at all times. This instinct accompanies them everywhere and everytime unawares. It expresses itself in all pervasive manner, while they walk, talk, work or involve themselves in any other activities. In case of men this instinct is not discernible enough to make any serious assessment. In women, this instinct operates very prominently, but neither cognizable nor palpable to anyone, including the women themselves. Surprisingly, even the men may not notice or feel at times, probably because they involuntarily grant or ascribe this phenomenon to the women. We, for example, do not notice, now and then or everyday, our great-grandfather's bust kept reverentially in our drawing room, though we are unconsciously aware of its presence there. Even while dusting and cleaning the bust, I wonder, the person may not remember him in the total perspective. This is human psychology—his cognitive system.

According to empirical studies I have evolved the following data, under (A), the age group of women, and under (B), percentage utilization of disposable time for the purpose of 'looking pretty, presentable and attractive':

(A)	(B)
10 to 20	40 to 50
20 to 40	50 to 70

Peak value of nearly 60% in the age group of 15 to 35, remaining part of only 40% earmarked for other 'important' matters. These data reflect an appalling predicament, I perceive. This instinct may be working on them consciously or unconsciously. The mind may be occupied fully directly in most of the situations, and at times indirectly. The indirect involvement of the mind is the result of having a second nature, which does not appear all of a sudden. It is the result of strong continuous conscious efforts on the part of the mind for long duration of time in early part of life. The mind is programmed for an automatic execution of the overt and covert intentions in this regard. This is the initial investment. We know that nothing is produced without an investment. For all this, that is to develop, maintain and utilize thoughts, the invaluable energy of the intellect as well as imagination will have to be expended. Well, abstract nouns like investment, expenditure, utilization, advantage with the usual connotations as well as relevance may be used in this context as well.

Another trait which stands-out in women is their insatiability as far as their appetite for praise and flattery is concerned. They have tendency to over-consume these. This glut can deprive anyone of sense of direction and just perception. It reacts like drugs do. An overdose of these, generally speaking, renders them easy 'victims' of vile males. History can provide ample examples and cases where this malady had played havoc.

To sum up, I have dwelt upon some of the salient features, as observed from a peculiar angle, of women's socio-psycho psyche, like their physical debility, sense of patience, shyness, over-cautiousness, self-preservation and security, beauty consciousness, morbid affinity as well as vulnerability for praise, flattery and appreciation, and so on.

"Behind every man's success", they say, "There is always a woman". This, again, is said by men to appreciate or appease the 'woman behind', trying to recognize her positive role in her man's success. These days the saying stands modified in many cases to "Behind every woman's success, there is always a man."

Understanding the Old

20

It is reckoned that nearly one-third of living humans comprise of old people. These 'oldies' are the older brothers and sisters, fathers and mothers and grandfathers and grandmothers of the rest of the population. One can include great 'grands' as well in the list. All of them have great problems in carrying on with their lives. Sympathy and care from the younger lot can alleviate their problems and help them die peacefully. Society has responsibility towards them in this regard. It is a bionomical activity.

It is often said, 'Old is gold'. It implies that the old is wise. During the process of living, man encounters and gathers abundant data about the world around him. He processes them and converts them into information. As he carries on with his life, this information gets further processed gradually and turned into knowledge. And again, when this knowledge is allowed to mature, it becomes wisdom. All these statements look simple, but these indicate involvement of processes which consume nearly half a century, more than three-fourths of his life. Artificial 'mutation' can, probably bringforth viviparity to some extent, but it is, then, a very rare phenomenon. But there is no guarantee that accumulated wisdom too will be brought forward in such cases. The natural processes happen without his knowledge and permission, notwithstanding he is now a wise but 'old' man. But by this time, he would have reached the 'destination' and awaiting the 'final whistle'. What, then, is the use of this output called wisdom coming up so late in life, when one does not get enough time to utilize and enjoy the benefits accruing from its utilization? One would suspect that there is something wrong somewhere and curse the system declaring that it is devoid of any sense!

One wishes if he could have acquired wisdom without ageing, through some shortcut methods or a system to 'rewind, reset and restart' the whole life-period, bringing forward with him, as inheritance, wisdom gained and 'saved' intact in his brain in his 'previous life'. The humans approached God and appealed for grant of necessary boon in this regard. But He rejected the appeal. If this process is allowed to perpetuate, all persons existing on this Earth would be turned into mere 'huge heads', without bodies and legs to support. They thus will cease to be 'ordinary' human beings. They would become immortal. If the present trend is any indication, this earth would be turned into a heavily crowded planet with sinners.

It is believed that 'sin' is more ponderous than solid rocks, and therefore it would be too unbearable, even for the mighty Hercules to hold the weight of the earth together with that of the sins for a long period of time. Moreover, such 'heads' would try to rule the universe, ignoring even the Great Custodian. The latter does not like this, and hence makes sure that this 'fantastic phenomenon' does not take place which otherwise would have rendered the already existing beautiful system unworkable and led to confusion. And even His authority would have been challenged and so also the existing control-system which He has purposely and thoughtfully designed would have perished. A great danger is thus averted! No boss, to bring in an analogy, would have liked his subordinates to be smarter or cleverer than he is. It is an important ingredient to be integrated into any system if it is to continue to sustain as an efficient organization.

Each part of the body loses its original shape and strength and they are turned into helpless, functionless, burdensome and redundant fitted items. The infirmity in the old is manifest in many respects. They are unable to maintain steadiness in their walking style. Their bodies take to a rhythmic oscillatory side-ward swing movement, while walking, depending on the degree of deterioration of a particular leg or side of the hip. While doing so, their hands get into an involuntary breast-stroke swimming action in order to balancing whole body system in its advancing action.

The old legs can not carry along the weight of the 'luggage' of bodies that they are destined to support, because they have lost their strengths. They send out some creaking sounds of protestations from somewhere in their mid-points, as though for want of 'greasing', while carrying out the various duties entrusted to them. In fact these protestations are addressed to the upper body-part who does not do anything positive to alleviating the burden of the legs. It expresses its regrets in its inability in doing anything positive in this direction due to many genuine reasons, and makes a petition for mercy and pardon. The legs grant pardon considering the over-reigning reasons. The legs start pitying the body and the body pitying the legs. They both thus become members of 'mutual pitying club'. As a result, they 'happily' suffer a lot of pain and discomfort, without any resentment. The legs take refuge in philosophic dictum, 'understanding people always suffer'. When one is in pain or sorrow, it is only 'Philosophy' that comes forward with its aid-services, offering their crusade brand of consolation-schemes.

The physical stature and structure of the old shrink. Tall ones develop hunch, and the consequential drooping heads. His seeing, hearing and chewing faculties too bid farewell to him gradually. Out of the thirty-two, only the early integers will shyly remain, here and there, in the ruins and remnants of a lost battle, as witness and proof of the existence of their 'once-upon-a-time' rich and well-to-do dynasty of brave members. His sensitivity of sensory systems like tasting, smelling, touching also fade. His appetite for food declines. His bodily warmth reduces and as a consequence he loses power of resistance especially in the cold season. He loses most of his beautiful hair, and whatever few 'disobedient' ones still hanging around will turn white. They too lose their struggle for existence and survival and finally give up, to follow the path which their seniors took. He is no more a smart, energetic handsome man.

When he was young he could jump high about one hundred centimetres, but now when old, the height reduces to five centimetres and gradually that will tend to zero. Once a Marathonian, now he starts, stops before he moves forward, and wins the race by standing at same point only. His mind wants to get there but the body refuses to co-operate, resulting in shortfall in performance. When he had joined the 'colours' in his prime of life, he could say, 'left', 'right', 'left', 'right' and march forward, but now he prefers to say, 'left', 'left', 'left', 'left' and performs stationary march only. He is left to accomplish all of his targets through his imagination only. While at the dinner table even if electric supply fails in between, the hand of a youth will have no problem in locating the food insertion point on the face. Someone of the old may find some difficulties in coping this involuntary co-ordination. It all happens to anyone and everybody, as a result of natural decayance and deterioration. The young can await their turn.

His only support for his infirm body comes from his walking-staff which reminds him of the fact that he is old. He is greatly grateful to this companion. His other companion is his spouse. Whenever both of them are together they forget about their age. They may even engage themselves in romantic conversations and pleasantries. They may chew like the cud the good old memories of their past pleasant experiences. They may talk about their naughty son and affectionate daughter when the latter were young children and relate that pattern of behaviour to that of their grand children. When one is survived by the other, the survivor feels lonely. It is observed in many cases that no sooner a wife predeceases her husband, than the latter follows her. The reverse too occurs but such cases are less common. It may be that survival instinct is more powerful in women than in men. It may be that built-in shock-absorption system in women is more tenable than in men. Women are generally, more affectionate and attached to their children and grandchildren than men are. After the death of their husbands, if their children are loving, affectionate and considerate, they would extend their earthly tenure. Moreover, women are better crises-managers than their counterparts. Even twilight-setting of the Sun can slightly be postponed or proponed 'on demand'!

At the embryonic stage and during early part of infancy, children sleep all day and night. They wake up only for short durations either to go for a re-fill of their stomach or to answer nature's call. This sleeping period starts reducing gradually as the age advances. In case of the old, it reduces to three to four hours a day. Some do not get sleep even for that much time. As they are physically inactive, they elect to remain lying on the beds and brood over on their past experiences, both good and bad, some delightful and some others depressing. Depressing ones cast their dark shadows on the delightfuls while they co-habit with the former. Depression is heavier by weight than delight. The delightful ones are lighter, finer and meeker. The heavier ones always succeed in dominating these lighter ones. It evolves itself as a result of natural mutual inductance. Hence, in the overall context, the net result is depression. There are many circumstantial factors like physical infirmity, 'departure' of spouse, hostile or uncongenial household situations, inadequacy of financial provisions too offer themselves as players in this. Net result is depression, and with it comes pessimism which can prompt them to pray for an early 'exit'. It is a sad and pitiable predicament.

It was when, it is said, Einstein was in the midst of discussions on his Theory of Relativity with other scientists, that an old illiterate infirm lady of eighty, his affectionate neighbour, came in interrupting, and asked him as to what this Theory which he was propounding was about. To make her understand, he then had asked her two counter-questions, one relating to her age at that time and as to how she had been spending her time then. She had said that she was eighty years of age and that it was very difficult to spend time. Then came his second question as to how she was spending time when she was sixteen. She replied, "O my boy, I had to chase time at that time. It was all fantastic". "Mama, my Theory discusses only about it. Nothing more", he replied. The old lady was satisfied and went away. In the old age time chases one and in the youth one chases time. It is very difficult to spend time in the old age. As naughty, nagging, nonchalant, delinquent and disobedient children to their parents, is time to these old people. Time teases. In their youth if they had developed love, taste or interests in any of the subjects of fine arts, like painting, music-vocal or instrumental, it would have come to their rescue in their ante-sunset period. Even listening to and enjoying music is highly desirable. Reading, again, is a good habit, but it can go on only till the eye-sight permits. These are some of the ways by which they can take refuge from monotony, dullness, depression and loneliness.

When someone looks at an old and physically infirm man, the former concentrates only on his physical infirmity and not on his intelligence and wisdom which are invisible. One should not forget that there is a wholesome volume of knowledge, sagacity and wisdom residing in this old infirm and frail form. Even the intelligence which one has been proud of in his youth wanes. Intelligence is kinetic and wisdom is static. The residual intelligence is no more kinetic to provide motive power to the mind. The mind gradually develops amnesia. It has been used up in the process of providing care and comfort to his children and probably to the entire society, and he acquires in return knowledge and wisdom as a bye-product of this process of living. Existence of the residual intelligence is not usually noticeable to any casual onlooker. Because of this, an average onlooker ignores such a person, even look at him contemptuously. None likes to transact with such a person. It becomes duty of the wise people to pardon, in the absence of any other choice, such onlookers, for, 'they do not know what they are doing'.

Any machine, due to long usage, will be subjected to wear and tear in the long run. In some cases it may be due to unfair wear and tear. In any case, they need periodic repair and servicing to ensure fairly long service. But at last it has to stop functioning. One can not blame the machine for its malfunctioning or disorder or abrupt collapse. This is quite a natural phenomenon. Similar is the case with all people. Deterioration gradually starts by the time the person reaches his middle age and then onwards it accelerates very fast as the age advances and reaches peak value when one is awaiting the 'final call'.

There is an old adage, 'the green leaves on the tree laugh at the fall of the withered yellow leaves from the same tree'. There is nothing wrong in this behaviour on the part of the green leaves, for it is in tune with Nature's great game-plan. Similar is the case with human beings.

'Golden old age' has to be managed. Its management has two dimensions; firstly, management by the old themselves and secondly by others. By and large the old may not realize that they have become old. At best it can be understood as a deliberate eagerness to avoid getting such a stamping on them. The main reason for this may lie in the result of their keen observation as to how old people are being treated by others, and they do not want to be in such predicament as those of such others. This attitude of theirs makes them adamant and uncompromising on various situations and issues. Maybe, in their younger days, their principles and value-systems have been relevant and the effects, results and impact of such things too were quite good and hence acceptable to others, at that time. But, even though situations and issues now are identical and the same as the earlier ones, none is ready to buy their same 'old' ideas. Hence there is no point in clinging to them fastitiously, for in the eyes of others they may be perceived as out-dated, old-fashioned and impractical.

The old must change. They must cast off their 'complex' attitudes, similar to the snakes doing an 'ecdysis' act by which they willingly cast off their integuments during certain seasons in order to rejuvenate and revitalize themselves. This attitudinal change will make them realize that they are 'old' and it will enable them to start taking care of by themselves. Once this is done they would start feeling internal freedom and relaxation which enable them looking inwards with a view to ascertaining their strengths and weaknesses. It is like unloading a loaded spring. The molecules in the spring would feei free of the artificial potential energy impregnated into them. It is also similar to neutralizing a high voltage of electric charge by 'earthing'. They gradually slip down from their stance of adamancy on their principles, and start compromising. This is a healthy trend which others would like to accept, and the old will benefit immensely from this in due course of time.

It is a good sight to see old people, both in urban and rural settings, congregate at appointed rendezvous to exchange notes. Mostly they would be talking about their woes they face in their evenings of life. It is but natural that they start criticizing those who are supposed to look after them. Some of them openly admire their sons and daughters-in-law, while some others curse and condemn them. In the latter case they ultimately take to a defeatist attitude and accept the predicament as their destiny and a gift from God. In any case through these interactions they are able to vent their sorrows. They get opportunities to compare each one's plight with that of others. It is like saying, "I have at least one leg, and I am better than the other who has none". They take special care to avoid monotonous reiterations of old stories. Some of them do not part with their sense of humour; they become a source of solace and cheer to others. Among them there would be retired cine and drama artists, professors, executives, sports personalities, defence personnel, bank employees, farmers, social workers and a lot many others. Notable absence is of politicians, as none retires in politics. Most of them prefer dying in harness so as to avail State funerals.

All of them come out to share their experiences with those of others. If any 'member' is absent on any particular day, he would be required to give satisfactory explanation as to why he was absent the previous day. It only shows how much they care for each other. Birds of the same feather flock together. There exists mutual admiration among most of them. To make fun they even resort to mutual derision, and none minds at all, all that. They have good sportsmanship. They go out on picnics where they engage themselves in static games and fun-making. They criticize all the governments, past and present, and their styles of administration. They may lament the 'changed-for-worse' administrative set-ups in the offices where they used to work. They perceive all-round deterioration in moral value-system, as compared to what they had in their time. They enjoy consensus in all these perceptions. They have heated arguments on politics, prevalent social norms and culture. They do not seem to have any bitter communal feelings. After all these interactions, their brain-cells get re-charged, rejuvenated and refreshed. It is known that bondage between and among individuals becomes stronger against a common enemy or in favour of a common cause.

They have their tea at nearby mini-tea stall, before they depart for their homes, after these deliberations on the day's unwritten unscheduled agenda. The owner of the tea stall is happy about the uninterrupted patronage he receives and hence offers cash-discounts to them. He can safely afford to supply tea on concessional rates, because most of them take t.s.s. (tea sans sugar)! He expresses his great concern about their health and welfare and does not forget to make enquiries in this regard, resorting to a random sampling method.

Some of these old people form some associations, registered or otherwise. They meet at appointed times and discuss common problems and their possible solutions. These are the forums through which they can make their grievances addressed to concerned authorities and seek redressal. They may be known by "senior citizens' conclave" or such other nomenclature.

It is imperative that these senior citizens must learn to look after themselves rather than expecting someone else to do that job for them. There is no substitute for the self-help. And this is one of the important methods. They should develop an attitude to perceive as bonus if someone of young alleviates their hardships when such gestures were never expected. One gets great joy when one gets what one never expected.

The physically strong and exuberant young people deride the old, as though old age has fallen on these people due to their thoughtless actions or mistakes. This attitude of theirs must change and grant them at least sympathy. That will help them a lot.

They must understand that the intellectual prowess of which people take great pride in their youth, gradually and slowly wanes as they advance in age. This happens without their being aware of. It is a helpless but sad predicament. In the younger days, none notices or realizes this phenomenon, because everybody is 'busy otherwise' in the process of living. None has time to look backwards to realize this fact. Some are even scared to do so. Those who dare look back realize it; they become philosophers, and you know that philosophy has no 'market' nowadays.

It is the co-habiting young who should earmark time for efforts to mitigate the miserable plight of these old ones. They should not be happy merely by providing good food and earmarking finances for buying sleeping pills for the old. They should allocate to these old hapless ones, at least half of the care that they lavishly shower on their animal pets!

In Indian societal context it is clearly understood that the old are to be looked after by their offsprings. Even old religious scripts prescribe such norms. All material assets, in certain cases even spiritual ones too, are handed down to the next generation. They take care of their parents and other seniors in the family, as though, fulfilling their divine duty. Non-fulfilment, if any, will be considered as sin. The word, 'sin' implies a heavy quantum of potential energy, like that of a bomb, capable of destroying one's most powerful asset called the 'soul' and denying entry into the most desired place called, 'heaven'. It creates fear-psychosis which will be of immense motivational thrust to those who are supposed to look after the hapless old.

Governments are too concerned about their welfare. They offer health schemes, travel concessions, old-age pension, rehabilitation and destitute homes and the like. Some governments enact social laws making it compulsory for the offsprings to provide adequate care and protection to their parents as a pre-condition for inheritance of the assets of their parents. If they fail in their duties, they could get punished under provisions of such Acts, besides their getting disqualified for inheritance. But there are some interesting facts and factors. There are rules and rules, but they usually lie hidden in the vast volume of papers. None should think that if the old are not being cared for by those who are supposed to, it will not be due to lack or absence of any rules or laws. Rules are only tools, and tools themselves cannot operate. It is the sincerity of the operators that makes things happen. There are no alternatives to sincerity. The implementation is nearly impracticable due to one or all of the following reasons:

(a) The affected old may not like to make complaints to the authorities against their offsprings due to false sense of pride and family reputation.

(b) The affected old are scared about the possible adverse consequential reactions or vendetta from those against whom complaints are being made. It would naturally be very difficult for them to cohabit with complaintees. Their lives could be rendered more miserable, if they are allowed to survive.

(c) They may be too old to understand if they are actually neglected.

(d) There cannot be any effective monitoring of any previous incidences.

(e) No law can enforce sincerity.

Understanding Idiocy—A Helpless Predicament

21

According to *Chamber's Dictionary*, an 'idiot' is "a person so defective in mind from birth as to be unable to protect himself against ordinary physical dangers: one afflicted with the severest grade of feeble-mindedness: a flighty fool: a block head, a foolish and unwise person." 'Idiocy' means "state of being an idiot: imbecile".

Idiots are the 'blessed ones'. They are by birth feeble-minded or having any thing worth naming minds. Mind is the creator of all problems to individuals and thereby to societies. Mind is considered to be brain, by some wise men. Mind is a blend of brain and heart according to some others. Mind stands for reason, and heart for emotions. In any case it is most dangerous thing that a person has. Mind is a manufacturing unit whose output is thoughts, wanted or unwanted, desirable or undesirable. It is heart-element of the mind becomes the source-centre wherefrom thoughts of hatred, hypocrisy and jealousy emanate. The brain or its thought-part tells us to do a thing, but the heart-part tells us the opposite. We are confused and obviously in trouble as to which way we should go. The result of our actions undertaken under the influence of either of the 'parts' would fall upon us later; or it may be too late to take any recourse or remedial actions, should our actions prove defective subsequently. So what do we do? Nothing. Eliminate the mind totally and become an idiot. It is the most difficult thing to do for a person having a mind.

We have heard many saints asking us to become 'idiots', because that is the way we can move God-ward, which is the ultimate goal of each one of us. They mean that such aspirants should be without any feeling of love, hatred, jealousy, egoism, hypocrisy, wickedness and greed, because, they say, these are hindrances while moving towards spiritual emancipation. We know that idiots do not have these feelings, and if at all they do have, then these will be in dormant, dilute, undeveloped or under-developed, faint and feeble state, depending upon degree, level or status of their idiocy. They do not have enough 'amperage' or 'motive force' to force their way. So if anyone wants to move God-ward he should cast off all such feelings and get 'neutralized', lust like a magnet getting 'demagnetized' In effect, he or she is advised to become an 'idiot', not merely 'idiot-like'.

Electric bulbs have various wattage ratings. Even a 'zero' wattage rated bulbs too have some minimal wattage to prove that they too are electric bulbs. They blink. Similar is the case of idiots. Some of them have this 'blinking' capacity. There is scope for some studies and research on them, because they form 'border-line' cases. It is wrong to say that all idiots have the same level of idiocy. They may possess intelligence from zero level to some detectable magnitudes. Accordingly, their behaviour, attitudes, and response to stimuli may be different. Some may have infinitesimal and some others have more than that, but definitely less than that of 'intelligent' persons. Their response to stimuli may be poor, but they respond to them to some extent.

The idiots too have some of the feelings like love, affection, hatred, sorrow and happiness. They exhibit as well as enjoy physical love and affection. They hate those who give them pain. When they are subjected to physical pain, they weep and cry, but in case of mental pain their response or reaction may not be perceptible enough. But they surely have. If at all it hits the little brain that they have, their reactions may be physical. They even enjoy jokes or humour, but their response may be very much less than that of an average person. They may laugh or smile in mechanical manner, as they observe other 'normal' members in the group. They laugh or smile because others do the same. In all this they exhibit their 'eagerness' to become 'part' of their 'intelligent' counterparts. They observe others and try to ape such behaviour of theirs. They laugh on certain occasions on misjudged or presumed humour. This behaviour can be because others around them laugh and this provides inkling to them that the matter talked about at that time by others may have been something to laugh about. And they laugh. "Let me also laugh, otherwise, I may not be identified with these others present there. I may be left out", the idiot instinctively realizes thus. This behaviour may not be due to some deliberations in their minds, because they do not have the needed 'amperage' at the disposal of their feeble minds. At best, all these can be called 'sympathetic vibrations'. Hence it is the instinct-element that prompts him to take a stand like this. In all these, their responses are similar to those manifest by children, even-though the idiot is an adult by age.

The idiots like to listen to music, preferably instrumental or highly rhythmic. They don't seem to enjoy it, the way intelligent people do. They enjoy, at the least, the rhythmic gyrations that the music would be offering. Probably they won't even mind manipulating and converting, to their advantage, classical to non-classical or anything else but only criterion is that they should enjoy or seem to enjoy some music. That is all about it. Here also they may be aping the 'intelligent lot', as mentioned earlier.

All 'wickeds' are not 'stupids', but some stupids are wicked. Similarly some stupids are selfish too. Their both wickedness and selfishness are employed only to the extent required to insure their physical maintenance as well as security needs. If one asks a child to part with the one piece of chocolate that it possesses, the obvious answer is a big "NO". This is selfishness 'unplugged', and it is justified through and through. An adult's behaviour at the same issue, obviously, would have been quite different. Both the child and the adult are equally 'guilty' of being selfish, but the society condones this guilt, because this is not beyond the permissible limits, granted to each and every member, by the society itself. This sort of wickedness and selfishness is rampant among other members of the fauna as well. Selfishness is prevalent among members of flora as well, at the same time there seems to be no evidence of their being wicked.

Some of these idiots develop and nurture good physique. The tendency is an expression of need for some sort of compensation as well as complementation.

Law of any country provides for the protection of these mentally as well as physically weak persons against harm or atrocities perpetrated on them by the physically and mentally strong persons. Law provides that no contracts can be entered into with them by other party. Such contracts are declared null and void *ab initio*. This is to protect their interests. The governments have responsibility towards them as they belong to the weaker section of the society. They are feeble-minded and as such they can not protect themselves.

22 Indulgence in Counselling—An Interactive Demeanour

Counselling is one of the best examples of social interaction. It happens sometimes voluntarily and some other times involuntarily, solicited or unsolicited. It could be an overflow of ideas one possesses which he likes to share with his fellow-beings as a gesture of goodwill, general benefaction or entertainment.

Counselling is the act of rendering advice, and this is the easiest thing to perform at a 'no-cost' basis. Advice is given to a needy who accepts it if he is convinced of its usefulness. He accepts, enjoys the fruits, and acknowledges his gratitude to the giver of it. He is happy. The giver too is very happy when he comes to know that his advice has really benefited the taker. He feels satisfied in the fact that he could be of some help to the other person. The service rendered in this way is usually considered a 'thankless' one, and it should be so in the eyes of the giver, even though the beneficiary might loudly express his gratitude, if he is benefited by it. If he is not benefited, the advisor will be severely condemned and criticized, even though the giver gave it in earnestness and goodwill, and without any malice. It is good for the advisor to anticipate such repercussions before rendering advice. In fact he should have carefully selected the right person to receive his advice *ab initio* itself to avoid a boomerang later. In any case, the advice-givers are advised to keep helmets with them to protect their heads, as a precautionary measure to meet any adverse eventuality, should the advice rendered backfires. It could be a dangerous game!

In a society where people live together with a common cause or goal, it becomes duty for each of its members to serve or help mutually. This attitude on the part of each and every member ensures the well-being of the society, thus ensuring its ideal sustenance and existence. Society consists of different types of people with varying levels of knowledge, sagacity and intelligence. There should be equitable distribution of these. Mutual interactions among members of the society ensure sharing this wealth of knowledge. It is obvious that only those who have can part with. In this, unlike in other cases, the giver does not lose the portion that he gives out to others. In fact his capability to give advice will be tested, and thereby his acumen will get sharpened. When the taker gets to know that he is benefited by the advice rendered by the other, he expresses his satisfaction. The gleam on his face depicts the level of satisfaction by seeing which the giver too gets fully satisfied.

Everybody would be having some specialized knowledge in some specialized field or other. A person with human and humane approach may share and induct these. Some people seek advice from others whether they require it or not. It could be a clever or clandestine move by them to enhance the latter's egoism and thereby create a rapport with them. It is an investment of insurance for any future exigencies. This may produce, sometimes, a recoiling effect. Such people may be thought of as vile or foolish by cleverer or more intelligent onlookers. This sort of behaviour is discernible in official relationships between officers and their subordinates. The subordinates utilize this frivolous method or pretext of seeking advice for non-existent doubts from their bosses to sublime the latter, obviously to earn their sympathy and subsequently undue favours from them. This also happens in this world!

Solicitation of advice comes about in different manner. Some people may not even know where to 'knock', when they are in real need of some advice, guidance or direction. They remain confused. Some others, on the contrary, dislike avail advice from others, even if they are in dire need of it. Advice is available, but one refuses to take it because of his dogged egoism. His egoism does not permit him to condescend from the high pedestal where he has placed himself on. He thinks it is below his 'dignity', as he equates taking advice to some sort of subjugation, dependency and obligation. This is sheer obstinacy borne out of misconception, misapprehensions and lack of mental development. This is a symptom of some psychological disorder. Such a person is apt to say, "Who is he to give me advice?"

A cynic will not like to share good things, if at all any, with others except, probably, his cynicism. He does not like to give away his expertise and knowledge because they might benefit others. This might cause indigestion to him. He is apt to say, "Why should I advise anybody? I have gained my knowledge by my hard work. If anyone wants it, let him also do hard work and undergo tribulations and thereby earn it. I am not here to make him happy." Similar is the case with selfish people. They are highly suspicious about others. If all members think the way the cynics and selfish do, then the society would remain stale. It will become a congregation of irresponsible members, a garbage heap. One should think that rendering correct advice to the needy is a noble cause. If people lived earlier on this earth too had thought the way these cynics and selfish people do, then humanity would not have taken so many forward strides, the positive effects of which we witness and enjoy today.

There are some people who think that they are highly knowledgeable and sagacious. They have some sort of a superiority-complex. They have a feeling that they can find solutions for any problem that anyone faces. They can not 'sit quiet' without giving advice to someone. It seems that such people have 'itching tongues'. It is their hobby to distribute, so to say, advice to anyone and everyone, irrespective of whether the latter requires it or not. It is unsolicited advice. The main reason for such a behaviour could be that they want concurrence from others to their feeling of self-superiority, and a stamp of recognition from them to that effect. It is also an attempt to assert their egoism and pride. They seem to underestimating and undermining the level of knowledge and competence which others possess. It is observed that some seniors in some organizations do this mistake of advising their juniors, on personal matters, without the latter's seeking for it. This too is unsolicited advice.

It is not always true that unsolicited advice is rendered just only to project the giver's ego-sense or superiority to the other person. Let us consider the case of two friends. The first 'symptom' of the existence of a good friendship between two individuals is that there will be no ego-clash. Another name for good friendship is compromising. There are certain conditions when unsolicited advice is exchanged between two equally intelligent and sagacious friends. It is, however, always possible that even a high intellectual could forget very important but routine matters. In such cases it is the duty of his good and understanding friend to render him advice or making him aware of the need for initiating some actions in some directions. Whether it is solicited or unsolicited, it is good if he takes his advice and implements it wholeheartedly, not rejecting it outright telling that it is an unsolicited advice. This rejection could be viewed as an unwise, crude and cruel demeanour on the part of that friend. Here it can be seen that more importance is attached to his egoism than to his friendship. He should have sacrificed his egoism at the altar of friendship, if, after a thorough analysis, it is proved that the advice is well-intended and worthy of adoption. One thing is clear; there is no place for malice or malfeasance in true friendship.

Communicative Interaction 23

Man is a thinking animal. This trait in him makes him different from other living organisms. His thoughts encompass all aspects of the art of his living. He is not living alone in this world. His thoughts, howsoever lofty, will have no utility in the context of societal living if he chooses to keep them preserved in his mind alone. When he leaves the world on cessation of his earthly innings, these thoughts would also be buried in his coffin along with him. On the other hand, if he leaves them behind, it would be of great help for others still left living in the world. So he has to communicate and disseminate his thoughts, thereby enhancing the quality of life of his fellow beings left behind. Group activities is the essence of societal living. In this it is imperative that information and knowledge acquired by him are shared among all the members of his society by interactional transactions. But for this, our societies would not have flourished and attained advancement as we witness today. This all is the result of communication.

Communication of any sort forms an integral ingredient of inter-personal interaction. Communication is a process. Oxygen and water are the two most important elements required for the very existence of all living organisms, but none is conscious about their importance except in their absence or inadequacy of supply. Similar is the case with communication. Communication comes to the rescue of a breathless patient asking for remedying breathlessness or a thirsty person for a glass of water. Communication forms, thus, an important ingredient required for the very survival of living beings. Communication takes place automatically without the consent or request of anyone. It is a process which most of us never think about analytically. Any breakdown of it culminates in all kinds of maladies. People, who analyse the use and the usefulness of this process, gain immensely in terms of an unusual insight into human nature. People cannot share knowledge in which case each person would have to learn everything himself. There are various ways through which living beings communicate with each other. They manage it by tongue, teeth, mouth, nose, eyes, face, head, shoulders, hands, legs, whole body, singing, laughing, dancing, weeping, touching and even by silence. In short, they use all the resources at their command for the purpose of communication. They share their ideas and emotions, actions and reactions through this communication with other members of their societies.

Communication is sharing information or for providing entertainment. Probably, the most important type of communication is personal communication which happens when people make their thoughts and wishes known to one another. Without personal communication parents would not know what their children want; teachers could not help their students learn; friends could not make plans with one another. In fact human beings could not have survived as a society so long but for communication. Another type of communication happens when messages are sent to large audience: we call it mass communication. The media for this are books, television, newspapers, radio and the like.

Development of Communication

In pre-historic times, people probably communicated with one another by sound and gestures long before they developed actual words. We can guess that the advent of spoken language must have come about as an imitation of sounds in Nature, such as howling of wind, sound from waterfalls, sonant notes emanating from friction among clustered trees, bird-songs, splash murmurs of rivers, barking, growling, howling and roaring of animals and the like. After the advent of language, people exchanged views and news chiefly by word of mouth. Runners carried spoken messages over long distances. People also used drumbeats, fires and smoke signals to communicate with other people who could understand those codes used. Paintings and drawings were the first step towards a written language. Pre-historic artists began to use a series of pictures to tell a story, such as the history of a good hunting trip or violent storm. Gradually they developed small pictures that stood for most common objects and ideas—the hieroglyphic or pictographic writing. For all these developments, it took millions of years; it has been a very slow evolution. It is surprising to see only in the last few centuries of human civilisation that human beings could make notable strides in its development. It would be sheer childishness, impiety and even blasphemy on our part to ask or even think as to what our ancestors had been doing till then. After a couple of centuries hence, if we, the present generation, survive, to state optimistically, our successors would include us too in the ancestral fold and might hold us responsible for not making notable strides, considering the present unimaginable galloping trend of development in the field of communication. Oh, Lord, pardon them then! It has been a natural organic evolution. It needs to understand that the evolution and development of communication have been a great impetus for the development of our brains as well, and that is how we are able to think now like that. After that, the process of development got accelerated. The sequence of evolution and development in brief is as follows:

> Paintings and drawings—hieroglyphic system of writing and communicating—invention of paper—invention of pencil of graphite—printing machine photography—electric telegraphy—typewriter—telephones—wireless telegraphy radio—television—Xerox—teleprinter—satellite communication—mobile phones—laser—fibre optics and God knows what more to follow!

Communication is the process of imparting information from a sender to a receiver with the use of a medium. Communication requires that all parties have an area of communicative commonality and mutual relevance. It is defined as a process by which we assign and convey meaning, in an attempt to create shared understanding. This process requires an inexhaustible inventory of skills in intrapersonal and interpersonal processing, listening, observing, speaking, questioning, analyzing and evaluating. Use of this process is developmental, and transfers to all areas of life: home, school, community, work, and beyond. It is through communication that collaboration and co-operation are elicited.

Communication vis-à-vis Other Members of Fauna

In many of its facets is not limited to humans, or even to primates. Every information exchange, transmission and reception of signals, between or among living organisms can be considered a form of communication. Animal communication is any behaviour on the part of one animal that has an effect on the current or future behaviour of another animal. Of course, human communication can be subsumed as a highly developed form of animal communication. The study of animal communication has played an important part in the development of ethology, sociobiology, and the study of animal cognition. Although animals communicate, they do not have language like what the humans have. They do make noises but these tend to be situation-related, for example, a loud shriek to signify fear or severe pain. Even humans also have situation-related noises. If an Indian, an Englishman and a Russian, standing blind-folded would make the same noise if anyone stamped on their toes. These are examples of the ways of communication. This is quite evident as humans are able to communicate with animals especially dolphins and other animals employed in circuses; however these animals have to learn a special modified means of communication. Animal communication, and indeed the understanding of the animal world in general, is a rapidly growing field, and even in the current century so far, many prior understandings related to diverse fields such as their emotions, culture and learning, and even sexual conduct, long thought to be well understood, have been revolutionized. Animals can learn human language to some extent as understood recently with respect to dolphin communication and teaching hand signals to apes. Some dogs are taught by humans to sing songs. It is a pity that the great humans with great level of intelligence are unable to learn the language of the less 'intelligent' animals, instead they have to force them to learn theirs!

It is interesting to watch hundreds of birds fly together in beautiful perfect formations, like our fighter planes do. There are a few cases wherein fighter planes in such air displays had met with accidents by collisions, whereas in the case of the birds, there have been no such cases. The latter unlike the former has modern devices of communication with the help of which they do a lot of manoeuvring in the air space. These birds maintain the same speed as well as distances between and among them while flying. They definitely have some communication system though incomprehensible to humans. It is, in any case, fascinating spectacle!

Birds communicate with one another in a series of ways. Vocal communication by means of calls and songs is the most important way. Generally, all birds have a voice and they use it to call or sing. Birds use their calls mainly as signals to other birds. Baby birds call in one way to tell their parents that they are hungry, and another way to convey if they are hurt or frightened. A male robin sings a song; it will mean for another male a call for fighting to defend its territory; a female listening to some other type will get ready for mating. They all may sound alike to humans. Even in a crowded colony a parent bird can single-out the voice of its chicks and the chicks can recognize that of their parent. Some birds mimic other sounds in the surroundings. Certain birds like parrots and mynas become mimics when in captivity. They can even be trained to imitate human speech and whistling. Some birds communicate by sounds other than vocal sounds. They resort to visual displays like flashing of tail feathers used in courtship. A peacock spreads its beautiful feathers into a gorgeous fan and dances during courtship to attract and invite peahens.

There are two very intriguing members of the fauna, two leviathans of the earth, the blue whales in the sea and elephants on the land. Both are very huge in size, but they are generally harmless with respect to humans. They do not show any aggressiveness against humans except on direct or indirect provocation on the part of the latter. Today we know them to be virtually harmless to humans and that they have quite a bit in common with us—they, too are warm-blooded mammals that must breathe air. They are highly social animals with complex languages and intelligence. Most importantly, they are not monsters at all, but gentle giants deserving respect, admiration and protection. In nature, the very largest of the large creatures in general have been virtually harmless to humans. In fact, magnificent creatures such as the great blue whales have suffered most at the hands of humans bent on destruction. Blue whales, as well as many other whale species, have been hunted to the brink of extinction by people from all over the world for centuries. It's only recently, in this century, that we as a species have begun to appreciate the value of all living creatures. This 'change of heart' is not due to their pitying of these creatures, but because of their growing sense of existentialism. We have come to feel that wiping any species of animal off the face of the earth forever is an evil thing for humans to do. Blue whales have been put on the endangered species list. In the last two centuries, these giant whales have been hunted by unscrupulous humans, thousands have been killed and brought them near extinction.

The most spectacular thing about the blue whales, probably, is the big sounds they make. Scientists have measured the low-frequency sounds they make when they communicate with each other by using a decibel meter. Some of their vocalizations have been recorded as loud as 188 decibels and can be heard as far as 850 km away. To get an idea of just how loud 188 decibels is, we can compare it with that of the sound of 120 decibels that a commercial jet makes at the time of taking off. Human shouting is 70 decibels; sounds over 120 decibels are painful to human ears. That makes whales, by far, the loudest living thing anywhere on earth! They emit very loud, highly structured, repetitive low-frequency sounds that can travel for many kilometres underwater. These sounds may be for long-range contact, assembly calls, advertisement for mates, greeting, location and availability of food, threat, or individual identification.

The way a mahout of sixty kilograms weight and of one-and-a-half metres height conducts and disciplines such huge animals is something awe-striking and unbelievable to anyone watching. The mahouts feed them. They love them and they reciprocate that love. The animals understand their language and expressions. These animals are sensitive to the changing moods of their mahouts who even punish the errant ones. They accept the punishments in right sporting spirit and earnestness. If they consider that the punishments are unwarranted or excessive, they pardon them once or twice but they debit these against their names, and later on they opt to clear that debit account once for all by resorting to retribution. They are very fond of bathing, and the mahouts bathe them as they do for their own children. They thoroughly enjoy the caressing that these mahouts do, despite their thick skin covering. They have high bodily temperature, and to cool it they love to roll themselves in mud and slush if they get opportunities for that.

The elephant has great power of memory. If any wrong or harm is given to it is not forgotten and it avenges it at appropriate moments in its style. There is a well-known fable. An elephant used to be taken everyday to a river for bathing it through a particular route. On this route there was a tailor shop. Everyday the tailor used to give it a banana. On a particular day he did not give, but playfully pricked its trunk by a needle. The elephant had filled its trunk with water after bathing, and on its way back, it went straight to the tailor and released the water on him, wetting the whole shop. The tailor learned a lesson, and the elephant avenged the hurt it received. This fable depicts of its memory as well as its revengeful nature.

An increasing number of incidents involving elephants attacking humans leads us to believe that the animals may be seeking revenge. They are prone to get angry when they do not get enough to eat. They are surprisingly vegetarians and they consume about a quarter of a tonne of food and drink that much of water everyday. They do not compromise on this quantity. If they are deprived of this, they go berserk, 'mad' and belligerent. The domesticated elephants, when subjected to full or partial starvation, run amok, and attack and kill their irresponsible keepers, and bring about total destruction all around. The keepers make them do hard work with the wrong presumption that these strong animals do not get tired and exhausted. An exhausted and starved elephant becomes the greatest of all threats. There are frequent reports of herds of wild elephants destroying villages without apparent cause; some scientists are speculating that elephants might be attacking humans in revenge for years of abuse, giving new meaning to the saying elephants are retributive and revengeful and they never forget or pardon misdeeds perpetrated on them by the humans. They are certainly intelligent enough and have good enough memories, the 'elephantine memory', to take revenge.

Communication is the cause and behaviour is the effect. Communication is the stimulus and the behaviour is its corresponding response. One is the action while the other is the reaction. If one watches a behaviour, one can reckon the communication process behind such behaviour, an indirect way of understanding. Moreso it is true of animal communication. Unlike in the case of the humans, animals do not have any 'hidden agenda' behind their behaviour. The behaviour seems to depend on patterns of reaction with which they are born, called instincts and reflexes, there being hardly any or no role for intelligence to play. After breaking out of its cocoon, a moth flies about and finds its food in the juices of plants without having to learn how to do so. Instinct directs the animal to do certain things to stay alive. Intelligent animals like apes, monkeys and dolphins learn to solve their problems with the help of their intelligence, besides the power of instincts. In this, they rely on previous experiences. Animals use their senses to receive communication from others of their kind and interpret them. Some other animals use their scent in the same fashion. Members of canine and feline families define and proclaim their territorial sovereignty by urinating on the boundaries. Some animals use their face and body to communicate. An angry gorilla may throw leaves into the air and beats its chest with its fists. Elephants communicate with one another in various ways of posturing and gesturing. They make different kinds of rumbling sounds; a hoarse loud one when they are frightened, a low humming one to calm young ones. Many mammals, in particular, have glands that generate distinctive and long-lasting smells, and have corresponding behaviours that leave these smells in places where they have been. Often the scented substance is introduced into urine; sometimes through sweat. Cats have scent glands on their flanks, and deposit scent by rubbing their sides against objects; they also have scent glands on their foreheads. Other instances include the warning cries of many monkeys, and the mating calls of many species of frogs.

System of communication prevailing in the community of ants is very intriguing. Ants that live inside plants or in the leaf-nests may tap their gasters against the outside walls of their nest when they discover food or enemies. Such taps arouse the insiders who rush out of the nest within seconds to carry food inside or fight the enemy. They may even produce squeaky or buzzing sound to complement the taping sound. Ants also communicate with one another by giving out a sensitive chemical called pheromones with different kinds of smell and taste, each kind communicating different information like food availably or presence of enemies. Often one can see ants conferencing and sharing information. Within seconds of the death of another living being including humans, a particular type of ants assemble at the spot for a sumptuous meal. One wonders at this spontaneous congregation. This behaviour of theirs gives ample proof of their unbelievable communicating capability. In the case of death of a human being, it is they who declare the person dead even before a doctor could do so. Hundreds of them assemble near the dead body abruptly to make and share a dinner or supper uninvitedly. Ants can tell a colony-mate from enemies by odour. When two ants meet they smell each other with their antennae. If they are nest-mates they stand mouth-to-mouth and exchange pleasantries. It is interesting to watch tiny ants with very 'hot news' about availability of their favourite item, sweets, somewhere in the vicinity, doing to-and-fro brisk walks between two points to convey the news to their kith and kin. Within seconds all of them reach the rendezvous to share the happiness.

A bee discovering a plentiful supply of nectar several fields away from the hive returns and gives directions to its fellows by flying in the direction of the source in a series of complex patterns in front of the hive. The other bees will then fly straight to the food source. Bees carry with them a pouch of material from the hive which they release as they re-enter, the smell of which serves as 'gate pass' for their safe entry into the home-hive. It is communication that has the final say.

It seems that these sweet and honey eaters—ants and the bees, do not contract the deadly disease of diabetes, despite their consuming them in large quantities throughout their lives! It is Nature.

Behaviour vis-à-vis Communication (Fauna)

Any behaviour indicates communication and any communication results in behaviour. Animal communication is any behaviour on the part of one animal that has an effect on the current or future behaviour of another animal. The study of animal communication, sometimes called 'zoosemiotics' (distinguishable from 'anthroposemiotics', the study of human communication) has played an important part in the development of ethology, socio-biology, and the study of animal cognition. The best known forms of communication involve the display of distinctive body parts, or distinctive bodily movements; often these occur in combination. So a distinctive movement acts to reveal or emphasise a distinctive body part. A parent bird bringing food, for example, and presenting its bill and tapping on the ground in front of the nest elicit begging response from its hungry chicks. It is the result of a learning process on the part of the chicks via rewards. Another important form of communication is bird-song usually performed mainly by males which is the best known case of vocal communication. Other instances include the warning cries of many monkeys, and the mating calls of many species of frogs.

Prey-to-Predator Communication

It is interesting to watch some of the systems of communication between prey animals and their predators. A wasp uses its bright colours together with attending gestures to warn its predator that it can cause harm to it. The predator chooses to keep away from it, succumbing to the threat potential in the warning. Its previous unpleasant experience too might become a deterrent. It is more interesting to watch hoverflies coloured in the same fashion as that of the wasps, but without having their stinging faculty, mimic the wasps and get away. Some of the members of the canine species adopt aggressive postures, such as growling with their teeth bared and successfully get better of their predators. Rattlesnakes rattle to warn potential predators of their poisonous bite. A few animals like chameleons change their skin colours smartly within seconds to match those of the surroudings and thus avoiding detection in order to hoodwink their enemies. Sometimes a behavioural change and warning colouration will be combined, as in certain species of amphibians which have brightly coloured bellies and capabilities of adjusting the colour of the rest of the body with that of the surroudings. When confronted with a potential threat, they show their belly, indicating that they are poisonous and they mean 'business'.

Another example of prey-to-predator communication, is referred to as a pursuit-deterrent signal. Pursuit-deterrent signals occur when prey indicates to a predator that pursuit would be unprofitable because the signaller is prepared to escape; "Here-do-I-go, catch-me-if-you-can" attitude. Such signals can be an advertisement of its ability to escape. Pursuit-deterrent signals provide a benefit to both the signaller and receiver; they might be able to prevent the receiver from investing in a costly pursuit that is unlikely to result in capture; they without wasting time and energy might be able to prevent the sender from clever fleeing. Pursuit-deterrent signals have been reported for a wide variety of fish, lizards, rabbits, rodents and birds.

Some predators communicate to prey in ways that change their behaviour and make them easier to catch, in effect deceiving them. A well-known example is the angler fish, which has a fleshy growth protruding from its forehead and dangling in front of its jaws; smaller fish try to take the lure, and in so doing are perfectly placed for the angler fish to eat them.

Communication vis-à-vis Flora

I had sprinkled some chilli seeds in an earthen flower pot kept in the balcony of my flat. Some of the seeds germinated and tiny little plants came up, and as they grew up they started flowering. The balcony is a closed one with sliding glass shutters. I had kept one of the shutters open, to allow a bit of sunlight and fresh air to come in. They had practically no direct contact with the mother earth, but for the gravitational force. I was worried as to how pollination would take place, as the pot was not in the open, which fact would have prevented the flowers from 'inviting' the pollinating agents. To my surprise, pollination took place. But, despite my keen watching, I could not see any pollinating agent arriving and doing the 'work'. I could get what I wanted—fresh green chillies from my 'mini garden'. Who called the pollinating agent to come there and do its 'job'? The invitation of the flowers to the pollinating agents to enjoy their hospitality is, again, a case of communication: with the favourable response from the pollinating agents a two-way communication is complete. None should wonder if there is some communication between flowers of a plant and the pollinating agents by means of some unknown media. The scent they send out, the colour they exhibit and the sweetness of nectar tasted earlier by themselves or the experience of taste relayed, recommended and communicated to them by their benefactor-friends could be the media. Whatever they may be, the receivers get the messages right, and they are motivated to perform the required 'duty' entrusted to them by Nature—pollination. It is the great Nature that has brought about this phenomenon. One would suspect if Nature has developed some sort of invisible website or resorted to some kind of clandestine communication! One would often get excited by thinking about the various games that Nature plays.

Plants too engage themselves in communicating. A 'touch-me-not' plant, for example, responds the moment anyone touches it, by folding all of its leaves spontaneously, to scare away its 'enemy'. We have known about how carnivorous plants behave. Communication is observed within the plant organism, i.e. between and among plant cells, also without between plants of the same or related species, and between plants and non-plant organisms, especially in the rootzone. Plant roots communicate in parallel with bacteria, with fungi and with insects in the soil. On a more basic level, there is cell signalling, cellular communication, and chemical communication between primitive organisms like bacteria, and within the plant and fungal kingdoms. All of these communication processes are sign-mediated interactions with a great variety of distinct co-ordinations. Fungi communicate to coordinate and organize their own growth and development. Additionally, fungi communicate with same and related species as well as with nonfungal organisms in a great variety of symbiotic interactions, especially with bacteria, plants and insects.

Social Justice and Welfare

24

All the countries are welfare states. Most of the governments in the world are run on democratic norms. Since the governments are 'by the people' and 'for the people', they concentrate on the welfare of people. They are keen to provide social justice as well. In order to achieve these twin-objectives, governments enact various social laws on various aspects of social requirements like health, education, and implement them in right earnestness. These are of paramount importance for the very existence of societies.

It all amounts to inter-relationships between the governments and their people, the people create the governments, provide them with authority as well as resources, and then rightly expect the former to perform adequately. The aspirations of the people are to be fulfilled. The governments have a duty towards this and the people have a right to realize the benefits. The performance of any government will be judged on the basis of success or failure in the implementation of the avowed policies. Governments and their various functionaries are accountable to the people in this. People have the power and they use it too to replace any non-functioning governments through democratic process of exercising their right of franchise.

'Social justice' refers to social, economic and political justice and equality of status and of opportunity. All these combined as conclave to define social justice. Although these phrases look simple, their contents are enormous with great ramifications. It is very difficult if not impossible, to understand the subject in its entirety. They are all genuine basic interdependent requirements that are individually and collectively relevant. Constitutions of all countries declare that these form the basic goals, objectives and aims that are required to be achieved. Social welfare can be guaranteed only when social justice is administered; both are synonymous in the ultimate analysis.

There are machineries created, governmental as well as non-governmental, that are meant to ensure that social justice is achieved. The former ones are formally created by law and they function like any other department of the government. They are impersonal and blatantly bureaucratic in their manner of functioning. There is hardly any 'human touch' discernible in their functioning. Most of such set-ups hardly manifest any sort of moral commitment. They 'achieve' social justice on paper. None can buy 'soft ware' items like sympathy, sincerity, mercifulness, magnanimity, loyalty, commitment to a cause and the like at a price. There is no way to instil or instal such qualities in anyone. An attendant hired on payment would not bring with him sincerity and such other qualities when he is to serve an ailing patient. He leaves his heart in 'safe vault' at home before he comes at the place of his duty. It is no blasphemy or calumny in case of governmental organizations.

Law of any country provides for the protection of the mentally as well as physically weak persons against harm or atrocities perpetrated on them by the physically and mentally strong persons. Law provides that no contracts can be entered into with them by other party for obvious reasons. Such contracts are declared null and void *ab initio*. This is to protect their interests. The governments have responsibility towards them as they belong to the weaker section of the society. They are feebleminded and as such they can not protect themselves.

Governments are concerned about the welfare of the old. They offer health schemes, travel concessions, old-age pension, rehabilitation and destitute homes and the like. Some governments enact social Laws making it compulsory for the offspring to provide adequate care and protection to their parents as a pre-condition for inheritance of the assets of their parents. If they fail in their duties, they could get punished under provisions of such Acts, besides their getting disqualified for inheritance.

Non-governmental organisations (NGOs) are self-sprouted and self-sprung. Their starting point is the genuine unostentatious sympathy on the part of some noble hearts for some of their brethren who are deprived of something that they deserve. Their commitment to the cause that they stand for is really sacramental and sublime. They offer dedicated, selfless and yeomen service. They establish 'home for the old', 'home for the destitutes', 'juvenile offenders', 'forsaken infants and minors', 'poor children and the like'. Thus they serve and help the old who are declared 'redundant, obsolete and hence no longer required' by their kith and kin, the destitute women and children, victims of social atrocities like rape and riots, severely mentally and physically handicapped and any others who require mercy, love and care. Some of the 'registered' establishments get grants from government, but the financial help thus obtained is insufficient. They get donations from benevolent individuals and corporate houses to supplement the government grants.

It is a fashion prevalent among the rich to take to charitable work in the society. They form Trusts and build hospitals for charity, and credit huge sums of money, mostly ill-gotten, in the trust-accounts. Donations are made with full fanfare in full public view with full press coverage for wide publicity. They themselves become managing trustees of such trusts. They mismanage the funds therein in clandestine manner. The money they donate to the trusts is exempted from tax-levies. In many cases, this becomes the way to hoodwink the government. Thus it is a safe way to divert their excess money. In the eyes of the public, they become good social workers. It is crass dishonesty and deceit and hence hypocrisy.

Of Humans and Other Animals 25

In the fauna, humans according to their own perception, at least, stand out as a special variety or phenomenon. They claim that they are more intelligent, imaginative and intuitive compared to other members of the fauna, whereas, as they concede, the latter is bestowed with more power of instinctivity. Thus they are compensated adequately by their Creator. Most of them are seen intuitive too at times. The humans are not apt to recognize and concede the presence of traits of intelligence and intuition in other animals. They consider themselves to be the most intelligent. The yardsticks and parameters of measurement of these traits are designed by humans themselves to measure and compare the IQ among themselves. In fact they are applicable only to themselves. It is totally unfair on their part to apply the same methods to measure IQ of other animals. They are bound to go wrong. Because of these 'extra' intelligence and high imagination, the humans have created 'hell' for themselves, and are thus moving towards extinction in the immediate future. The tip of the index finger of some erratic person is only a few centimetres away from the Control Switch Panel of Nuclear devices earmarked for total annihilation of this 'intelligent' mankind. There is enough number of such erratic and cynical people available amongst us to perform this sacred act of 'pressing' the red button on the panel, and bring about holocaust. Global warming is another case of self-infliction, causing great concern. In religious scriptures there is a mention that the end of the 'world' would be caused by devastating floods. Global warming makes it possible, and humans do everything to warm up the globe. Animals other than humans live happily and harmoniously following all the rules laid down by Nature, and it is the human beings who flout all these rules and seek self-destruction. Innocent animals too will have to face the brunt of all these thoughtless misdeeds of these 'intelligent', 'imaginative' and 'intuitive' human beings.

Let us compare certain characteristic traits of human beings and other animals with a view to understanding and ascertaining how 'superior' or 'inferior' each is in respect of the other:

Anger

Man gets angry on multifarious situations many of which may be self-arising out of his own built-in physical, physiological or psychological system. In some other cases, it may be due to the socio-psycho system into which he is integrated. This anger is the result of some accumulated irritation or frustration that he has experienced due to his having been really or virtually deprived of an object, person or an ideology which he likes to hold for himself as valuable belongings. The anger may be explicit or implicit. Its intensity may vary from covert simmering to overt belligerence. In any case the result could be disastrous. It is difficult to understand as is integrated. In any case the result could be disastrous. It is difficult to understand as well as forecast the complex behaviour of the human beings in this regard.

In the case of other animals, they also get angry. The causes are only physical or physiological, not any psychological or socio-psychological situations. They express their anger explicitly by mounting abrupt attack on the object of cause, and hence it is very easy for others to take cognizance.

Behaviour

Human beings at their infancy behave like animals do. Their behaviour is later modulated and conditioned by their elders so as to make them 'fit' as members of the elders' society. Thus their behaviour will be made to conform to the prevailing standards of societal system of behaviour.

In the case of other animals, their behaviour is, by and large, natural. Elders in their case too provide them with some training just enough to enable them to survive and lead an independent life. There is no perennial elaborate conditioning training system being followed by them, as in the case of human beings.

Communication

Communicative system is a developing field in the case of human beings. Communicative skills are very efficient in case of other animals.

Courage

Man is generally not a courageous animal. He becomes 'courageous' when he is badly cornered by an impending serious danger. This can be called 'desperado-psychosis'. Even those who venture adventure sports are not really courageous. They collect 'courage' bit-by-bit right through the various stages of practice, and accumulate them to make it a part of experience. For those who undertake such 'courageous' or 'adventurous' acts, it is sheer expression of experience, but for spectators, they form courageous pursuits. Fear of death or very serious injuries dissuade man from taking-up any activity which might involve potential danger to him. That is to say that man is basically a coward. Even in the face of an enemy, a soldier exhibits courageous demeanour because of the dictum, 'before you kill me, I have to eliminate you'. Yes, in some respects it is a courageous act. Illiterates or uneducated men can be seen to be more courageous than the educated. They can be more easily indoctrinated and conditioned to behave in a particular fashion than their educated counterparts. The level of courageous behaviour is inversely proportional to the level of education. It is the 'education', formal or informal that renders persons less courageous or cowardly.

The animals other than human beings are courageous. Even a weak animal puts up a brave fight against an attacking lion. It does not surrender without a proper fight, even when it is aware that it is a losing game. Man gets frightful at the very sight of such dangers and succumbs without a fight.

Creativity

Human beings are highly creative. This skill is quite often used to seek self-destruction. Other animals too are creative to some extent.

Crying

Human beings cry when they are in pain, physical or mental. They express grief by crying. Crying invites sympathy from fellow members of society. Tears shed by fellow beings are not 'always' crocodile tears.

Animals other than men generally do not cry. Some of them with higher intelligence level do cry when in pain or at the demise of a fellow being. Even if they do not virtually cry or shed tears, they demonstrate agony in their own way. It is, in fact, more pathetic to witness such a behaviour than a crying scene of human beings.

Curiosity

Humans are highly curious in many realms. Their so-called advancement in many fields is as a result of this. They misuse often this faculty to avail sinister sadistic pleasure. Other animals too are curious, but only to the extent in search of their food.

Cynicism

It is the domain of human beings. They are expert cynics. Cynics envy their fellow-beings for the latters' achievements. They condemn the whole of humanity. Cynics seek sadistic pleasure.

Other members of the fauna do not have this dangerous trait.

Derision

People laugh at other fellow-beings. Deriders too, like cynics seek sadistic pleasure. By resorting to derision, they hide the same trait or perpetrate an escapade. Other members of the fauna do not have this trait.

Discipline

If a society is to sustain and survive, its members should follow certain norms of orderliness in their behaviour. Some of the human beings, due to their being intelligent, imaginative and egoistic, turn delinquent and erratic, falling not in line with the laid down norms and standards. They are indisciplined. Society tries to correct them, and if they get corrected then they are accepted, otherwise rejected.

In case of other animals, the situation is quite different. If one elephant, for example, goes out of its herd and gets in touch with human beings, he is never admitted back into the herd. He would be socially boycotted. This is somewhat similar to the human social behaviour, especially of some human tribes or aborigines. A male monkey, again for example, keeping a harem of two or three dozens of females does not allow any male offspring to be a part of his 'house-hold' once the latter becomes an adult. He will be either killed, or allowed to escape and form his own family or harem.

Dramatics

Humans enact many a drama in their real life. No sphere is spared in this: Sorrow, happiness, sincerity, friendship, sympathy to others, etc. Other animals do not know this form of 'art'.

Egoism

This is the greatest malady being faced by humanity. No cure for this. Man minus egoism equals a naught.

There is no evidence to suggest that other animals are egoistic.

Exploitaion

Humans exploit their poor. They exploit Nature too. Other animals do not do this.

Frustration

Human beings get frustrated on deprivation of anything that they desire or crave for. They pursue efforts till they get satisfaction. Frustration is manifest in the form of irritation, resentfulness, anger, belligerence, crying, or going psychic. Some easily succumb to it, while some others can absorb a lot of it.

Other animals too get frustrated due to deprivation of objects. They too get restless and agitated, and try and retry to achieve them. They make unusual sounds and move about aimlessly.

Happiness

Man's happiness can be clearly understood from his facial expressions as well as his body language. He smiles or laughs, or sometimes even sheds tears when he is happy. Other animals manifest nothing of this sort, but some of them like lambs and dogs, though rarely, jump about and play. This behaviour is not seen when they are sad or having pain. This contrast in behaviour is the key to understand their disposition.

Hatred

Human beings hate objects, situations, ideas and ideologies, besides other human beings, for good or bad reasons. It is more psychological than physical or physiological. Their demeanour in hatred is full of complexities. Sometimes they choose to keep silent, and while doing so they accumulate and nurture it till it becomes strong enough for a 'showdown' at an opportune moment. Their imagination and cleverness offer them tremendous 'help' in this.

Other animals do have hatred, but it is more of a physical or physiological nature. They 'settle the score' on the spot. This demeanour is less dangerous.

Hypocrisy

Human beings are highly hypocritic. They speak what they do not mean and they mean what they speak not. Hypocrisy is stealthily pervading in most of what they do and speak.

Most of them believe and take for granted that it is an inevitable evil as an integral part of their societal life. It is quite a convincing excuse! Other animals are never hypocrites.

Imagination

Man is bestowed with imaginative prowess. He uses and misuses it at will. An amalgamation of imagination and intelligence forms-up creativity or destructivity, depending on the way he uses or misuses this amalgamation. Egoism comes into a major role in the employment of imagination.

Other animals, it seems, do not possess this imaginative power.

Immunity

The present-day human beings, among the entire fauna, are, perhaps, the only ones who have hardly any immunity towards diseases. They become easy preys in front of even micro-organisms that cause diseases. Their 'intelligence' has been pressed and stretched into service to find remedies for these maladies, so far with little success. Probably due to 'wrong' adaptive systems followed by men in the early stages of life, millennia ago, they are unable to protect themselves from the vagaries of Nature. To protect themselves from cold weather, for example, they borrow sheep's fur and skin, and in return they offer or promise to offer their intelligence services. If they expose themselves to Summer-heat, Winter-coldness or rains, they fall ill due to lack of protection or immunity. They flout all the Laws of Nature. They destroy the purity of Nature and hence they are left to atone for their mischievous behaviour.

Other animals are better equipped with immunity-systems. They, in fact, are naturalists, who live and move about in Nature. They are true representatives of Nature. They love Nature and obey all Her Laws.

Instinct

Human beings immediately after having been born rely on instincts for their very survival, in the absence of a developed brain. As the brain develops gradually, the dependence on instincts also reduces accordingly, but its role is not totally eliminated in their lives. Other animals do primarily depend on instincts for their survival. The role of intelligence has been made secondary for them. Well, it is reckoned that this asset of instincts can effectively replace that of intelligence, in this case, considering the lifestyle of these animals. As a matter of fact, to lead a natural life there is hardly any need for intelligence.

Intelligence

Man is bestowed with intelligence in abundance. He is very conscious about it, and he is apt to look down upon others who, he thinks, has less of it. He has made use of it to make his life comfortable. He has found its destructive use as well. Imagination clubbed with intelligence forms up creativity. He may use or misuse. Other animals too have intelligence, but it may be of a different kind. Man should not try to define their intelligence in terms of his own. He can go wrong. Animals exhibit their 'intelligence' in quite a different way. When he does not understand their way, he declares that animals do not have intelligence. Man must leave them in their way without wasting time and efforts in comparing and contrasting the quantum of intelligence at his possession *vis-à-vis* that available with the other animals.

Intuition

Man has intuitive power. This power is the outcome as a by-product of continued joint application of intelligence and imagination. Familiarity and experience are two essential ingredients bringing about intuition. It is not *per se* a quality that is originally bestowed upon man; it is a faculty that is subsequently acquired. A small child, for example, may not experience this power, he may have instinctive power only, and as he grows-up, he acquires this faculty of intuition. This 'item' appears in 'reserved category' for humans. Other animals seldom possess intuitive power, even though a few with the 'human's kind of intelligence' have intuitive power. They have replaced intuition with instinct, a fine arrangement, so to say. They, in fact, do not require the human's kind of intelligence for their happy and harmonious existence. Their instinctivity can stand for adequate compensation.

Jealousy

Jealousy is one of man's biggest enemies. Selfishness, greed, cynicism, unhealthy competitive spirit and a bit of sadism form the root cause of jealousy. It emanates from inter-personal interactions between and among members of a society. Jealousy can be avoided by sedulous unbiased self-analysis. Other animals are lucky that they do not have this problem.

Laugh

Man laughs when he is encountered with wit and humour, through words or situations. He laughs at others, and very rarely at himself. Laughter is good medicine. It is an expression of genuine internal happiness, and it transmits cheer and goodwill in contagious manner. Other animals do not laugh.

Love

All members of the fauna experience and share love. From love, affection is generated. Love-sharing is part of a healthy social living. Different beings express love in different ways. Love should be unselfish and absolute, and love should be only for love's sake. Man's ideas about love are sublime, but what he practises is generally not in conformity with his sublime idealistic thoughts. In some cases, love is found to be negotiable and conditional.

In the case of other animals, they practise love undilutedly and unconditionally. There are no *quid pro quo* arrangements.

Loyalty

Most humans are loyal in their friendship to other humans, for some others it is negotiable and conditional. They are largely found to be faithful to their religious faiths. Their behaviour often does not conform to expectations.

Animals domesticated are very loyal to their 'masters'. They are dependable and their behaviour conforms to the expected standards of loyalty.

Megalomania

Human beings are megalomaniacs. Other animals do not have this trait.

Revenge

Man likes to avenge any wrong done to him. It is more of a mental activity. Other animals too resort to taking revenge. It is more of a physical activity.

Sadism

Most men are sadists. They take pleasure in troubling others. Sarcasm, cynicism, derision are all expressions of this sadistic mentality.

Sadistic behaviour is totally absent in the case of other animals.

Selfishness

Men are quite selfish. They even think that the whole world is 'created' for their enjoyment, and they don't allow other animals to have their due share. They are conscious of the fact that selfishness is an undesirable quality and hence each one of them claims that he is unselfish. This is a natural tendency to be selfish. Infants do not hide their selfishness.

Other animals too are selfish but in very limited way only.

Sexual Behaviour

Man's sexual behaviour is covert. Mating takes place throughout the year. Males try to ignore unwilling responses to their sexual advances from females and force their way in order to satisfying their voluptuous urges. In a civilized society this behaviour on the part of the males is termed, as 'rape'. This sort of a behaviour is an aberration.

Sexual behaviour of other animals is overt. Mating is seasonal only. In their world, there is no such incident as rape. A bitch, for example, expresses its unwillingness to copulate by different gestures like using its tail to cover the 'area' or just lying down flat on its chest. The male understands and co-operates. Incidents of rape do not occur among other animals because of theirs is a permissive society. Unlike in case of humans, they do not practise paedophilia or other unnatural acts.

Sincerity

Man is sincere, but he is seen to be quite hypocritical, at times. Other animals are sincere and unhypocritical in their behaviour.

Shyness

Man is basically a shy animal. His shyness on some occasions may not be genuine, but hypocritical. Shyness may be mental or physical. Most of the other animals are not shy.

Smile

Man is capable of smiling when he is happy. Other animals do not know how to smile.

Society

Man is a social animal. Society provides him with security. He is to follow the norms laid down by the society. His disciplined behaviour ensures the very existence of the society. Society punishes him for any misdemeanour. Most of the other animals too have a social living.

Strength

Man is basically physically weak and delicate. He is unable to protect himself physically but by using his intelligence he is able to exist and survive.

Other animals are physically strong, and they rely on their physical strength for their survival. Animals like elephants do not even know that they are very strong and that is how a mahout of meagre strength and size is able to discipline even a huge elephant.

Sycophancy

Humans tend to be sycophants. Other animals do not practise this.

Sympathy

Human beings express sympathy for those among them who are in discomfort or pain. In most situations the sympathy shown is genuine. Other animals too show sympathy to their fellow-beings.

Terrorism

Terrorism is resorted to by humans among themselves. Other animals use this technique only to the extent to intimidate their preys while hunting. It is not purposive.

The above accounts reflect some of the characteristic traits, as I could conceive, of all major living beings. I have tried to compare and contrast these, in human beings *vis-à-vis* the other members of the fauna. I have been able to highlight the fact that other animals too are having certain superior qualities. The difference comes about because man has 'more' intelligence and imagination, as they are apt to boast of. But these special traits have not helped them in leading a happy and harmonious life, whereas other animals, in the absence of these, are a happy lot. Some of the traits like egoism, hypocrisy, sarcasm, cynicism, derision, jealousy, social indiscipline and prejudice are very serious adverse elements discernible in human beings only which make them inferior to other animals. The genesis of these lies in the misuse of their special traits of intelligence and imagination. These form burdensome curse, so to say. The human beings are unhappy and are unable to lead a harmonious life. Other animals love Nature, and follow Her Laws. Human beings do not follow Laws of Nature. They pay heavily for this callous and indignant attitude towards Nature. It is a pity that others on this Earth too have to share the brunt.

Alcoholism—An Avoidable Malady

26

It is seldom that anyone consumes alcoholic drinks alone. He needs company if he has to enjoy them, because enjoyment multiplies in geometric proportions when he is in the company of like-minded individuals. Any enjoyment in viewing alone of any spectacle, for example, beautiful Nature or celestial phenomena/occurrences like shooting of stars, a solar eclipse or meteoric fly-past or sports activities like a football match gets enhanced manifold when it is done in the company of others, especially of like-minded persons or friends. Drinking alcoholic concoctions, similarly, in the company of friends brings-forth greater enjoyment than doing it alone. Enjoyment enjoys enjoyment. Hence drinking alcohol is one of the ways of incidence of human bionomic activity. In the case of alcoholism, onlookers enjoy more than perhaps the alcoholics themselves. Unfortunate!

Alcohol is "essence, a distillate, a liquid generated by the fermentation of sugar or other saccharine matter, and forming the intoxicating element of fermented liquors." An alcoholist is one who favours the use of alcohol or who drinks in excess. Alcoholism is alcoholic poisoning.

Alcoholism is as ancient as human civilization. Millennia ago human beings like other members of the fauna used to be living in forests. They lived on fruits and roots available in the forests. Some of the fruits were sweet and fresh while some others were sour. Due to scarcity of these, at some point of time, they were forced to eat over-ripe or partially rotten ones. The sweet juice in those fruits turned sour due to fermentation. They thus had the opportunity to taste some that made them feel tipsy. Some of them got fainted. They thought that some evil spirits were casting their vile will over them. Initially they had got confused and did not know what to do. They had declared that such fruits as dangerous hence forbidden. Many others too had such experiences. They became curious and had a lot of discussions among themselves on the subject. They had again tasted, this time deliberately, for experimentation, and found such fruits and the juice they tasted were not harmful. On the other hand, they had started enjoying their taste. They understood that the intoxication that they had experienced was only of a temporary nature, right contrary to what they had suspected. This was great revelation to them. Having found that intoxication could provide them with lots of relief from physical fatigue experienced while hunting and performing various types of hard physical work during the day, they started preparing such drinks and drinking in the company of their friends. Even their women also started enjoying the drinks in the company of their men.

Drinking alcoholic drinks in social groups is what we see generally. It only shows that the manner in which the human beings behave has not undergone any change over many a millennium. They had always believed in collective social living because of the great physical and psychological advantages that is used to be attached with, like security, sharing of sorrows and happiness, alleviating both physical and mental tensions, facing common enemies and hunting. One can get proof of existence of such behaviour in their earlier period of life, when he observes the living styles of some of the aborigines and tribal people still left behind in the forests and jungles by the modern man. They are ‘unpolluted’, ‘untouched’ and ‘chaste’ with regard to their social fabric and culture. They are exceptions in the present day context, but ‘exceptions do always prove the law’. They help us to go back to many millennia and understand as to how they all had lived then. They form the original specimen for our research work. Most of these aborigines and tribal people have special liking for alcoholic beverages and concoctions. They drink and make merry on their various social occasions. They have developed their own music which we call now tribal and folk music. They are fond of dancing with musical accompaniment of high sounding rhythmic drum beats. They were peaceful, frank, unhypocritical, simple, innocent, fun, music- and peace-loving and caring. In fact all the epithets with good meaning could be ascribed to them. The modern man envies them and shows hypocritical love for such music and culture, and they yearn (or pretending to be so) to be like their worthy ancestors.

To begin with people began to drink alcohol for socializing. They consumed only limited quantities in the social congregations just only for company's sake. Alcohol like many drugs gradually created 'drug effects' on these people without their knowledge and consciousness. Some of them got addicted to it gradually. Then it became alcoholism. It is observed that people who are emotional and sentimental are more prone to get addicted to it. People who are frustrated in their personal lives too become preys to such addictions. They think that drinking can help them in providing relief. It is proved that this feeling is nothing but illusion, and further, an expression of escapism and so also an excuse for drinking. In fact, the presence of alcohol in the body-system makes one to the worse; the extra courage that one collects under its drug-effects is purely notional and his emotional equilibrium gets disturbed, to the worse rendering the person erratic. People who are 'matter-of-fact' and sagacious desist from falling preys to alcoholism. They use their head more than their hearts. Habitual drunkards are too aware and conscious that drinking is no solution to solving their personal physical or psychological problems they face. An alcoholic takes pledges not to drink anymore, just only to break these pledges on the very next day or next occasion. Their subconscious minds always anticipate advent of such occasions; occasions always befall on them. Such people continue to do this game of 'make-and-break' of pledges throughout their lives. Some of them make record number of times and get their names appear in record books. They are, probably, helpless or pretending to be so. Whatever may be the case, they become experts in this game.

It is a fashion among youngsters belonging to the so-called aristocratic and affluent social strata to 'enjoy' having a 'peg' or two for company's sake. If anyone in the group resists, he will be declared unfit and unworthy to be in their group; he will be ridiculed and derided. He gets influenced and succumbs to such pressure tactics and obliges his good friends. He has fallen! This is the beginning of an impending disaster.

Alcoholism is a universal disease. It exists in all countries of the world, in all races, in all the climates. In spite of researches, present and past, nothing explains vividly as to why certain people do become victims of alcoholism while some others never do. It is a disease and nobody knows the causes of it. Patients give an account of problems they 'face' in their lives such as worries, loneliness, unemployment, and problems in married life which pushed them to alcoholism. These 'problems' are sheer alibis. It is true that everybody, during his life, goes through bad times, but all people do not turn alcoholics. Even though many 'enjoy' a drink or two, all of them do not become patients; they regulate their drinking. Since the origin of the disease is unknown, there is no treatment as well, except their accepting the fact that the 'problems' they cite are artificially created and felt and they can be 'solved' by self-analysis and self-possession or by sincere counselling by sagacious men. The alcohol-dependence itself is not curable easily except by total and final abstinence employing one's will power.

Alcohol is not an essential food item for sustenance of life; normally it is superfluous, but some people perçeive it to be otherwise. It cannot remedy the hunger nor quench the thirst. Alcohol is a food that is drunk. Unlike other liquid foods, it fails to give signal of satiety despite the intake of a large quantity; in fact, the need for intake goes stronger; the built-in 'satiation meter' malfunctions. Here lies the real danger of the disease since it goes in contrary direction of biological laws, therefore, of life. Alcohol functions in the wrong way. If one does not eat food, the need for food or the hunger increases and when they take-in food, that need will be adequately satisfied, whereas in the case of alcohol, the need for more arises even after sufficient quantity of it is present in the body system. If there is no alcohol in the body, there will hardly be any demand for it. Here the situation goes against the theory of 'supply and demand' and the concept of 'marginal utility'. Normally an appetizer is consumed to enhance appetite for another food item, but in this case, this appetizer increases the demand for more of the appetizer itself. Alcohol attacks adversely the performance of liver. Alcohol too contains carbohydrartes. Apart from this, a tendency to consume food more than the requirements of the body also develops. Undigested proteins too will be converted into fat. All these pose too much of a ponderable task for the liver to undertake. The result is obesity.

It is interesting to watch an inebriated person walking and conducting himself in public. He would be a comic in human form. He struggles hard unsuccessfully to walk erect and straight, making maximum efforts to pretend that he is not drunk. He talks to himself modulating and manipulating his voice at will. He asks questions to himself and answers them incoherently with irregular pauses. If anyone asks him if he is drunk, he retorts, "No, not me. You must be drunk." He is in another world, floating like suspended particles, instead of walking. Onlookers will like to donate two additional legs for him, seeing that the two he is having are over-worked and that they are inadequate in their efforts to take him to places. If none donates additional legs, he becomes self-reliant by 'earthing' his two hands to alleviate woes of his legs. His mind will be working on a single point agenda. He might have had many thoughts, both good and bad, just before his 'attack' on the first 'peg', but all of them would have vanished into thin air except, probably, one, the one that he is holding on while walking back to his resting place which may not be his own home. He is not choosy in selecting his bed; may be on the road-side near drainage gutter. He does not select them deliberately and consciously, but the alcohol in him does that job for him. He keeps pondering on the one agenda he has unknowingly selected. He forgets even that too for a while in between, but by applying his full mental might he brings that point back into his memory domain. After all, man is a thinking animal, and he thinks. It is on this topic that he feverishly discusses with himself. His is an audible soliloquy. He murmurs frequently, "I will kill you; I will kill you." He may have somebody in mind. The poor fellow would not be remembering that name after a good sleep. An inquisitive passer-by stranger on the road, with a good intention to give testimony in the court of law against him, like any responsible citizen, if he murders someone, asked him as to whom he would kill. "You, You. Now you clear off from my way" would be his reply. While replying he has unsuccessfully been struggling hard to point his shivering disobedient right index finger at that stranger to specify the individual. If what he was uttering were true, the stranger understood, he would not get a chance to give testimony in the court of law in case he himself would be the actual victim. None can testimony after one is dead! An inebriated person would be incapable of acting in the manner he would like to act. For the successful culmination of any act needs co-ordination among all of his physical and psychological assets, his limbs and the whole body, besides his senses and the mind itself. An inebriated person does not have any faculty of co-ordination. A knife he would be wielding to kill someone would kill himself. A hunter becomes the hunted.

An inebriated person never likes to be advised. If he is told not to drive his vehicle in that condition, he refuses, "I am not drunk; I can drive; do not interfere" would be his reply. He takes out the key of the car and tries unsuccessfully to insert it into the ignition hole which is 'missing'. It might have been a wrong hole. When he locates the insertion point, he finds that it is the wrong key. How can anyone start the car with his house key? "Oh, this is not the car key, it must be the one", he murmurs and takes out the other key-bunch. He manages to start the car. He presses the accelerator pedal as though he is taking revenge on an enemy and drives it very fast, probably to prove to himself, at the least, that he is not drunk. This behaviour is also addressed to onlookers. Now onwards alcohol takes over driving, unmindful of the width, twists and curves of the road and the traffic signals *en route*. Alcohol does not have eyes. When he regains his consciousness, most probably in a hospital, he realizes that a few of his limbs are no more capable of functioning in the usual old manner. They are in 'plasters'. He wonders as to how all this happened. The friend who had advised him not to drive is seen sitting near him in the hospital room. He feels ashamed of facing him.

All said and done, it is popularly believed that alcoholics are simple-hearted. The greatest quality discerned in them is their compromising nature which they extend to whatever they do in their lives, even when they are not drunk. It becomes a second nature. They do not exhibit 'stiff-neck' attitude and obstinacy. Most of them, who consume alcohol in limited quantity, that too occasionally, are sober and soft in their attitudes and behaviour. Some of them engaged in work that requires precion and concentration like medical surgery, painting, works of art and artistry, creative writing and poetry accost the needed ignition and stimulation when they keep a 'glass' filled with his favourite drink near them. There are many cases where eminent and expert surgeons perform commendably very complicated surgeries after having their throats a bit 'wet'. Some of the very highly imaginative persons genuinely make their minds fly in high altitudes, the abode of lofty ideas, with the aid of a 'couple'. Some of the eminent singers had produced their best recitals after their having emptied a few glasses. Also, often it is fashionable for these intellectuals to take to alcoholic drinks for the sake of nothing. It might also not be a mere expression of their psychological need or an excuse for drinking. Many of them 'get drunk and sunk' in the work they do, even without drinking alcohol, manifesting commitment and devotion in whatever they do. Commitment and devotion too cause intoxication, of course, of a different kind.

Alcoholics are shy, weak-minded and cowardly. It seems that alcohol provides them that extra mental energy needed to surmount these weaknesses. They speak out what they otherwise would have hesitated to say, they behave as they would otherwise have never done. They cast off their shyness and reservations. They let out secrets; air their real or virtual grievances; behave in uninhibited manner; unwind and release the undesirable impregnated potential energy of their minds, thus lightening them. They manifest tendency to exaggerate or distort facts that they want to express. They are also apt to make a mountain out of a mole and *vice versa*. Alcoholics illogically and inappropriately accord stress to irrelevant points. In retrospect they repent for some of their utterances, actions and behaviour. Alcohol enlarges four-dimensionally one's sorrow, anger and happiness. One gram of each these feelings swells to one kilogram. A sad person keeps weeping; an angry one becomes very angry and aggressive; a happy one keeps on laughing, while some others opt not to utter any word. They become rock-solid.

Alcohol is supplied to members of armed forces of almost all countries. The troops operate in hostile terrains in high altitudes all along in order to guard the frontiers of their motherland. Their families and kith and kin would be living separated from them hundreds or thousands of kilometres away from them, that too for months together. There is every reason for these soldiers to get frustrated, despite their having been conditioned to live like that. They have only the sky up, barren snow-clad mountains all around, and enemies to face in front. Moreover, they have to fight inclement weather conditions. They have hardly any source of entertainment or sports. From all these adversaries they have no escape. They engage themselves in communion with Nature, in lieu of their families. A few of them become poets, painters and writers. It is this alcohol that provides them with some sort of physical and psychological warmth thus serving to alleviating their miseries *vis-à-vis* the bitterness of cold. In extreme cold conditions, even animals like horses, camels and mules employed by the army are provided with alcohol. 'Prohibition' rules are relaxed and made inapplicable to these troupes by fact-facing governments.

Policy on prohibition of alcohol consumption adopted by government draws a fair amount of criticism. Government will also be criticized for not enacting laws on prohibition. The approach of the people towards their governments is "If you did, why did you do? And if you did not do, why did you not do?" There are arguments in favour and against. It is argued by antagonists of prohibition that consumption of anything is alright when viewed in the context of individual choice and it is to be conceived and perceived as an expression of individual freedom. Such people strongly believe that individuals should be allowed to decide as to what to eat or drink, and that government must not interfere with this fundamental right of citizens. It is all fine in a democracy. Can this argument be extended to consumption of poison in suicide cases? An attempt to commit suicide is punishable in the eyes of law. The state as well as the society has responsibility towards its members, firstly, in the angle of health of all members and, secondly, welfare of community. Here we have to draw a line in between. The debate can continue. Certain governments have, however, taken an antagonist approach to these arguments; they go about implementing prohibition from the standpoint of welfare and health of their people. In a country like India where *per capita* income of people is very low *vis-à-vis* the global context, such a law would enable the lot especially from the low-income groups to earmark more or most or all of their meagre earnings for the bread and other essentials for the subsistence and survival of their families, rather than spending on non-essential items like alcohol. Most of the antagonists of prohibition belong to the rich and affluent class. They can be allowed to maintain their 'antagonism' to prohibition. Governments can earn large amounts of revenue from manufacturing and selling of alcoholic drinks, in terms of various taxes and the revenue thus accrued can fruitfully be utilized for the general welfare of the masses.

There can be laws and laws, but their implementation is more important than their enactment. It is very difficult to implement a law like the one on prohibition. "Forbidden fruit always tastes sweeter." When someone tells another not to look in a particular direction, the immediate tendency for the latter is to look in that prohibited direction only. In fact his curiosity increases; curiosity causes uneasiness which becomes his strong motivation. This is human tendency. Those who want to consume alcoholic drinks will always find loopholes in the system of implementation of this law, and avail advantages. It fosters corruption at all levels. Alongside the law, there is a need for creating awareness among the citizens of the ill-effects of alcohol consumption. This can be done by social philanthropic organizations. Their efforts can not replace any legislation, but their contribution in this direction will complement the spirit of the provisions of the law.

'Sincere' governmental authorities cleverly but infructuously put-up messages for the public, "Alcohol Consumption is injurious to health" on bill boards, posters and signs of advertisements, all over the places. Such labels printed in red ink are glued on the bottles containing alcohol. The contents of these bottles feel uncomfortable. It is deemed to be 'statutory warning'. And for whose benefits anyway? Governments are to satisfy majority of electorate; the manufactures of alcohol are to satisfy their controlling governments. Governments are happy because of large chunk of revenue they get; the manufacturers are happy because they can expect to thrive well in their business. Alcohol manufacturers meticulously print the 'stuff' on all boxes, cases and cartons or wherever they could find some space for it. They over do it. "Government wants us to write like that and we are doing the same meticulously mainly because we do not want any provisions of law should attract us and get ourselves 'booked hooked and cooked.'" They do it, because they are told to do so, not that they want to do. Drinkers as well as non-drinkers enjoy reading this red-lettered warning; drinkers getting the 'kick' out of the happiness they extract from flouting the spirit of such messages and the non-drinkers aggrandizing their share of happiness in the fact that they have not compromised with anything causing 'injury to their health'. "Thank God, we are healthy", the non-drinkers say with a sigh of relief. There are reasons to believe that some non-drinkers envy the drinkers, when the former see the latter enjoying themselves with intoxication. They even openly say so, probably a case of expressing derision or subtle contempt towards the drinker. Or is it 'sour-grapism'? It is an accepted fact that a drinker can not stop drinking and a non-drinker can not start drinking.

Alcoholism among men, young or old, brings about malfunctioning of the brain. It is the nervous system that will be affected severely. Alcohol in excessive quantity consumed regularly over a period of time weakens the nerves communicating information to the brain. The two-way channel will become inefficient or ineffective, resulting in incapacitation of comprehension of any new information on the one hand, and inability in retrieving the information already stored in the memory, on the other hand. This is what we call neurasthenia which culminates in amnesia. The social behaviour of these alcoholics is pathetic and erratic. They become highly emotional disproportionate to the perceived causes or stimuli. In many cases they become insensitive and incognitive. They lose their cool and become irritative. The timid become 'bold and courageous', and cast off their inhibitions. Secrets flow out of their minds and hearts helplessly. Their latent criminal instincts find expression and commit crimes that they would never have perpetrated but for adverse effects of alcohol. Often when they come out the effect of intoxication, they repent for such acts of commission.

There exists a wrong notion that consumption of alcohol enhances sexual urge. The truth, in fact, is the opposite. More often than not, males become inert and their sexual behaviour will be rendered wanting. The co-ordination between mind and body will cease. The mind says, "Yes, you can", and the body says, "No, I can't". They will gradually develop impotency and psychological disorders in this respect. Alcoholism among young women can be linked to delayed childbearing and host of problems of dysfunctions like risky sexual behaviour, a greater risk of delayed reproduction, menstrual and sexual disorders, and pregnancy complications that include spontaneous abortion or miscarriage. These complications may become more pronounced with time. Higher rates of reproductive dysfunction in adult women may reflect the cumulative effects of longer exposure to alcohol for older women than for female adolescents.

Smoking too is as old as human civilization. It might also have been an accident similar to the way our ancestors got introduced to drinking. It might have been accidental that some of the men while resting after their hunting pursuits of the day might have been forced to inhale smoke coming out of nearby forest fire. In the forest all kinds of plants were available, some of them being good and beneficial, while some others bad and harmful. They were experts in identifying and linking the various types of smell contained in the smoke they were forced to inhale with type of plants or their leaves which contributed to each type of constituent element in the smell. Inhalation of some type of smoke might have given them a smoothening effect and intoxication. Slowly they started enjoying such smells. Their curiosity encouraged them to be creative. They made proto-type 'cigars' and started smoking them. The initial accidentality was thus gradually got converted into purposiveness. The drinking and smoking have thus become part of their habits though both of them were introduced to them accidentally. It is interesting to note that human beings have great affinity and proneness for things that are bad, evil and harmful. They prefer listening to obnoxious, acrimonious and negative assertions made by devilish people to positive sacramental statements made by wise men. They are highly prone to evil-doings. Some good people get fed up of being good and they experiment on bad things, in search of a 'change'.

Governmental approach to 'smoking' tobacco by the public is identical with that of 'drinking' of alcoholic drinks by them. In this case, none voices his protests to statutory labels, "Cigarette smoking is injurious to health" appearing on cigarette packets and cartons. These warnings do not have any punitive content; they form mere harmless literature. Smokers do not notice such statutory warnings because they do not want to. Can any government stop manufacturing of cigarettes? Not abruptly, gradually it may be possible. Similarly, can any government prohibit manufacturing alcohol? It is not probable in the near future. Till then, let us be happy with these labels of statutory warnings only. A literary reading material, indeed!

If we undertake a sedulous scrutiny of the genesis of various habits, interests, inclinations and general behaviour of the 'modern' man, we would be convinced that there are only infinitesimal modifications taken place; all these traits can easily be traced back to those of our ancestors. We, the modern variety, have not changed much; we are intrinsically the same, notwithstanding our replacing their clothing items and style like tree-barks, leaves and animal hides with our present-day trousers and jeans made out of cotton and synthetic materials. The 'see-through' variety of our present-day clothing is nothing 'new'. It seems that our present-day nudity-syndrome is a true copy of what our ancestors had practised; the only discernible difference is that they never had considered 'nudity' as a 'dirty' word and had practised innocently, unlike what we the modern type do. Similarly, we have changed or modified the proto-type hand tools made out of rock pieces to metallic ones or replaced arrows used for hunting with huge arrow-shaped hollow devices filled with explosives, we call them missiles. There can be hundreds of examples like these. When we consider these changes, modifications or revolutionisations as mere extensions of those old things, we would realize that we as humans have not changed from the prehistoric state. There are hardly any changes in our psychological propensities and philosophy of life; if perceived otherwise, they are purely notional and virtual. The characteristics of genes too are not changed. All apparent changes are extrinsic and not intrinsic. We have nothing to boast of as our achievements.

"Consumption of alcohol is injurious to health" and "Cigarette smoking is injurious to health".

Ragging as an Expression of Bionomics

27

Ragging literally means "to tease", and was originally supposed to be a set of activities undertaken by the seniors to break the ice with the juniors. *Ragging* is a form of abuse on newcomers to professional as well as general educational and training institutions in many countries.

Ragging is an important ingredient of the culture of any organization. It is a form of performing art, and the senior members in the organization are the performers. It is similar to a puppet show where juniors are cast as puppets. It is the duty of those who have served a particular organization for a fairly long period of time, to maintain high level of performance, and so also perpetuation of the already existing cultural ethos. It is this cultural element that enables the organization to move forward. In it are included uniformity in the pattern of behaviour of all its members, orientation in singleness of objectives and the like. Ragging is one of the means through which the organization achieves all such objectives. It is like pruning and cutting of hedges to make it even and beautiful.

Ragging is a universal feature. It is prevalent in universities, institutions of higher education, professional institutions like management, medical, engineering colleges, military academies, police training establishments and even in schools. Though it has both a beautiful and an ugly face, it is usually ignominious for the ugly face. Individuals come to the organizations or institutions from different social strata, some coming from urban, some others from rural settings. They belong to different religions and castes, different economic and social backgrounds with different philosophies and habits. They all are to be brought to behave in one particular pattern. After the training programme, all of them would be rendered as 'finished products', and they behave in one particular standard and pattern only. Their responses to stimuli, their actions and reactions, and their propensities will all be rendered co-planar. That is necessary to keep all of them together as a unified entity. It is this ragging that can do the job. Even though initially all dislike and detest ragging, but later on in retrospect, however, they are bound to concede that it is a necessary evil. This is the beautiful face of ragging. It is worthy.

Ragging, however, if not perceived in the correct perspective by the operators, will lead to great losses. It is a very interesting game, especially for those who have latent propensities to take to sadism. So when they are in this business they often lose their heads and go almost eccentric. The heads and those others in the administrative set-ups of the organization seem to believe in the doctrine, 'hear no evil, see no evil, and speak no evil', and choose to remain unaffected and nonchalant. This is tantamount to permission. The 'raggers' start adopting a Don Quixotic type of heroism and bear a tendency to over-do the act. They perceive the targets, the helpless juniors, as toys to play with. 'As flies to wanton boys, are these hapless juniors to the seniors; for, they tear them for their sport.' Many a time, this 'sport' has created devastation for many. Some of the 'victims' are made to suffer from all sorts of physical inflictions; some of them develop even psychological disorders, even though causing harm, as such, might not have been an item in the pre-meditated agenda of ragging. This cannot in anyway be an excuse or justification for the perpetration of crimes. When the agony becomes frustrating and unbearable, rampant ragging results in suicides. Because of this, some responsible governments have taken positive steps of banning ragging by suitable legislations. Law considers ragging as any other criminal offence. Thus ragging is banned *de jure,* but may not be *de facto*. All provisions in the Indian Penal Code such as 'causing hurt or serious hurt', 'abetment to suicide', 'culpable homicide not amounting to murder' *et cetera* will be attracted, and made applicable in case of ragging. This is the ugly face of ragging. It is unworthy.

Let me make you share the experience of an officer, Ramesh, a friend of mine, who served in the Indian Air Force during sixties to eighties of the last century. This account is to be considered as ancient, and as such it will have only historic value. Some of his surviving contemporaries might be able to relate this account to their own personal experiences, and derive some sort of nostalgic pleasure. I would like, on his behalf, to make them rewind their memory of that period and rejuvenate and elevate their spirits, and if anyone of them wishes to join him in his delight, he would wholeheartedly be welcomed. He has preserved their photographs in his heart alongside sweet memories. If anyone comes forward, then he will be captured and placed in his heart in order to replace his photograph. Any emotional person would prefer his physical presence in such group photographs.

The story as told by Ramesh runs thus. The Air Force Academy where he had undergone induction training was situated in the southern part of India. At the local railhead at the academy, an Air Force coach would wait for the arrival and reception of the new 'in-take' of 'Flight Cadets' (in the Indian Army, they are known as 'Gentlemen Cadets') for indoctrination and induction into the training programme. Many of them would reach and alight from the same train, and only after boarding the coach, would they realize that all of them came for the same training programme. All of them would be driven to the academy like goats taken to a slaughter house! Ramesh too was one of them. No sooner had the coach arrived at the academy than a group of people clad in some uniform with Rank badges of Corporal and Sergeant, moving briskly, surrounded them as though they closed-in to provide their services in off-loading their luggage. They felt very happy to see that they were being cared for very well.

There was one Master Warrant Officer (MWO) also, as one among the new arrivals. Some serving Airmen were too given chance to become commissioned officers, if they pass the requisite written examinations, and clear successfully through other selection procedures and processes. It is similar to the system being followed in the police organizations. Some among the state-level police officers are elevated to the elite Indian Police Service (IPS) on merit considerations. He was clad in lounge suit, and he was standing there three metres away from the coach, looking as though he was supervising the off-loading work. He had probably thought that he had already become a commissioned officer. One sergeant approached him and enquired, "Sir, what will you have, Coffee, or tea?" With a great pose, he expressed his preference, "Coffee". A cup of coffee was brought in and offered to him. He was impressed with the efficiency. No sooner had he had the first sip of the coffee than he heard the same sergeant shouting at him, at very close range, at the top of his voice, "Idiot, you stupid fool, what you think of yourself? An officer?." And there were a few filthy abuses too hurled at him. Ramesh hesitated to re-utter those high-potency abusive expressions. The strong abuses made the fellow to don a lost look; and the entire coffee drenched his lounge suit, the coffee cup and saucer falling on the ground. He as well as the onlookers like Ramesh could not understand that it was part of 'ragging', clandestinely sponsored by the directing staff. Their abetment to such unholy deeds, he had realized later, would ultimately help those directing staff in their efforts to inculcating sense of discipline in the new entrants. The iron rods are required to be placed in furnace to get them hot or melted as a prerequisite to make them into the required shapes by hammering.

The 'sergeant' was a senior Flight Cadet. And till the end of the next three months, none of these new entrants could set their compasses in the proper direction. The conspicuous MWO and some others like him were the selected targets of the senior's teasing for the rest of the period of their juniority. As all the cadets had strictly followed the joining instructions they had received, they had packed the boxes with many items which included a few blankets, mosquito net, sports shoes and gear, tennis and badminton rackets, his 'lucky' cricket bat, two or three pairs of civilian shoes, a few dress items and some special pickles and 'eats' that their beloved and proud parents had sent with them. All these had, therefore, rendered the boxes very heavy. The seniors then asked those bewildered lot to carry their luggage on their head and proceed to their respective rooms. Those who hesitated, had to face the ire of seniors, who mercilessly asked them to carry the huge and heavy boxes on their heads and jump like frogs till they reached their rooms. Punishments for any sort of 'disobedience' would be decided and executed on the spot, according to the whims and fancies of particular senior cadet who used to be 'in charge' of that particular unfortunate junior. There would be many seniors who wantonly rushed-out to their fancied junior cadets who would be too totally 'lost' to understand as to what was happening to them. The seniors pounced upon the juniors like wild ferocious lions on hapless lambs. They all had joined together to create commotion all around.

Creating commotion and confusion among the target group would ensure success of missions of those who create it. It was like weird villains attacking heroines; or a group of dacoits creating commotion by resorting to shouting and sporadic shooting in the area where they have planned to plunder, as depicted in cine pictures. One would be remembering the old parable of the wolf and the lamb. The wolf would falsely implicate the lamb of dirtying the water that he was to drink, even when the lamb was standing down stream and drinking water. Both of them knew about the scientific truth that water does not flow against gravity. The wolf had determined to kill and eat the lamb, and for that he had made excuses. In fact there was no need for his entering into any dialogue with the lamb. Most probably, he wanted to avail sadistic pleasure too as a bonus. It is also like the cat trying to kill the rat after playing many a cruel and teasing game with it. In the case of cadets, the seniors were trying to kill the ego of the juniors.

All the above-mentioned activities consumed only the first three hours of the first day of their training programme. After occupation of the room, they were forced to clean and re-clean the already clean areas. That process would go on till it would be time for evening tea. All sorts of perpetration of harassment would continue till late in the night by which time most of them would have even lost sense of direction and balance of mind. They even forgot their own names. It seemed that there was a

'Research and Analysis Wing' attached to the seniors. They used to spend a lot of time in finding out new methods of ragging, even at the cost of their own studies. Some of them seemed to have got addicted to ragging. Some of them were cynical and mean-minded. These are all against the 'rules of the game'.

In the evening on the first day, all of them were taken to the hair-cutting saloon established in the academy premises meant only for cadets, and they would be given nearly 'zero-haircut'. Hairdressers took instructions only from the seniors who used to accompany them to the saloon. The nexus or the 'unholy alliance' between the hairdressers and the seniors was very conspicuous. The cadets were reminded of their good old younger days when their parents used to take them to the nearby hairdressing saloons, and passing instructions to the barber as to how the hair of their wards was to be cut. Even at that time too, the children used to express their fanciful ideas on hair dressing. Parents invariably used to oppose, most of the time for the sake of sheer opposing, and exercise their 'veto' power, overruling any suggestions from their wards. It was a pity that even when they were grown up, their condition was worse than that of those younger days. Most of the cadets had lovely 'film star' type hairdos and elegant mustaches. All that became stories of the past once when they came out of the saloon as 'finished products'. All false senses of pride, prejudices, prestige, complexes, egoism and all sorts of inhibitions which were permanent residents in them would have vanished by then. That was the aim of that exercise, forming an integral part of the ragging 'syllabus'. They might have silently cursed seniors and the hairdressers. All of the cadets looked, after this ordeal, like premature babies or chicks coming out fresh from hatchery or sheep after having their wool been pruned. At this, they used to make fun of each other privately, when the dreadful 'cats' would be away.

They were used to be woken up at three in the mornings and asked to get ready for health run. That was not part of the official training programme but designed by the seniors. It was all easy for the seniors. Only two or three of the seniors were required to be awake for that purpose and others could continue with their sleep. They used to detail by rotation by making their own 'duty roaster' for such 'harassment squads'. They were like sheep controlled by ruthless shepherds. Thereafter, they would be required to report for the official health run at five. Then they were allowed to have quick freshening-up and thereafter they were guided to the dining hall for fabulous breakfast which most of them could not enjoy at that time, for obvious reasons. The food served was very rich. The day started with 'bed-tea'. Then they had to chase time with the daily routines before they attended official 'health run' and physical training (P.T). After that, they had to report for a two-hour session of parade and arms drill, before which they would have had their breakfast. That sort of routine continued for three months, till their cursed 'juniority' ceased.

The breakfast used to be consisting of porridge, milk, eggs, bread or toast, butter, jam and fresh fruits, besides coffee or tea. Again, after the parade session, there would be a break for light refreshments. After that they would attend to a three-hour academic session in classrooms. During this, the directing staff would impart knowledge on military services, Air Force in particular, general management and all allied subjects. Many of the cadets used to drowse off during such classes, because of the physical fatigue that they had contracted while doing parade. They had to keep their eye-lids open to avoid embarrassment to the directing staff. Slowly they would acquire mastery over the techniques for that, an expression of their survival instinct. Thereafter, they would have their rich and heavy lunch which comprised of rice, chappatis, vegetarian and non-vegetarian dishes, curds and puddings. They were then allowed to take rest for nearly two hours. They used to sleep like uprooted trees helplessly lying on the ground.

The 'second bed coffee' would wake up Ramesh; Peter, his orderly, telling, "Sir, please have your coffee. It is time to get ready for games. The games gear is ready." He woke up and sat on the cot, and had his coffee, and again laid himself on bed. When Peter came back after a few minutes, Ramesh was still in bed sleeping. None could hoodwink Peter. He once again called

Ramesh. "You go to hell, let me sleep for some more time" was his response. Hearing the pandemonium around, however, he had no option but to get up and get ready. The orderlies like Peter were quite elderly and mature. They used to be very affectionate and caring. Peter did not get irritated or infuriated ever on such outbursts by those cadets. It was like an affectionate father, trying to wake up his very loving teen-aged son, urging him to get ready to go to school. The father would not feel bad at his son's rude behaviour on such occasions. Similar was the case with Peter too. He had been seeing such behaviour from cadets like Ramesh in the past too. So he only used to pass smiles.

In the academy, every activity that was to take place had a name suffixed with the term, 'drill' or 'parade'. There were, for example, hair-cutting, measurement for stitching uniforms, trial of stitched uniforms, inspection of hand nails, table manners, freshening in bath rooms, going to bed, arrangement 'kits' in rooms, cleaning of surroundings, attending to washermen, going to classrooms, even attending to nature's call, and what not, were all treated as such parades. The term 'parade' is considered sacramental to any 'tightly-held' organizations such as the Air Force, and it stood synonymatic with 'discipline'. They are good enough to bring in psychological conditioning, especially to those like the cadets who have given implicit willingness to join such organisations and thereby having no choice other than getting conditioned, and toe the line. None of them was allowed to do anything in individual capacity. There used to be various such parades whenever and whatever activities they were to do collectively.

During resting times, the cadets used to form random groups and indulge themselves in singing, sharing jokes of both 'vegetarian' as well as 'non-vegetarian' and merry-making. In all the activities, sense of collectivism could vividly be discernible. As what was taught while doing physical drills, each cadet was made to shout, "One-Two-Three" to achieve collective timing at these drills. Borrowing and extending this idea, at the end of such sessions, it was customary for all to shout the same "One-Two-Three" , but this time only to give timing to the collective effort to say, "Hutchch, Hutchch, Hutchch", the sound everyone makes while sneezing. It was done without any prejudice to the established system of training. It was all sheer merry-making and innocent enjoyment. It could have been a fantastic time!

No junior liked being ragged by their seniors. 'Ragging' was not offered as an 'optional' subject in the syllabus. Before anyone could realize, the 'business' would have started, leaving no chance for anyone to think of it. Surprise is an important element in warfare! But 'every dog has its day' is a meaningful adage in the case of juniors. Every junior becomes a senior one day when some others come-in as juniors. It is a perennial phenomenon. One has to await one's turn. Today when the juniors have become seniors, they get all the chances of experiencing what their seniors had at their cost.

After a few months, the seniors 'pass out' on their commissioning. Just a few days before their 'passing-out' ceremony, they would grant the juniors a boon for ragging them back. It was known as 'anti-ragging'. The seniors would condescend from the high pedestal of seniority to become ordinary cadets and mix with the juniors as good friends. This was to enable the latter to forgive and forget the possible residual ill-feeling left in them. The potential energy of hatred would be brought to a naught. Even though it was a chance for the juniors to avenge the misdeeds meted out by the seniors, it became only a formality in essence. At the time of parting, the whole lot of seniors and juniors used to sink and bury all their mutual unpleasant experiences, and only ever lasting friendship and relationship would be left behind as precipitate. Those seniors will have developed 'an-older-brother' syndrome for ever.

Later on, when all these young officers moved out to different bases during their service career, they would feel at home in all the places because of the standardized pattern of behaviour that they could muster during training period, thanks mainly to the devil, Ragging.

Forgetfulness—A Curse or Boon?

28

Mind is a concept. It is conceived as a combination of two elements, viz. one of heart and the other of head. Heart is a unit that concentrates on mass-scale manufacture of sentiments, and the head is the centre of analytical reasoning. They operate in two diametrically opposite directions and planes. Thus it is the combination of uncombinable and uncompromising elements. In the context of minds, let us assume that the 'mix' contains only a small part of heart and a major part of the brain, the former having only a limited role to play in the working of the combination called mind. Theoretically, the combination should work in smooth and balanced way. The combining trend varies in respect of different individuals, and hence there are various types of people and personalities in the world.

One has to manage his mind. Managing mind is management of thoughts, because it is in this mind that all thoughts are generated. Minds may be conscious, or subconscious. Consciousness is awareness, having the feeling or knowledge of something. In this state all our activities are performed by our five senses, relating to sight, sound, smell, taste and touch, and so also time and space. Any thought or action by the conscious state leaves an indelible impression on the subconscious mind and influences our subsequent actions and thoughts. It is the seat of intellect, logic and reasoning, and works only when one is awake. Subconscious mind is the seat of intuition, creativity and emotions, and it works even when one is asleep. It does not relate to the five senses, and time and space. The storage capacity of the conscious mind is quite meagre as compared to the subconscious mind which can store huge quantum of information which becomes mental software.

Information that we get through our various senses is not allowed to be lost. All the pieces of information coming in are collected, collated and consolidated by the brain, the Central Processing Unit (CPU) of human computer system. It behaves like a miser who likes to receive, accept, and hoard wealth as much as possible. It sorts it out into different classes and categories taking into consideration of its futuristic relevance and utility, and preserves all what it thinks fit to be kept back with it and sends the remainder to subconscious mind for storage and safe custody. All this will be further classified and segregated by the brain and subconscious mind independently, and stored them in their appropriate shelves separately available with them, a system similar that of a library of books. In fact, conceiving the reverse order, that the system being followed in libraries is only an adaptation and imitation of the already established one in the brain, would be more appropriate. It is blasphemous for the great mind if someone tells that the brain has borrowed and adopted the idea from its own creation, viz. the computer. It is not similar to the interesting controversy existing in case of chicken and egg as to which is the first to be born; the chicken or the egg. With the help of the key board or control panel, the brain has total instantaneous accessibility at any point of time to any particular piece of information at will.

This is the phenomenon what we call memory. The memory is a blessing, but for this, whole system of living would be paralyzed. If one loses his power of memory, he ceases to live as a human being. He will be like an uprooted tree which continues to breathe involuntarily for a few more days. Memory is an asset for all the members of the fauna. In the case of the flora, due to lack of adequate information, it may be unfair on our part to presume that they do not have this faculty. Among the animals other than humans, elephants have strong powers of memory, hence the phrase 'elephantine memory'. Memory is the ability to connect past with the present, or project or superimpose the past impressions onto the present situations to provide a new lease of life to the old ones. It prevents the death of the past, in other words, it perpetuates the past. Life becomes wholesome only when the past and present are inter-woven.

One is apt to condemn another who lives only in the past. One must believe that the past stands for falsehood and the present for reality; to come to this conclusion, one must remember the past. He must chew it like the cud.

The memory can be a curse too. There could be many an unpleasant experience which might have cast dark shadows on one's life. In this case, forgetfulness is a blessing, and unforgetfulness is a curse. The more one tries to forget some unpleasant and distressing experiences of one's life, the more vehemently they come forward to make him more conscious of them and cause distress and sorrow. Memories about pleasant experiences are more transient than those of the unpleasant ones. It is a saddening, but, all the same, interesting as a philosophical phenomenon. Unwelcome guests outnumber the welcome ones.

If one does not utilize the memory-system that one has, it becomes dysfunctional; it gets 'rusted', so to say. With the advent of electronic calculators and computers, people have become hesitative and lethargic in putting the memory into use. The very existence of the built-in computer in the brain is ignored. Even for simple calculations they depend on such gadgets. They seem to be conserving and accumulating the energy of the brain! Nowadays children are unable to add or multiply, for example, two simple figures, two and two without the help of a calculating devise. They develop a sort of artificial 'dependency syndrome'.

Centuries ago, before humans started using paper for writing, they used to store the entire information in their 'memory box' in the brains, though its quantum, variety, volume and magnitude of such information had been meagre in those days as compared to those of our present time. In the present time we are exposed to large volume of information inputs, most of which are irrelevant and trash. As one puts this faculty into optimal use, its capacity gains enhanced elastance and efficiency. The entire volume of knowledge handled by ancient religions like the Hinduism was being stored in the memory of saints and sages who handed them to their disciples and followers, and in turn to their successive generations. This process used to continue uninterruptedly for many millennia. Later on they started writing on special type of dry leaves with the help of pen-like pointed metallic implements, and preserved them. Written on them, for example, are the most sacred scriptures. The writings cover revelations made by godmen on yogic practices and the *Ayurveda*, the ancient system of medical practices. Most of these are transferred to paper and electronic devices, keeping pace with our technological advancement. Interestingly, many of the old manuscripts written on leaves are also kept preserved as precious treasures.

Some people, saving the old, remember only those things that can serve their private ends. Young people, for example, do not forget the names or even minute details of likes and dislikes of their girl or boy friends. Similarly, they do not forget the names of their enemies, the exact amount of money receivables and so on. They consciously or otherwise forget those that are of 'no use' to them, for example, the amounts of money payable to others by them, the names of friends who are no longer beneficial to them, good moral lessons that they had learnt in their childhood and so on. This is part of their artificial style of living, a tendency of selectivity designed and fostered by them to suit to their selfish motives. These are purposive and deliberate forgetfulness. Here hypocrisy and untruthfulness are the underlying factors.

Some people make out lists of things to be done on a particular day, when they go outing. That means that they have decided not to use the faculty of memory. They depend only on the list. But they forget to take the list with them when they go out. Despite their best efforts to recollect the particulars of items in that list, they are likely to forget all except probably the first one or two. Even the faculty of memory also needs to be employed to activate its nerves and cells, a sort of an exercise. A dormant or hibernating memory can not be reactivated at will and hence it may fail to function adequately when one wants it to.

Let me come out with some typical behavioural transactions involving forgetful oldies. When such an oldie happens to meet someone of his type at a familiar and frequented rendezvous,

'Sunset Park', he would accost him and say, "Hello! We have met somewhere earlier. I am not able to recollect where exactly. Was it at the Eros cinema or the children's park?" A prompt but nonchalant and genuine reply might come, "I too don't remember. I think it was probably at the Kaypees. But, when was it? Not definitely, yesterday. I think you had asked me the same question yesterday when we had met at the Superstores. No, No, sorry, I didn't visit there, it was at Havmor Restaurant", or "Aren't we brothers living in the same house?" or "We are meeting first time now. Aren't we?" At the same place, he happened to meet a young man. The old man thought that he definitely knew him, and therefore accosted him and said, "Aren't you the son of my good friend, Ramesh? How is he? I haven't met him for a pretty long time. Your name is Gopal, if my memory is correct. What are you?" The youngman was terribly embarrassed, because he was neither Gopal nor his father was Ramesh. He was a good sport. He politely replied, "Uncle, My father is fine. He often talks about you. I shall convey to him of your loving regards." The young man had understood the situation very well and tackled it very well. The old man was made happy because of that harmless lie, and apparent frankness. He could have said, "Uncle, I am not Gopal and my father is not Ramesh. You have gone wrong"; or some rude words to show his irritation. All these are the signs of amnesia on the part of the old man.

Let me cite an incident. A father had fathered twelve children at fifty-fifty sex ratio. He had used twelve alphabets, A to L, to start their individual names. Thank God, he did pot have to use all the twenty-six! The birthday of the 'twelfth-man' of the team, Laxman, (the name begins with "L", the twelfth alphabet), coincided with that of his own fiftieth. Once when a distant cousin of his visited him, one of his beautiful daughters came in near them. The visitor asked his cousin what his daughter's name was. Promptly with a proud smile he replied, "Molly." In fact that was not her name. Having realized the gross mistake, he issued an amendment, "I am sorry, her name is Sweety. Molly is her next senior." Seeing the embarrassment of the cousin-host, the cousin-visitor 'consoled' him by saying,

"Don't worry, this sort of mistake can naturally occur in cases such as yours." The visitor had a hearty laugh. It was not a case of amnesia and ignorance or mischief and fake. It only shows his lack of concern and love for his children. He had, probably, maintained a strong belief that all those children belonged to his wife only, and it was a chance that he became their father!

In most houses, time available in the mornings of working days is totally inadequate to attend to all the tasks required to be done. Time chases the housewife more than anyone else in the family. Her children have to be sent to school. They have to be got ready before the school bus arrives. At the same time, her husband has to go for work. While she is busy in the kitchen, she has to answer a frantic call from her younger son, "Mama, where is my tie? My shoes are not polished". The elder one joins him, "Thank you for doing my homework, Mama, but where did you keep my work-book." "I am coming", she shouts back. Now it is the turn of her husband to flash out SOS, "Darling, I don't find my watch. I think I had kept it on the table. Did you take it?" She answers that too, "I did not take it and I do not know where it is. I am coming." There could be no wonder if she goes mad. But she does not go mad because this sort of things happen everyday, providing a conditioning effect on her. She is so much used to all these, and but for these she would have gone mad.

In this case, the husband and the children are exploiting the lady of the house. The lady is fully aware of her present plight. The love and care she was showering on them have been mistaken for weakness. Her husband undoubtedly is a self-centred man. He does not want to see the woes of others, because it may not be convenient for him. So he deliberately chooses to pretend to be forgetful and careless. All children like to imitate their father, especially if it is beneficial to them. As it is, all human beings have a tendency to pick-up bad habits, and an affinity for evil things.

There are two simple methods by which the confusion in that household can be circumvented: conditioning training for limbs and organs of the members of this family, and implementation of time management concepts. It is good to train and condition one's whole body as well as organs like hands, eyes, legs to behave in some mechanical ways. When the children come back from school, they should be told to freshen-up. They must be insisted upon to keep their shoes and school uniforms in fixed places. They should be given some food, and after that they should be asked to do homework and read lessons for the next day. Then only they should be allowed to play. This routine must strictly be followed everyday so that it becomes their second nature, and thus their mental as well as the bodily system get into die-hard habits. Similarly their father after he comes back from office should keep his wrist watch, shoes, hand bag and others in fixed places everyday. His hands, legs and eyes will always be conditioned to do things in the same way everyday. It is good to make the organs slaves of these habits. This strict training will be required to be done only for a few days, after which both the father and the children will continue to do all this involuntarily. With this practice they all become good time-managers of their available time. They will no longer be forgetful. Now onwards they can switch off their conscious mind in all these. These habits make them self-reliant in their old age as well, and the ill-effects of a possible future amnesia can be circumvented.

An inebriated person, a case in point, had to drive a twenty-kilometre-stretch of road in the dead of night. Next morning when he woke up, it took some time for him, due to hangover, to realize that he was in his house, safe and sound, and he could see his car parked in the garage exactly in the same manner as he used to do when he used to be 'normal'. Moreso, he had kept his shoes at the designated place, and hung his lounge suit on coat-hanger and kept in the wardrobe and slipped into his normal night gown, perfectly as usual, before he had gone to bed that night. It was due to the involuntary co-ordination of his sensory organs and legs that brought about that perfect job. The training and conditioning of these only came to his rescue. He did not do all this as a conscious person. The case is very identical with that of an old person in the grip of amnesia.

So the moral of the story is that if one wants to circumvent difficulties in old age due to a possible amnesia when his sensory organs and conscious mind are likely to fail, he should have to form good habits when he is still young and healthy. For this, everyone should have to presume well in advance in his youth that he would surely be a victim of amnesia one day when he would be old. A wise young will be making adequate financial provisions to cater for subsistence and sustenance of his self in the evening of his life. Together with this, he has to train, condition and organize the behaviour of his physical and sensory organs and prepare them to behave involuntarily by the time he becomes an old man. At that time, there will not be 'stimulus-response' system working properly; in the absence of mechanism for sensing or detecting the presence of a stimulus itself might be insensitive, dysfunctional or absent.

Amnesia is a general term describing loss of memory. Symptoms include general memory loss, confusion and the inability to recognize familiar faces or places, and to recall the recent past. It comes on some slowly, whereas in others it appears suddenly. Symptoms of amnesia may be temporary or permanent. Initially, the 'memory box' is empty. At that time, any input of information about persons, objects or situations will be totally accepted and assimilated by the brain. But gradually, the entire space or 'bytes' will be utilized in this process; a situation of saturation. When the capacity of this 'reservoir' is thus fully utilized, people experience difficulty in acquiring new information. They face difficulty in recalling previously learned information. They are prone to malingering and try to exaggerate and dramatize their symptoms. They fail to recall important personal information like address and location of their home, names of their dear ones and even their own names.

Amnesia has several root causes. Most are traceable to brain injuries related to physical trauma, disease, infection, drug and alcohol. The nervous system connecting to the memory 'box' placed in the brain gets weak, insensible or damaged, and because of this, the continuity of conduction of impulses of information suffers impairment. It is similar to what we experience in very old houses in respect of electrical wirings and the resultant disturbances and interruptions in electric supplies due to short-circuiting. It is interesting to see some old individuals remembering very vividly some incidents occurred when they were in their early youth, but they fail to recollect details of recent events occurred even a few minutes earlier, despite their being key players or witnesses of such incidents. In youth, normally the memory is quite sharp. The storing capacity of the 'memory box' is under-utilized during that period. At that time, they will be able to remember the names and other details of all persons they have met. As they grow-up, they happen to come across hundreds of people, objects and situations, and gradually the storage space will be totally utilized. No new inputs will be accepted for storage. It is not possible to make more space available by replacing or erasing the information already kept 'saved' therein. They would remember only the initial inputs which have been given status of 'permanent residents' in memory.

When people are very old, they get disoriented. They become inept in remembering the basic details like the location and address of their residences, even their own names. It is a very dangerous problem especially when they venture to go alone out of their homes. It is advisable not to allow them to go out unescorted, and even then they should be in possession of their identity particulars safely held on to their person like we do for our minor children going to their Kindergarten. People who are suffering from amnesia may not even be aware that they are in such a condition. It is good enough if others are aware of the fact. At that time, there will not be 'stimulus-response' system working properly, in the absence of mechanism for sensing or detecting the presence of a stimulus itself might be insensitive, dysfunctional or absent.

It is interesting to see some old individuals remembering very vividly some incidents occurred when they were in their early youth, but they fail to recollect details of recent events occurred even a few minutes earlier, despite their being key players or witnesses of such incidents. Even the faculty of memory also needs to be employed to activate its nerves and cells, a sort of exercise. A dormant or hibernating memory can not be re-activated at will and hence it may fail to function adequately when one wants it to. When people are very old, they get disoriented. They forget even the basic details like the location and address of their residences, even their own names. It is a very dangerous problem especially when they venture to go alone out of their homes. It is advisable not to allow them to go out unescorted, and even then they should be in possession of their identity particulars safely held on their person like we do for our minor children going to their Kindergarten. People who are suffering from amnesia may not even be aware that they are in such a condition. It is good enough if others are aware of and considerate to those who are facing this problem. They need sympathy and help from others, because they can not help themselves.

People adopt some simple techniques to remember things. Housewives before their shopping errand, for example, formulate some codes made out of the first letters of the articles they want to buy from market. For example, for items of sugar, oil, flour and soap they make some word, "SOFS", and try to remember that word by reiterations many times in their minds, while travelling towards the market in their vehicles. Different people adopt different methods. Some others keep black boards and keep writing on them with chalk during their daily chores, as and when they remember of something which they would want to purchase in their next outing for shopping. Some of them entrust their husbands with the job of reminding them at the appropriate time. Husbands invariably forget the details, and knowing this, they would be carrying a list of items secretly with them. This would embarrass the husbands; and the wives do not spare such opportunities of scolding their husbands for the lapses. Scolding is resorted only to cement bondage of love-between them!

The Husbands and Their Wives 29

One of the most intriguing relationships is the one between the human males and the females, and in this, is that between husbands and their wives. In many respects it is considered a sublime, sacramental and spiritual relationship—a "made-for-each-other" arrangement. They say, marriages are arranged in the heaven. It is the solemn duty of either of them to make the other happy. For that, each of them should possess certain qualities considered antonyms of egoism, selfishness, hypocrisy and the like. The *de facto* situation more often than not is contrary to this concept. Fault, if at all one would like to unearth and ascribe, is to be attributed to both the partners. The husbands on their part fail to impress and convince their wives, either by actions or words, that they are a genuine lot, sincere, trustworthy, lovable and dependable ones. This is due mainly to a twin set of factors, viz, the nonchalant attitudes on the part of the husbands on one side as well as the non-corporeal, fanciful, unrealistic expectations and demands of their wives. Normally it is the nonchalant lot who would be facing ire and brunt of the clever, careful and determined lot; it is philosophy. Nothing can be done to repair and retrieve the situation.

Some wives consider their husbands as ornamental possessions while some others perceive them as 'bonded labours' or employees "at their majesty's service", while many husbands subscribe to the idea that women, their wives, are mere objects of sex. This is an incompatible predicament. These are perceptive and cognitive aberrations on the part of either of them culminating in disharmony in their relationships. It is the women that 'marry' men and not that the latter 'marry' the former; men only just 'get married' to women. Even though women clamour vociferously that they are not given equal opportunities and status by these 'men-dominated' societies, (in some realms it may be true), even when the fact is that men always believe in a 'ladies first' attitude. This attitude of the men make the women ask for 'more'; immature children too behave this way; it is natural tendency of human beings. In the social outings and gatherings, one can see men taking utmost care in looking after the interests of women, even ignoring their personal comforts. In the civilized and developed societies like those of the Armed Forces, one can see when a young officer's young wife enters the venue of the social gathering, all the senior officers irrespective of their rank or position get-up from their seats and greet the lady with great respect and regard, even at the embarrassment of that lady.

This is the era of 'woman's lib'. Liberation is required only in cases where someone is subjected to subjugation. The outcry about women's liberation is itself *prima facie* evidence of the existence of a serious vexed problem. In our societies, subjugation of women is prevalent, though in somewhat sporadic manner. The main reasons could be illiteracy, superstitions, economic backwardness, economic dependence of women on men, social customs, inaccessibility to new ideas, and so on.

Man is a social animal. When we started on an organized social structure, millennia ago, able-bodied men were required at the helm of affairs to provide physical protection to weaklings under their care, from attacks from wild animals as well as vagaries of Nature. Men were 'invited', so to say, to do those jobs, and they 'willingly accepted' the responsibilities. So, probably, protecting weaklings or any needy has become a strong instinct in them, and without their knowledge it has become second nature in them. None can eject himself from this syndrome very easily. Since the societies have grown bigger and stronger and the overall security situation also underwent changes, this job has been rendered redundant. Men have lost all their initiatives, and they are left confused and lost at loss of 'employment'.

Knowledge about the physical world was at first acquired by men, naturally, due to their exposure in the various fields of activities. They then gained sagacity. Through their interactions with others in the 'close-net', which we named later, 'family', and so also with others in the social group, they started sharing mutually the knowledge, wisdom and sagacity each one of them individually and severally acquired. Women initially received information indirectly, but later they too participated in the interaction processes. This way the level of information, knowledge, wisdom, competence and skill in everybody could become nearly equal. Thus men have 'brought-up', so to say, their women by giving enough chances for their growth and development. This has immensely helped them in realizing if they have been subjected to subjugation or not. It seems that they have realized it and hence they want to get liberated and elevated themselves. They even want to 'take over' the society as well as the world by one snatch. This is similar to 'taking over' of business establishments or companies by their own employees.

In rural rustic settings, there is ample evidence of the continuing trend of subjugation of women. Their role in the family as well as society is secondary to that of men. We should not debate on the merits or demerits of this situation. There are advantages as well as disadvantages vying with each other for better projection. In urban settings, people are educated on 'modern lines' on 'codified' norms and they are aware or not aware of each one's role in the prevalent social systems. Here both men and women are on equal footings. Women should push themselves forward to realizing their proper position in society.

One word, 'henpeckery' has been sent to oblivion. It is no misnomer. Henpeckery is a reality in actual life of husbands. Women, as though they want to avenge their 'subjugation' to which they allege to have been subjected over millennia want their husbands to be subjugated. This, in a way, is a part of organic revolution. But it is nothing but a natural tendency of vendetta. They have 'hundred-and-one' ways of accomplishing this goal. Men are generally nonchalant, and appear before these women as useless, timid, lethargic and good-for-nothing.

Women's perception about men also undergoes a change, once when men's utility as 'men' follows the 'law of diminishing returns', especially after women's achieving their *raison d'etre* through them. The men, the husbands, are turned into like 'crushed sugarcanes'.

In this world of hypocrisy, hardly anyone admits that he is hen-pecked. To begin with, none may be consciously aware of this fact. Only a person who is given to self-analysis can realize its existence, otherwise he would carry on, without any awareness, living in his 'paradise'. Realization comes about on a fine day, but it is too late to take any remedial or retrieval action. Much water would have flowed under the bridge by then. If anyone reveals in public that he is henpecked, he becomes a laughing stock, and therefore, he chooses to keep quiet. It is like a person, who was beaten up by some people, telling about the incident, after looking around, in a twisted manner and trying clearing his name. Even the 'hen' will not admit the fact in public that her man is 'pecked' by her. This is quite an interesting thing.

If we analyze the scenario in rural and urban settings, we will find the following: In rural settings, men do not admit this fact at all. In the presence of other friendly couples they agree for a meager percentage, whereas rural women, up to about 20%. In urban settings, about 20% of men strike the deal generally, and in presence of friendly couples up to 60%.

Women seem to admit privately up to 90% in presence of other women, to score a point or two therefrom, but they totally deny such a thing in presence of other men or couples or in public. It is all hypocrisy galore!

Now let us analyse the better side of henpeckery. A henpecked husband can enjoy certain advantages too. He can safely 'switch off' his thinking machine. Whenever any issue crops up in household context, he does not have to take any decision on any matter, as he is afraid that his opinions or decisions will find their place in the garbage can. In any case, she is going to 'think' and take decisions either directly by herself or indirectly by way of rejecting or overruling his. Some difficult decisions, however, will be left for the husband to 'take'. This will enable her to scan through such decisions with a view to finding out mistakes. If she 'solicits' his opinion on her scheme of things, the husband should adhere to answers like 'yes' or 'no' or 'I don't know'. This is playing safe. But she will get frustrated at this and will come out with insults. Be prepared. In fact all this behaviour of hers is to find out his 'wrong foot'. For her, every foot of her husband's is a 'wrong foot'. The wife does not like this evasive attitude on the part of her husband, because she loses the chance of a possible 'post mortem' criticism, and most importantly the 'fun' attached to it. This only shows that men are a hapless lot.

Another advantage available to the henpecked ones is that it is possible for them to improve their health. They will mostly be in charge of the kitchen, as their wives are busy with other more important matters. Such husbands are made, of course secretly, to do physical labour at home. These two engagements provide them with good food on one side, and the needed exercise and rest on the other. And these are the requirements for acquiring the 'primary' need of good 'bodily' health.

In the initial stages of married life, there is no scope for henpeckery. Wife stays at a low key, and she spends most of her time in observing her husband thoroughly, in order to take stock of both good and bad traits in him. Interestingly, men are quite slow or not interested in observing their wives, probably because they take things for granted, because of their 'self-confidence'. Slowly she focuses on 'bad' points, and starts advising him to change them. At the same time, it is concluded that she has 'no adverse' points to be rectified as 'unofficially confirmed' by her husband, based on some hunch, imagination or presumed or deemed observations. Here there is no room for any advice to be given to his wife. As he is nonchalant and care-free, he ignores her advice. This is the first step towards the 'grip' she wanted. She tightens it, thereby 'kick-starting' the 'pecking' business. My boy, you can't get away from this.

Every woman's need is that her husband is captivated and controlled; otherwise, she is afraid, she might lose him, because Nature has made him a LLB ('Licentiate Loafer Beetles').

Making him 'henpecked' is one of the ways of controlling him, thereby assuring an insurance cover, in her favour, to protect against any possible threat of 'theft, fraud or misappropriation' of her 'dear' husband.

If we undertake to go for a confidential opinion-poll among, say, one thousand married men, at random, in order to grab their 'confessions' or otherwise, and work out some statistical data, we are sure to get nearly nine hundred and fifty confessions *id est* 95%. The 5% less may have been caused, probably because, they were fast asleep or pretending to be so, or they could not understand the question, or they are so henpecked that they could not get permission from their wives to talk to public on such sensitive subjects. Let us first of all thank those 'brave' 95%, and 'excuse' the remainder 5%, as they are innocent, and 'they do not know what they are doing'.

With scientific inventions, it may be becoming a reality in the near future that woman would be able to bear children without the help of man, and to that extent, man will be deemed or rendered redundant. *Prima facie* it would be welcome news for women, who do not want husbands, but only children. But what do they do for 'other benefits'. If such a phenomenon comes through, it is more advantageous to men than to women. Men can 'officially' become 'loafer beetles', with no 'responsibilities' whatsoever. The words, 'husband' and 'henpeckery' would become defunct and hence get expunged from Dictionaries. Word, 'cockpeckery' would replace 'henpeckery'. But, in case they could beget only female children through any new process then it results in 'value addition' to 'awaiting' men.

A Dog's Musings

30

Man establishes and maintains relations with his fellow humans through his interpersonal transactions. He is conscious as well as concerned about the manner in which these transactions take place. He comprehends their holistic relevance by relating them to the overall situations in which they take place. He objectively as well as subjectively and consciously or unconsciously analyses the bionomical impacts of such transactions on each individual and on his society at large. By and large he is quite successful in his endeavours to understand and analyse the effects of his behaviour vis-à-vis others, because he has effective two-way communication system which provides him with feedback. Every action has an equal and opposite reaction. It is this reaction to his actions, that is, response to stimuli of his behaviour that brings forth the vital feedback. This action-reaction nexus provides the key to his ability to assessing and understanding the result of his behaviour. He undertakes similar transactions with other members of the fauna too and with those of the flora and the very Nature herself. But in all these cases, as he gets only inadequate or insufficient feedback, such analyses would not be feasible. It is worthwhile to reckon and know their responses to these stimuli of interactional transactions together with their bionomical impact. This is possible only through his imagination. As for example, let us imagine as to what his most favoured pet, a dog, reveals of its perceptions in respect of the behaviour of its master towards it. This revelation is in an autobiographical mode.

From time immemorial, we dogs have been the best friend of the human beings. Millennia ago all members of the fauna were wild. The human beings used to live in caves or improvised huts in jungles. In fact, the earth used to be covered with either forests or naked deserts. Rivers used to flow through the forests. For the very existence of both flora and fauna, they needed water, besides air. Hence forests came-up near water resources and the fauna settled down where both water and forests were available. That is why all human civilizations had flourished all along-side the courses of rivers. None of members of the fauna could settle down in the deserts, for obvious reasons. All of them had the same kind of living style. They lived mainly on fruits and roots of plants; and some of them on their hunt-proceeds.

Most of the wild among wild members of the fauna used to hunt and kill other animals and ate their meat for their livelihood. Initially, the homo-sapiens used to be hesitant hunters. Gradually they too took to hunting small animals. They ate raw meat probably in the absence of fruits and roots. There used to be forest fires which killed many animals, besides mass destruction of the flora. It was, probably, accidentally that they happened to taste meat of some animals that were roasted alive by such forest fires; and so also when they found that there were no plants to provide fruits and roots or living animal-preys seen anywhere in their neighbourhood for hunting. It was the survival instinct that made them to eat this roasted meat. They found it very tasty. That marked the end of their eating raw meat. We dogs belonged to the canine clan. We were physically weak as compared to other animals in the jungle. Our only weapon we had, besides our canine teeth, was our capability for loud barking which we employed in scaring our enemies. But our enemies knew, as you too, "Barking dogs seldom bite". That was what our plight was. The tigers were very fond of our flesh, and, therefore, they never allowed us to live in peace. All know that cats and dogs always maintain belligerent stance with each other. In fact, this truth can be extended to the entire feline and canine species.

We found that humans, though small in size and weak in bodily strength, as compared to many other animals like the elephants and horses in the forest , by their high level of intelligence, were able to conquer and make all of them their slaves. The greatest surprise we experienced was when we saw the huge and the mighty elephants were tamed and trained by those humans and made them their most obedient slaves. It was a great sight when they used to discipline these mighty elephants with the help of a stick of nearly a metre in length. Mounting on them, the humans used to take them to the forest and utilized their services while they went hunting. Unbelievable!

Understanding all this, we decided to depend upon the humans. For this, we had to prove that we meant no harm to them. We had to struggle hard to convince the humans in this regard. It might have taken many centuries for that. Initially, after mustering courage, we had started sleeping outside their caves, once they went inside to retire. Through out nights we used to be awake, as though we were guarding them. Many a time, we had raised alarms to those humans sleeping inside their caves about the presence in the neighbourhood of a tiger or some other enemy. They had thought initially that we were a nuisance and were chased away by them. But we were not discouraged. After some time they had realized that we had meant all good. It was nothing but a mutual benefit scheme. We were terribly afraid of such ferocious creatures, and we knew for certain that the humans would chase them away. This sort of things had happened many times. The humans thus recognized our sense of sincerity and loyalty, and understood that we had the quality to become their security advisors. They also understood that we would one day become their loyal servants. We used to eat their left-overs', proving that we never had any intention to interfere and snatch their food. We had proved to them that we were at their mercy only.

It all took many years before we could muster and win their confidence. We did all this at the cost of losing our hunting skills. We slowly developed a dependency syndrome *vis-a-vis* the humans. There was not even an iota of sense of sacrifice in whatever we did at that time, only a *quid pro quo* arrangement under a *sine qua non* situation. The human beings, in this respect at least, were not hypocritical, and they called a spade always a spade. That was how we dogs earned a permanent place in their hearts and with that we had cast off our initial cautiousness, skepticism and hypocrisy and became genuine beings. We would never vacate that place in their hearts, nor would we be allowed to do so by them. Our bondage of friendship is millennia old, and it has stood the test of time.

These humans asked us to help them in hunting. They used to take three or four of us with them into the forest. It used to be quite a thrilling experience. They made use of our sniffing capabilities to their good advantage in locating their hiding preys. We used to walk a few metres ahead of them, leading them, giving an impression that we were the actual hunters and they were only our followers. We all used to spend the whole day hunting, and in the evening we all used to return with our fortunes in the form of those unfortunate victims. We all then shared the hunt-proceeds happily. The life went on like this. We had our own language and we used to discuss all hunting strategies among ourselves. The humans could get an inkling of what we wanted to convey to them. We could not talk the language they spoke, but slowly we developed some sense to understand what they wanted to convey to us. We became experts in understanding their body language and gestures, and they started understanding ours too. It was all a happy situation through and through. We had developed identical understandings on most of the issues.

Both of us started enjoying our companionship and comradeship to a very great extent. Millennia rolled off, and friendship too carried on. The human nature underwent a lot of changes. Their concept about their dwelling places too changed drastically. They gradually developed first-hand scientific knowledge on the changing climatic seasons and day-to-day weather conditions. They started cutting trees of the forest, making the land naked and barren. The vastness of the forest contracted and shrunk, and the wild animals kept retreating, keeping pace with the backward movement of the forest. The humans started constructing their houses with solid materials. Then onwards they did not have to be afraid of the attacks from those wild animals. There used to be sporadic incidences of attack by the wild animals, mainly to give expression to their displeasure and anger due to what the humans had done to them. If any one of a human, venturing to undertake an independent analysis, would come to realize that he has caused irreparable damage to Nature due to his thoughtless acts. He atones for all these now, though belatedly.

The humans cultivate friendships also with some other animals like cats, cows, buffalos, horses, elephants. The cats belong to feline clan, other members of this being *felis leo* (the lion) and *felis tigris* (the tiger). The cats are *felis domestica.* They are highly ferocious and they normally do not like to contract long standing friendship with anyone including the humans. They can, probably, be tamed to be good companions only if they are adopted in their younger age. We are not like that. The humans know this fact very well. The human beings attach a bit of philosophy when they claim that they foster these other animals just because they are also created by God, and that they love them for love's sake only. Here we suspect a bit of hypocrisy on their part. They love them, but their love is not unattached. They seem to be attached to the benefits they reap from those relationships. The cats help the humans in eradicating menacing rats and rodents, the cows and buffalos give them milk, the horses give them entertaining sports and travels and the elephants help them in doing hard labour. These animals are docile and good-natured, and they all thus serve the humans in various ways. We have no competition with them in any area. Our clan is a very special type, and none can be compared with us. That is why the humans have given us a very special status. We are greatly grateful to them for it.

People say that our name often stands as synonym for high degree of loyalty, friendship and trust-worthiness. All have respect for us. We are not cunning like cats, *felis domestica,* and with which we have occasional fights. The cats tease and deride us. We are physically stronger than cats, but in our fights we don't win as they cunningly climb nearby trees and escape defeat. We can not climb trees. We are simple and innocent in nature, unlike jackals, foxes or wolves of our own canine family.

Human beings keep home-pets most common of which are dogs, cats and rabbits. We dogs become the obvious first choice. They keep us in pairs. We often request them to keep both the sexes of the same breed in that pair, enabling us to have some sort of romance and married life. It is our right. Don't you agree with us? Mostly they oblige us. Some of them do not have any sense, and to their liking, they keep a male Alsatian with a female Pomeranian thus depriving us of a possible alliance. We have our strict ethical and moral codes prohibiting us from such relationships. It seems that keeping home-pets serves as status or fashion symbol among urban affluent human families. The urban human females are very fond of us. It is generally observed that the madams take us out for walk through the streets of the city, probably because it is a way to 'show off their vanity. They provide us with very rich food. It seems they bathe us in warm water, applying some special variety of soaps. The manufacture of these 'special' soaps is the monopoly of some particular type of firms who carry out aggressive marketing strategies by advertisements, addressed mainly to these madams. They claim a lot of advantages in using the particular soap. These madams fall in their traps; and purchase such soaps; they do it without consulting us. We have no problems. We enjoy the bath; needless to mention about their soft touches and the humming of some light music. They get us clad in expensive and beautiful outfits. Even the belts fastened around our necks are well-decorated and attractive. These innocent and thoughtless lots do not understand that we do not enjoy these things. OK, we ignore these!

They love us and treat us members of their family. The 'man' and his 'woman' in the house become our foster father and mother. In fact we become their children and they our parents. It is needless to say we too love them. Whenever visitors come, we will be formally introduced to them, "Look, Goldie and you, Mildie, meet your uncle and aunty. This is your uncle, and this is your aunty. Come, shake hands with them." After obeying the instructions, we wag our tails and sit near them for a while, till we get marching orders, "OK, now you can go away to your room and play." Thus we get opportunities to practice what they had taught us earlier. We could hear their appreciative words about us and our behaviour, "They are very cute and lovely. You have trained them well It is fantastic", they offer their appreciative commends and comments. Our 'parents' feel elevated and satisfied. Some people feel jealous of our life-styles. They consider us to be very lucky, and they would have wished themselves if they could also get a life like that of ours. Even some humans too cursed their bad luck in not having been born as dogs like us. In any case, other members of our canine family would definitely have been very envious of us. When Goldie fell sick, our 'parents' sat near her through out the night, nursing and attending on her. A veterinary doctor was summoned; and got her treated. But unfortunately she died. I felt very sad, but more than that, our 'parents' could not bear the loss. They did not eat any food during the entire mourning period of three days. They had withdrawn themselves from all entertainment activities in or out of the house. They wept in front of her photograph that they had taken only a few days before her death. Some visitors came to the house to condole the death of their loved one as well as to console their friends at these trying and grieving moments.

Most of us are chained whenever we are taken out for a walk, usually by our young 'mother', and the ends of such chains are held in her left hands while walking. She is afraid that we would run away from her. Why should we run away when we are cared so much by her? Where else can we get such royal treatments? She is unimaginative and short-sighted. Poor lady! She keeps on talking to us in some incoherent language, which we sometimes take for soliloquy. She gives commands to us, loudly, "Goldie, no, no, get away; come this way". We obey those commands to oblige them. These madams, nay, 'mothers' are happier in the company of those of us who are huge and ferocious-looking or tiny and cute. There is a hidden agenda in this. They too can get a lot of attention from the human male onlookers. A handsome onlooker might enquire as to what the age, height, weight, breed and so on about us, knowing fully well that these topics would please the young lady. He might not be interested in the answers to the questions; at best, it would be an excuse to 'gate-crash' into her heart. They make us look down upon those of our less fortunate and destitute members of our clan, moving around aimlessly on the streets. They are unable to hide their contempt for them.

Most of us have the good or bad luck to share their beds. Young ladies in the house get into arguments among themselves as to who out of us should share their beds. We can understand if unmarried girls fight among themselves in this matter; but to our surprise, young married ladies too get into competitive spirit. It is blasphemous to think that they prefer our company to that of their husbands. Anyway, it is more than pleasure to be sleeping with them. They caress and kiss us. Our saliva left behind at places where we lick can cause infections. Knowing this, we hesitate to kiss or lick. Their expression of love sometimes gives impression that they are trying to compensate or supplement the love they receive elsewhere. It is wrong to suspect that it is case of sublimation.

Childless parents normally like to adopt a human child from some orphanage. This is done probably to fill-in the existing vacancy of a child in the family. Or is it because they are very fond of children, or is it because that they want a successor to inherit their large assets, or throne in case of kings, once when they would cease to exist? Whatever may be the reason best known to them, they adopt children. It is the lady who has to take a final decision about 'whats and whens' of adoption. Some of them may not like to adopt a human child at all, as some of these barren ladies go cynical and decide to adopt one or two of us dogs instead of human babies. They do not mind declaring that they prefer puppies to human babies because they perceive that the former will be more affectionate and grateful. We are lost to understand as to why they expect or demand gratefulness from the adopted. Only those who do favours should expect the favoured to be grateful. None of the adopted would have requested anyone that he should be adopted as a favour. Adoption is done to satisfy the adopters' own interests. This fact should be clearly understood by them well before the adoption. There is no *quid pro quo* arrangement in this. This is no commercial transaction. Humans are requested

We remember some funny incidents. We don't know if this is really that funny, it probably happens to a lot of others too. One day we saw Lina keeping staring at herself in the mirror! It was a tall mirror, set up against the wall and there's a space behind it, and she kept staring at herself and barked and scratched and thought another dog was there! The cute part was that she went behind the mirror to check of the dog was actually there! Though we also had similar things when we were also young puppies, we laughed and laughed.

Once on another occasion, she hid an ice cube in her blanket and was very upset that it was gone a little while later. She kept moving and dragging the blanket looking for the ice cube. She did not know that ice would melt and vanish. Poor girl!

While at the vet, Dr. Vetman was holding Lina and talking to her about what a well behaved little girl she was. He was supporting her bottom in his hand. As he gave her a treat, she peed in his hand. Silly girl!

The hospice was established by the Monk Bernard of Menthon in Switzerland near Alpine pass, a few centuries ago in the service of travellers getting trapped in heavy snowfall or avalanche. The monks who maintained it, discovered that the St. Bernards, that was the name given to them then, were good companions to have with them during the night searches and during storms. They had learnt to find the paths with unerring accuracy. They had great agility among the rocks and boulders of this mountain region, and could carry loads of supplies for the monks and the hospice. And they possessed such an acute sense of smell that they could locate victims of avalanches three to six metres under snow. They made huge contributions to mountain rescue work, by augmenting the work done by the monks. After-all, they are some of us. We salute the memory of the great St. Bernards!